LIFE
BEYOND
COLLEGE

LIFE BEYOND COLLEGE

EVERYTHING THEY DIDN'T TEACH YOU ABOUT YOUR FIRST 10 YEARS AFTER GRADUATION

KEVIN P. COYNE

CASTLEREA

PRESS

Published in 2020 in Atlanta, Georgia, USA, by:
Castlerea Press Inc.
8 Old Paces Place, Atlanta, Georgia 30327
www.castlereapress.com

ISBN Number: 978-1-7345080-0-0
Library of Congress Control Number: 2020900982
First Edition

Manufactured in Canada
Book designed by Burtch Hunter Design

NOTICE
While every effort has been made to ensure that the information herein is accurate within the constraints imposed by brevity, the publisher and author make no representations to the reader, either expressed or implied, of any kind. Neither the publisher nor the author shall be liable for any damage, loss or expense of any kind arising out of information contained in this book.

Many of the subjects covered by this book involve legal considerations, which vary by jurisdiction (such as Federal, specific state, or specific city), and which may have changed between the time that the underlying information was prepared or accessed and the present date. Every case is different, and any particular case may be affected by multiple laws or regulations.

Further, many of the subjects covered in this book involve financial subjects. Such subjects are also case specific, and every case is different.

Therefore, any discussion or description of laws or financial considerations contained in this book must be understood as intended to provide only a general orientation and a framework for readers to use in conducting further research if they deem it appropriate. The book does not represent itself as providing advice on any individual situation or case, and cannot be relied upon for that purpose. The author is not an attorney or certified financial planner. The author and publisher specifically disclaim any responsibility for the applicability of any statements in this book to any particular situation or case.

*This book is dedicated to
my father, Edward J. Coyne, Sr.;
my wife, Gergana K. Coyne;
and my daughters, Jennifer Coyne McIntosh,
Patricia K. Coyne, and Krista A. Coyne*

PREFACE

A s a new college graduate, you will face many significant challenges and high-stakes choices during the next 10 years. Get off on the right foot, and you'll give yourself a head start on the entire rest of your life—but make even a few early mistakes, and you could set yourself back for years.

The purpose of this book is to enable you to say, when faced with one of those challenges or choices, "Aha! I understand how this works—and because of that, I have a path toward making a decision that will serve me well."

To that end, the chapters of the book are designed to do three things:

- Orient you about how commonly a certain situation arises

- Educate you on the most important issues and considerations in that situation

- Provide you with data on how others typically respond in those situations, as well as some "benchmarks" regarding typical financial or legal consequences.

Of course, it will ultimately be incumbent upon you to tailor your decisions or choices to the specific governing laws and specific options available in your particular situation—but I hope this book will provide you with substantial, practical information to get you started as you begin to make your way in the world.

One final note: As you've undoubtedly experienced already at certain points in your life, sometimes things in the "real world" don't go as smoothly as they should, and sometimes people don't behave in ways that conform to societal norms. Throughout this book I will occasionally insert sidebars, using the headline "Just So You Know," to make you aware of such situations and the behaviors you may encounter when facing them. This information should not be mistaken (and cannot be construed) as constituting a recommendation for how you should behave—it is included only because I believe it is in your best interest to be fully informed.

ACKNOWLEDGEMENTS

The author would like to thank a "crew" of thought partners, reviewers, editors, administrative assistants, and other supporters without whose help this book would never have come to fruition, including in particular: Robert E. Witt; Shawn T. Coyne; Gergana K. Coyne; Krista A. Coyne; Edward J. Coyne, Sr.; Edward J. Coyne III; and Ed Curtis.

TABLE OF CONTENTS

PART I: Immediately After Graduation

PART II: Your First Year Out of College

CHAPTER 5

Establishing and Managing Your Credit
• Establishing a Track Record
• All About Credit Scores
• How to Improve Your Credit Score in 30 Days
• Common Credit Traps to Avoid
• Personal Bankruptcy

CHAPTER 6

You Need to Start Saving Right Away
• How Much to Save
• Before-Tax Savings Versus After-Tax Savings

CHAPTER 7

Investing for Retirement
• The Basic Idea of Investments
• Types of Investments
• Restrictions on Investments in 401(k) Accounts and IRAs
• Appendix: Understanding Finance in 30 Minutes

CHAPTER 8

The Legal and Health Aspects of Sex
• Informed Consent
• Unprotected Sex: What is the Real Risk of Contracting a Sexually Transmitted Disease?
• Pregnancy: Rights, Roles and Financial Responsibilities

PART III: Potential Early Setbacks That Are More Likely Than You Think

CHAPTER 9

You Quit or Get Fired
• Long Before It Happens...
• If You Get Fired (or Laid Off)
• If You (Plan to) Quit
• Moving On With Your Life
• Better Résumé, Better Job Search

LIFE
BEYOND
COLLEGE

PART I

Immediately After Graduation

CHAPTER 1

Your New Legal, Financial, and Personal Relationship With Your Parents

The day you turned 18, you earned a number of legal rights and privileges and took on a number of legal responsibilities, whether you knew it or not. However, your relationship with your parents probably did not change noticeably—and your parents may well have retained de facto "supervisory" status in your relationship, at least in part.

At the time of college graduation, relationships inevitably shift. However, for many families, the parents and the graduate are on different pages as to *how* they should shift and when. You and your parents need some explicit discussions about how the family's financial, supervisory, and advisory relationships should adjust to your new status.

Most likely, it is not going to be a clean break. A 2015 University of Arizona study indicated that, two years after graduation, 70% of recent college graduates were still at least partially financially dependent upon their families. In fact, another 2015 study by the Pew Research Center reported that 61% of parents still paid for recurring expenses (such as cell phone bills) or covered special circumstances for their 25- to 34-year-old children.[1]

Do you know all the legal rights and responsibilities of adulthood? Do you know your parents' expectations about the degree and time limits on financing your transition to self-sufficiency? Does that assistance come with any expectations of how you will (and won't) spend the money? Is it a gift or a loan? Do your parents expect you to check in with them on big decisions?

At a minimum, you should consider four sets of changes that will be happening. In order for you and your parents to be on the same page, you might even want to use this chapter as a discussion guide.

Specifically, we will cover:

- The legal changes that already took place when you turned 18
- Issues surrounding continued financial assistance
- Issues surrounding moving back home
- Your evolving personal relationship with your parents
- An additional administrative item that could cost or save your family over $1,000

WHEN YOU TURNED 18

· · ·

On your 18th birthday, your parents ceased having legal responsibility for you. (It happened even earlier if you were legally *emancipated,* which means you were given legal adult status at a younger age). To some degree, you probably already knew this. However, you may not know all of the ins and outs of this simple change in status.

- First, as of that date, your parents were not legally obligated to financially support you in any way. Absent a legal contract between you and your parents, everything they have done for you since that date, with very few and narrow exceptions, is out of the goodness of their hearts.

- For the first time, you could sign a contract that legally binds you. (You could technically sign a contract before age 18, but in most cases, the contract could not be enforced against you, meaning you could legally ignore it, even if you lied about your age when you signed it. And your parents could not be legally forced to honor the contract unless they co-signed it.) However, if you signed a contract as a child, and formally or informally ratified it after you turned 18 by continuing to take actions based on that contract, you are legally bound by it, regardless of the age at which you signed it.[2]

- Your parents could no longer sign contracts for you, and any contracts they signed on your behalf before you turned 18 are no longer valid, with very few exceptions.

- Your parents can no longer be sued based on your actions, including your negligence. However, there are some exceptions to this general statement. If your behavior constitutes a danger to society, your parents have the same duties to report you as would anyone else. If your behavior involves using an asset owned by your parent (e.g., a car), and your parents are negligent to allow you the use of that asset (e.g., you habitually drove it while being drunk), they can be sued for negligence. Or, as with anyone else, if your parents themselves were involved in the negligent act, they too could be separately liable for it.

- Finally, if you are lucky enough to be the beneficiary of a trust fund, then the rules of the trust fund (such as when you are entitled to certain monies) continue regardless of your age. Many trust funds provide for disbursements at age 21, 25, 30, or even older. If your parents are the trustees, they continue to control those decisions.

CONTINUED FINANCIAL ASSISTANCE
• • •

As noted above, most parents of college graduates continue to support their child, even long after college graduation. In mid-2019, CNBC reported a study by Merrill Lynch and a research company called Age Wave that surveyed 2,700 millennials and parents about the nature and level of financial support.[3] 58% of early adults (i.e., those below age 34) surveyed said that they could not sustain their lifestyle without parental support. In a separate part of the report, for every one of the reported categories (i.e., food and groceries, cell phone, car expenses, school, vacations, rent/mortgage, and student loans), between about a quarter and a third of early adults reported receiving at least some support from their parents. Between 10% and 20% reported their parents covered that particular category completely.

Providing such support can be quite expensive to the parents. For example, if a 50-year-old parent supports a recent college grad with $459 each month (a figure explained in the next section) for five years, and that parent could have earned a 7% return on his/her savings (through interest or investing in the stock market), then that parent would have sacrificed over $66,000 in retirement savings at age 65.

An obvious first question is this: What amount of support is appropriate? The answer, of course, is dependent on your circumstances and your parents' circumstances. What can they afford? Are you going to go to graduate school (either now or soon)? Are you employed? If so, are you fully employed at a job that matches your skill levels or are you underemployed? (A 2018 study reported that 43% of recent graduates' first jobs did not require a college degree.[4]) Does your career require a period of low earnings while you build your base, as is usually the situation with people such as real estate agents, actors, stockbrokers, and artists?

Even finding benchmarks to calibrate your thinking is difficult. The best data available comes from a University of Michigan study conducted from 2005 through 2009[5] on persons between the ages of 19 and 22. That study reported:

- About 42% received help in paying bills, with those receiving help getting an average of $1,741 (about $2,100 in 2019 dollars)
- About 23% received help with vehicles (about $9,682 on average, equal to about $11,500 in 2019 dollars)
- About 22% received help with their rent away from home ($3,937 on average, or about $4,700 in 2019 dollars)
- About 11% said they received loans from their parents ($2,079 on average, or about $2,500 in 2019 dollars)
- Nearly 7% said they received financial gifts (average amount of $8,220, or about $9,800 in 2019 dollars)

(All figures are annual, except for the one concerning vehicles.)

Caution: Given that the recipients studied were mostly still in college, do not take these figures too seriously. Further, note the figures are not necessarily additive. The percentages of respondents who received assistance collectively added up to 105%. Therefore, it is theoretically possible that only 5% received assistance in more than one category or, conversely, that 7% received assistance in all five categories, or any combination in between.

Therefore, the appropriate amount of assistance (if any) in your case will need to be worked out between you and your parents with little outside data to go on. You should expect these conversations to be uncomfortable for all involved. Further, a single conversation will not reach a conclusion. Plan for a series of conversations spread over a couple of months.

Separate from agreeing on the amount of support, you and your parents will also need to discuss several key aspects of the form of the support. Specifically:

- Will the support come in the form of covering specific items (such as your cell phone bill, or vacations) or will it be a single amount each month, leaving it to you to allocate the funds?

- Are your parents comfortable with you taking time off before you start working?

- Will your parents require any documentation of how the money was spent (e.g., providing receipts)?

- Is the support strictly a gift, or a loan, or a mix of the two? If some or all of it is in the form of a loan, what are the repayment expectations?

- What defines the time when some or all of the assistance should end? Is there a particular date or a particular milestone? Is there some expectation for what progress you must make in terms of reaching financial self-sufficiency? What conversations should take place if you fall off track along the way?

- Are your parents willing and able to serve as a financial safety net if you experience financial setbacks, such as job layoffs, health emergencies, legal issues, etc.?

MOVING BACK HOME
• • •

If you decide to move back home with your parents, you will not be alone in doing so. A 2014 Pew Research Center Report found that 34% of 18- to 34-year-olds were living with their parents.[6] A 2019 study by TD Ameritrade found that fully 50% of millennials planned to move back home after graduation.[7]

There are many reasons graduates move back home. Some do not have jobs lined up and therefore cannot afford to live separately. But others simply want lower rent so they can save money, pay down loans, or care for their parents or siblings. The first important consideration about moving back home is for neither your parents nor you to feel the least bit sheepish about it. However, a successful move requires a meeting of the minds between you and your parents on several subjects that are best discussed explicitly at the outset. Your views and those of your parents may divide sharply on the following:

- What (if anything) are you expected to contribute to the household expenses by way of rent, paying for certain items or expenses, or sporadically paying for household items out of your own pocket? While there is no specifically right amount, some facts may help your discussion. The U.S. median monthly rent for a one-bedroom apartment in 2019 was $1,219.[8] If you believe a more appropriate comparison would be one-half of the cost of a two-bedroom apartment, that would be about $703 per month.[9] According to one study,[10] the average net cost to parents of having an adult child live at home is $459 per month.

- What living space is considered your (and conversely your siblings' and parents') private space?

- What duties do you have with respect to caring for yourself? Must you do your own laundry? Are you expected to keep your room clean and neat? Do you have to buy your own groceries?

- Are you assigned chores for the household at large? Is the list the same as it was when you were in high school, or are there changes as a result of your current age and status?

- What are the rules with respect to boyfriends/girlfriends? Do these hold true if your parents disapprove of the person and indeed do not trust that person being in their house? How do your parents feel about their house being the scene of casual sex? Are you allowed to have your (short-term or long-term) lover spend the night? If so, is he/she expected to stay in your private space or is he/she allowed to watch TV and play video games with your siblings? Are you allowed to have him/her move in with you?

- For how long is this arrangement expected to last? Is there a time limit, or is the move-out time to be based on some milestone, or will you just see how it goes? In fact, the most difficult aspect of this issue is unlikely to be achieving an agreement at the time you move back. It will come later, if the deadline approaches or if one party is becoming tired of the situation. How will you and your parents handle raising the subject when one party (either you or your parents) wants you to move on but the other does not?

THE FAMILY'S EVOLVING PERSONAL RELATIONSHIP

• • •

Even if there is no continuing financial support and you do not live at home, your relationship with your parents is about to undergo some stress. Conversely, if there is such support or you will live at home, there will be even more stress.

First, you may individually suffer from post-college depression. One common cause for this is unemployment or underemployment, which can cause you to think that your college career was wasted. A second common cause is the sudden departure from the relatively safe cocoon offered by a college environment and the sudden disbandment of one's close circle of friends. Symptoms include an abnormally negative perspective, decreased motivation to get out of bed, a general sense of hopelessness, and, occasionally, substance abuse. Systematic studies about the prevalence of this affliction are difficult to find, but it is believed the condition is underreported because graduation is supposed to be a joyful time, which makes it difficult for someone to admit that he/she is actually feeling the opposite.

Even if there is no individual depression, some families have difficulties adjusting to shifting roles and responsibilities and lifestyle patterns. For example:

- Some parents have developed unrealistic expectations over your high school and college years about the level of success you will enjoy immediately upon graduation. They will subtly or not-so-subtly communicate their disappointment over your choices and level of success. This can obviously be hard to take.

- Parents may be used to checking in with you quite often. As long as they were paying the bills, both you and they accepted their implied supervisory role. But when you are living away from home and are at least mostly self-sufficient, you may not want any feeling of supervision. Your parents may take time to transition from supervisor to advisor to peer.

- When you were in college, the default option was to come home for most holidays, vacations, etc. You may not have come home every time, but if you chose no place else, you would go home. Now, your definition of home may have shifted to your separate residence. Your parents' definition will not. They still think of the same old place as home, and they may have difficulty adjusting when you think of it as a place you will only go when you specifically choose to.

While it is beyond the scope of this book to delve into the psychology of your family's relationships, know that most experts recommend the best way to alleviate these problems before or after they arise is to hold explicit conversations about the substance of the issue(s) with your parents.

ONE LAST ADMINISTRATIVE ITEM

• • •

As your employment status changes, the difference between good and poor coordination between you and your parents can cost the family hundreds or even thousands of dollars around a single issue: healthcare insurance.

Most college students are covered under their parents' healthcare insurance as part of the family. Under current law, you can generally elect to be covered under that insurance until age 26. But you and your parents can also elect for you to no longer be covered by their policy, and you may obtain a policy that covers only you, either through your employer or through national or state-specific healthcare insurance exchanges established under the Affordable Care Act (a/k/a Obamacare). You collectively need to coordinate on what will be best for your family.

How much money is at stake? To find out, you will need to make some calculations for yourself, as premiums differ from plan to plan, and so do deductibles and coverages. (This is described in more detail in Chapter 3.) However, to illustrate, let's use some statistical averages.[11] In 2018, the average healthcare insurance premium for an individual covered by a group insurance policy (i.e., one obtained through their parents' employer) was $574 per month. The average premium to cover an entire family was $1,634 per month. Roughly speaking, the average premium for two parents alone would have been about $1,167. That means, if you are an only child or the last child to be covered under their policy, your healthcare insurance cost your parents about $467 a month.

The worst uncoordinated outcome is if your employer mandates you be covered under its policy, and you and/or your parents delay in adjusting their policy. That would waste $467 per month (or over $5,600 per year).

The other source of waste comes if you do not have employer-provided group healthcare insurance and, perhaps because of that, your parents do not at least consider removing you from their policy and looking into an individual policy for you. Because you are young, and because you may not need as thorough coverage as a typical family member, you can probably purchase an individual policy for less than the $467 your parents are currently paying for you. For example, the national average monthly premium paid for an individual policy on the insurance exchange market is $310 for males and $332 for females. That could represent a savings to your family of about $140 per month (or over $1,600 per year).

Be careful—policies provide different coverages, have different deductibles, etc., and the cheaper alternative may not be a good idea in your particular case. But, as the figures above show, it is worth investigating, so look into the details for your particular case before deciding what to do.

∿

Most new college graduates and their parents have an image of graduation as a "flash cut" to independence. It rarely works out that way, but rest assured, your path will get you there—and in the long run, that's all that matters.

ENDNOTES

[1] Cited in Tammy LaGorce, "The Long-Term Cost When Graduates Move Back Home," New York Times, November 17, 2018, nytimes.com/2018/11/17/business/the-long-term-cost-when-graduates-move-back-home.html. Accessed November 11, 2019.

[2] USLegal, Contract by a Minor," n.d., contracts.uslegal.com/contract-by-a-minor. Accessed November 12, 2019.

[3] Megan Leonhardt, "Here's how many millennials get help from their parents to pay rent and other bills," CNBC, May 2, 2019, www.cnbc.com/2019/05/02/how-many-millennials-get-help-from-their-parents-to-pay-rent-other-bills.html. Accessed November 13, 2019.

[4] Preston Cooper, "Underemployment Persists Throughout College Graduates' Careers," Forbes, June 8, 2018, www.forbes.com/sites/prestoncooper2/2018/06/08/underemployment-persists-throughout-college-graduates-careers/#1c649d4b7490. Accessed November 13, 2019.

[5] Institute for Social Research, University of Michigan, "How much money parents give to college-age kids: U-M study," May 3, 2012, https://isr.umich.edu/news-events/news-releases/how-much-money-parents-give-to-college-age-kids-um-study. Accessed November 13, 2019.

[6] Richard Fry, "For First Time in Modern Era, Living with Parents Edges Out Other Living Arrangements for 18- to 34-Year-Olds," Pew Research Center, May 24, 2016, https://www.pewsocialtrends.org/2016/05/24/for-first-time-in-modern-era-living-with-parents-edges-out-other-living-arrangements-for-18-to-34-year-olds. Accessed November 11, 2019.

[7] Zack Friedman, "50% of Millennials Are Moving Back Home with Their Parents After College," Forbes, June 6, 2019, https://www.forbes.com/sites/zackfriedman/2019/06/06/millennials-move-back-home-college/#4ea7e23e638a. Accessed November 11, 2019.

[8] Libertina Brandt, "Here's how much it costs to rent a one-bedroom apartment in 15 major US cities," Business Insider, July 24, 2019, https://www.businessinsider.com/cost-of-one-bedroom-apartment-rent-major-us-cities-2019–6. Accessed November 13, 2019.

[9] Rachel Layne, "U.S. housing rents hit record-high average of $1,405 per month," CBS News, July 6, 2018, https://www.cbsnews.com/news/u-s-urban-rents-hit-all-time-high-at-average-1405-report/. Accessed November 13, 2019.

[10] Maurie Backman, "Here's How Much It Costs Parents to Have Adult Kids Living at Home," The Motley Fool, December 7, 2018, https://www.fool.com/retirement/2018/12/07/heres-how-much-it-costs-parents-to-have-adult-kids.aspx. Accessed November 13, 2019.

[11] Kim P, "Study: Average Cost of Health Insurance," CreditDonkey, June 19, 2019, creditdonkey.com/average-cost-health-insurance.html. Accessed November 13, 2019.

CHAPTER 2

Renting That First Post-College Apartment: Seven Issues You May Overlook—and Later Regret

In college, you may have lived on campus all four years in dorms, in a fraternity or sorority house, or in a university-affiliated apartment. Even if you lived off-campus for a year or two, it was likely in a student-oriented apartment compound, where perhaps dozens of other students currently or previously lived. The prior student tenants implicitly performed all the necessary due diligence for you—after all, they voted with their feet by living there. Hence, you simply assumed that the apartment complex and surrounding area were safe (enough), and that the landlord and student tenants had long ago reached a meeting of the minds about various landlord-tenant arrangements.

After you leave college, rental life is very different. Although there are no statistics available, it's probably safe to assume that most college graduates end up with at least one major regret about their first rental experience. It may be that the neighborhood was sketchier than they thought; that their roommate was surprisingly difficult; that there were issues with the landlord; that it cost more to break the lease than they imagined; that they did not get their security deposit back; or any number of other painful experiences.

In this chapter, I hope to help you minimize the odds of such regrets, or at least reduce their severity, by highlighting the most commonly overlooked causes of later regrets and discussing what you can do to avoid them. They are:

- Paying too much (or too little) in rent
- Failing to find out about the worst aspect of this particular apartment before you moved in
- Choosing the wrong roommate
- Incurring legal issues due to your roommate
- Signing a lease with unusually bad provisions
- Failing to take a few steps at the outset to improve your chances of getting back your full deposit
- Mishandling the process when you have to break a lease early

HOW MUCH SHOULD YOU PAY IN RENT?

Assume for the moment that you will be moving to a city where you have never lived before. You do not know the city particularly well, and you certainly have no inside information regarding the best apartment complexes for someone of your age and tastes. What should you do first?

A good first step is to estimate how much you want to spend on rent. At first, that may seem counterintuitive, because your first instinct is to say you have no idea what landlords charge in a specific market. While that is true, there are two pitfalls to looking before you establish a general budget. First, unless you know approximately what you hope to spend, you might waste a lot of time looking at areas you can't afford or areas you will later be happy you can afford to avoid. Why waste the effort? Second, and more important, there is an old adage in real estate: If you don't want to buy, don't look. Translated into apartment hunting, if you visit apartment complexes you can't afford, you will certainly like them better than the ones you see later that you can afford. That will result in either being disappointed with the apartment you eventually settle on (yuck!), or ruining your budget because you overspend on your rent and don't have enough money left over for other things (yikes!).

Here's how to estimate how much to spend on rent:

- Many experts say your starting point should be to plan to spend 30% of your take-home pay on your rent (which, by the way, includes parking fees and/or storage unit fees).[1] That means 30% of the amount of money left in your paycheck after the withholdings for income taxes (both federal and state) and FICA. Now, if you also deduct funds directly from your paycheck for retirement savings into a 401(k) or IRA (see Chapter 6), you can add back this year's contribution as part of your take-home pay for purposes of this calculation.

- Next, multiply your take-home pay by 30%. This is your first estimate. Next, adjust this figure up or down by as much as five points (i.e., make it somewhere between 25% and 35% of your take-home pay), based on whether you tend to spend the large majority of your evenings at home with dinner and television or gaming, etc. (in which case, you may want a nicer apartment and can afford to spend a little more on it), or whether you tend to spend as little time as possible at home, preferring to eat out and spend your evenings with friends, etc. (in which case, you need to save on the apartment rent in order to have more funds available for entertainment).

- Next, decide whether you plan to live alone, or with a roommate who can share the rent with you. In Chapter 1, we saw the U.S. median monthly rent for a one-bedroom apartment in 2019 was $1,219,[2] and that one half of the cost of a two-bedroom apartment was about $703 per month.[3] Analogous figures can be found easily on the internet for most U.S. cities.

Knowing how much you might spend compared to the average rents in your chosen city then allows you to know whether you will be looking for an average, way above average, or budget apartment. That should help target your search.

If you will be looking for an apartment in conjunction with a roommate, insist on the roommate performing the same calculation for himself/herself, and on the two of you sharing your results with each other, before you go hunting. You need to know if his/her limits are different than yours. It will avoid fights over where to live and/or problems later when one of you decides he/she cannot afford the choice you jointly made.

Finally, do not make the mistake that millions of Americans made leading up to the real estate debacle in 2008. Some apartment complexes (like some mortgage lenders in 2006 and 2007) use teaser rates to attract you. In your case, these may be discounts for your first year of rent. (This is a particularly common offer when buildings are new, and there are dozens or hundreds of apartments the landlord is trying to find tenants to occupy. The discounts can run as high as 25% or 30%.) Now, the discounts themselves are great. But when you are calculating whether you can afford that apartment, be sure you use the full rent in your calculation, not the discounted rent. You are very unlikely to receive a raise in your salary that fully offsets the increase in your rent at the end of the discount period, and you do not want to be in a situation of being forced to move because you can no longer afford your apartment. From 2007 through 2009, millions of Americans lost their homes, many due to the fact they found they could not afford their mortgage once the teaser rate had expired—don't let the analogous issue happen to you with your rent.

WHAT IS THE WORST ASPECT OF THIS APARTMENT?

• • •

Most apartments, except perhaps really expensive ones, have something about them that is annoying, unpleasant, or problematic. Most tenants don't find out what that something is until they live there, because most tenants don't take some easy steps that would reveal the problems ahead of time.

Most problems fall into three categories:

• How is the neighborhood? Is it safe? Is it incredibly noisy at night? Is it located next to a smelly industrial park? What is the neighborhood and complex like at its worst time of year (such as the dead of winter or during flood season)?

- How is the landlord (whether the landlord is a specific individual or a large corporation)? Does he/she/it keep the building in good condition? Does he/she/it respond quickly when repairs are needed? Does he/she/it plow the snow promptly? Is he/she/it fair when it comes time to refund the security deposit?

- How are your specific prospective neighbors? Are they loud, particularly when you want to sleep? Do they show respect for the property, or are they messy or destructive? Do you care if they (and/or their children) are friendly or not? Will they be comfortable with the noise you make?

Each of these categories of issues is surprisingly easy to check out before you sign a lease. Most obviously and important (but usually not done), knock on the doors of two to three prospective neighbors and meet them. Ask a lot of questions. They will know all about the first two categories, and they will demonstrate much of what you need to know about the third. If the apartment is gated, such that you cannot get to your potential apartment without the rental agent, wait by the gate and ask a few questions of tenants who pull up to the gate or who are about to go out for a run, etc. Yes, it will feel a little awkward—but the vast majority of people will be helpful, and a few minutes of awkwardness is better than six months or more of a lease you wished you had not signed.

See the local police department or precinct to ask about the safety of the neighborhood. They have, and will share, a variety of key statistics (which are probably also posted online). Be friendly, and they may also tell you any specific history and issues related to the specific apartment complex you're considering.

Finally, drive by and through the neighborhood and the complex late at night a couple of times. You will be amazed at how much its character can shift based on the time of day.

WHAT MAKES A BAD ROOMMATE?

• • •

If you're lucky, you already know your prospective roommate. If not, and you need to find one, you can take any of the obvious routes (i.e., networking through friends, asking at work, checking with the complex, searching online, etc.) to find one.

But what should you know and discuss with a potential roommate before deciding to move in together? Even if you know and like someone, there are still a number of reasons why he/she may not be a compatible roommate for you.

Here's a checklist of topics you should consider when assessing compatibility:

- Are you just splitting the rent, or are you jointly running a household (e.g., sharing groceries etc.)? Do you agree on what is the right split of the rent and other common expenses, given that one of you may have a larger bedroom, one of you travels a lot, etc.?

- Do you exhibit similar reliability when it comes to paying for joint purchases? The most toxic roommate situations arise when one person manages his/her money badly and therefore fails to have his/her share of the funds available when the rent and/or utilities are due. If one of you has a steady job and the other does not (e.g., if one of you gets paid by the gig as a musician, or is between jobs), you need to have an explicit discussion about how the two of you are going to handle any temporary cash shortages.

- Are your work times, sleep times, and "let's crank the music" times compatible?

- Do you have compatible views on the thermostat setting?

- Do you have compatible views on private spaces versus common spaces, and on how neat and clean to keep the common spaces? What will be the split of chores?

- Do you have similar views about whether you are looking for a roommate only or whether the two of you plan to become best friends who will constantly socialize with each other?

- Do you like or dislike your roommate's friends coming over a lot?

- Is it okay if a boyfriend/girlfriend spends the night? Is it okay if he/she starts hanging out at your place much of the time, even when your roommate is not there?

- Do either of you have personal attributes or habits that result in strong odors? For example, does one of you cook exotic dishes, smoke, enjoy incense, etc.?

- What will be your agreed policy on pets?

CAN YOU INCUR LEGAL ISSUES DUE TO YOUR ROOMMATE?

· · ·

When you have a roommate, you take on certain legal responsibilities. Two categories are most important.

First, how the lease is signed determines who is legally the tenant, and that affects both who is in charge and who bears what financial responsibilities. Basically, there are two options when more than one person will occupy the apartment.

- In the first case, only one tenant signs the lease. That person then becomes the master tenant, and the landlord's contract is with that one person only (unless someone such as a parent co-signs the lease as a guarantor ensuring that the rent will be paid).

  » The bad news about being the master tenant is that you are the only one bearing any responsibility for all the payments due under the contract, as well as any damage that is done. The landlord will look to you (and only you) for payment. He/she will not care whether your roommate left in the middle of the night, or that you are looking for but have not yet found a new roommate to cover part of the rent.

  » The good news is, you are in charge. Your roommate can remain in the apartment only with your permission. That means, unless you and your roommate have a formal written sub-rental agreement between you, which you would be violating, you can kick him/her out. If he/she resists, you can go through the process of legally evicting him/her.

- In the other case, both tenants (or all tenants if there are more than two) sign the lease as co-tenants. This is the form that most landlords prefer and many require (by having a no-subletting clause in the lease). Now, you might logically expect such an arrangement would subject each of the tenants to half of the financial responsibility—but you could be wrong. In most co-tenant contracts, each tenant bears 100% of the financial responsibility. That way, if either tenant were to leave, the landlord can look to the remaining tenant for full payment of any obligations. In fact, if a parent were to co-sign for one tenant in a co-tenant situation, the landlord may be able to go after that parent for the full amount of the obligation. Thus, that parent has effectively co-signed for all the tenants. Now, in a co-tenant situation, no one tenant has legal standing over the other tenant(s). So, a tenant cannot kick out a bad roommate without that roommate's agreement. By the way, just because the two roommates agree does not mean the departing roommate is automatically freed from the rental contract. He/she still bears full responsibility for all financial obligations unless and until the landlord agrees to release him/her from the lease!

The second group of legal issues can have dire consequences. If your roommate engages in illegal activities (such as theft, or possessing or selling illegal drugs) and he/she comes to the attention of the police, you are personally at risk from several legal angles.[4]

- First, if the police obtain a search warrant, it will most likely involve the entire apartment, including your private spaces. So, if you too have a stash, it will likely be discovered. Further, there is a legal concept called constructive possession, which means that if your roommate's contraband is found in a common space, you can be said to have exercised some control over that space and therefore be considered to share ownership of the contraband.

- Second, there is the issue of being an *accessory* to your roommate's crimes. It is illegal to help someone, even just a little, to commit a crime. An *accessory before the fact* is someone who assists, incites, or encourages another person in the commission of a crime. An *accessory after the fact* is someone who shelters or assists another person after a crime is committed. That illegal assistance can be any financial, material, or even emotional support of the criminal.[5] If you share an apartment with a person who falls into trouble with the police for activities in your home, you will likely have to convince the police you were unaware of your roommate's illegal activities. The more time and ties you have to your roommate and the more evidence found in the apartment, the more difficulty you will have avoiding being charged as an accessory.

WHAT SHOULD YOU
WATCH OUT FOR IN THE LEASE?
• • •

Landlords have the advantage when it comes time to sign the lease, which is the only legal contract between the tenant(s) and the landlord. Said another way, verbal promises that accompany a lease are generally not legally binding. It is the landlord who has drafted the document and can claim, "This is our standard lease, so we cannot make exceptions for you." Further, even the standard wording for leases has been built up over many years to the benefit of landlords. Every time there is a report that a tenant has successfully won a large lawsuit against a landlord, real estate attorneys get busy amending the standard lease forms to close that loophole.

Therefore, be sure to read your entire lease, in detail, before you sign it. Yes, leases are boring and full of legal-speak designed to obfuscate what is being said. And, yes, you've probably gotten used to signing an End User License Agreement for every app on your phone without ever reading it. Nonetheless, take time to read the entire lease, in detail, or you may regret it.

Lease agreements usually have a number of strict provisions, but most are not unduly onerous—so if you spot something in a lease that sounds a bit extreme to you, that should be a red flag, in and of itself. Before you sign any lease, Google "typical apartment lease." The results will provide you with several examples of average leases, including all the major clauses. If the lease you are considering has clauses that deviate significantly from those, you may not want to sign. I obviously cannot tell you when you'll encounter a lease provision that is so bad you should walk away, because every market is different—i.e., a provision that would be extreme in one locality might be the norm in another locality where housing is in short supply—but here are some clauses that you should pay particular attention to:

- Who signs? As discussed above, even if two of you will be living there, you personally should still prefer to have only one tenant sign—and you can figure out whether you would rather have that person be yourself or your roommate—but only if the lease allows sub-tenants.

- How long is the lease term? What are the penalties if you break the lease early? A typical lease is usually six months or a year. Beware of signing up for a longer lease your first time, because you will learn a lot about whether you like your job, your roommate, and the particular apartment over the next six months. If you must sign a long lease, be sure the penalty for getting out of the lease early is reasonable (e.g., a provision that says your maximum penalty is two month's rent and/or one month plus the security deposit; even better is if the landlord also commits to trying to quickly re-lease the apartment and reduce your penalty if they succeed in doing so). If the lease is longer than six months and does not limit the penalty for leaving early, that is a poor lease from your point of view.

- Does the lease have an automatic renewal clause? If so, read the clause very carefully, and think about whether you are comfortable with it— and not just about any stated increases in the monthly rental rate. Also pay close attention to how long ahead of the renewal date you must notify the landlord to prevent automatic renewal.

- How onerous is the security deposit? What are the rules for determining whether you get it back? Most important, can the landlord withhold the deposit even for normal wear-and-tear or for the need to re-paint or re-carpet the apartment when you leave?

- If the apartment needs repairs or refurbishment before you occupy it, what are the provisions to protect you if they are not completed to your satisfaction by your move-in date?

- What are the rules about landlord access to the apartment? Specifically, under what circumstances can they enter, and what amount of notice is required before they can enter?

- What if you are late with the rent or miss a payment? How onerous are the late fees? Does the lease require the landlord to abide by all local laws with respect to eviction?

- What are the provisions around excess noise, both yours and your neighbors'?

- What does the lease say about the landlord's required responsiveness for repairs? Do you have any leverage to push the landlord if he/she is unresponsive?

- How will significant disputes be resolved? Does the lease require you to submit to arbitration rather than taking the landlord to court? The landlord tends to have the advantage in arbitration—and be especially careful if the landlord gets to choose the arbitrator, as he/she would likely have the overwhelming advantage in any dispute.

FOR THE LGBTQ COMMUNITY
Dealing With Potential Housing Discrimination

Members of the LGBTQ community face a decidedly mixed bag when it comes to finding housing. On the one hand, there are bigots everywhere, and you may well meet one in your discussions with landlords. There seems to be evidence that the landlord community is slightly but not overwhelmingly biased against same-sex couples and transgendered persons, at least in large cities.[6]

Fortunately, it is rare the bigots hold a monopoly on available rental units. There may be plenty of alternatives out there. A number of resources on the internet are specifically devoted to helping LGBTQ persons find rental units. And while I have not found studies to prove this, anecdotally I have heard you are less likely to be confronted with discrimination from large institutional complexes (particularly those who are part of multi-complex apartment chains) than you are at smaller, more intimate complexes (e.g., those containing only four to six apartments) that are run by an onsite owner. In fact, some larger chains have their own anti-discrimination policies.

Should your situation come down to a legal fight, there are laws against discrimination in housing on the basis of sexual orientation in 21 states and the District of Columbia.[7] Some cities have human rights ordinances that can also prohibit such discrimination. More broadly, although there is no federal law that directly protects you on this issue, there are laws prohibiting discrimination on the basis of sex, and many times the behavior that accompanies housing discrimination (such as harassment) has been held to have violated these laws.

CAN YOU IMPROVE YOUR ODDS OF GETTING BACK YOUR FULL DEPOSIT?

• • •

Perhaps the single most common anxiety in renting an apartment is the looming sense of dread about whether you will get back your security deposit when you move out. After all, because the landlord is holding your money, you are trusting that he/she will be fair and reasonable. But there are several things you can do to improve your odds:

- First, before you sign the lease, be sure to scrutinize the wording of the lease around expectations about the condition of the apartment when you move out. The more specific the expectations, the lower the chances for a genuine difference of opinion. If the basic lease is too vague, you might even suggest adding a clause that spells out expectations.

- Next—and here is where most renters blow their opportunity—take a ton of photos of the apartment before you move any furniture into the space. In particular, take close-ups of any pre-existing damage. Most important, email those photos to the landlord before you move in, and be sure to keep a copy of that email. That way, when you move out, you will have documented proof (based on the date of the email) that you were not the one who damaged the apartment. Simply knowing you have the evidence available will cause most landlords to avoid any argument. And if things do turn nasty, remember that lawsuits are won or lost on the basis of the preponderance of evidence (i.e., who has the best evidence)—and your photos, plus a copy of the email you sent to the landlord, will obliterate any "he said, she said" problems.

- When it comes time to move out, about two weeks ahead of time, compare the current condition of your apartment to the move-in photos you took. That way, you can tell if any minor repairs are needed. You will almost certainly want to make any repairs yourself, and you may even consider hiring your own handyman for the small problems you cannot fix yourself. This is because the landlord's way is almost always the most expensive way to fix anything. If he/she employs a crew, he/she will set the hourly rate for the labor required, which would be equal to the actual hourly salary he/she pays the crew plus some enormous overhead costs. If the landlord has to hire an outside contractor, he/she will care much less about finding the lowest bidder than you would, because it's your money, not the landlord's money, that is being spent.

- Next, clean the apartment really well—far better than the "broom-clean" standard the lease typically requires. Otherwise, some landlords will charge you a cleaning fee, claiming a difference of opinion on what constitutes "broom-clean."

- Finally, insist on a final walkthrough with the landlord. Have a physical copy of your original email with the photographs of the initial condition of the apartment. If the landlord does not raise any issues during the walkthrough, then you should get your full security deposit back. If he/she does raise issues, you are in a position to point out cases where the issue is actually related to a condition that already existed before you moved in.

WHAT SHOULD YOU DO IF YOU HAVE TO BREAK THE LEASE EARLY?
• • •

There are two categories of situations when you are moving out: those situations that are the landlord's fault, and those that are not. How you should approach this topic depends on the category.

Let's begin by looking at the first category—things at are the landlord's fault:

- There are many things a landlord can do to annoy you. But to rely on the landlord's behavior as a legitimate basis to break the lease, you must show that he/she has violated the terms of the lease.

- Therefore, start a written record. Document the violations, including the dates. Compare them to the terms of the lease, just to refresh your memory on whether it is truly a violation. Then, start sending written requests by certified mail (so you can later document the fact that you did indeed give him/her a chance to address the problem before you took more drastic action). In the letters, be specific as to what is wrong, how that is a violation of the lease, what you want him/her to do about it, and by when.

- If the landlord fails to satisfy you, you must decide which of two broad courses of action you prefer to take: (1) moving out—thereby forfeiting any prepaid rent and security deposits, and essentially challenging the landlord to take you to court if he/she wants more money; or (2) legally challenging the landlord. The first option is a bet that the landlord will not chase you, because pursuing you will be expensive and time consuming, and he/she will have to defend his/her lease violations in court. The second option is more involved. You will likely want to hire an attorney to create a credible threat that you will sue the landlord. If that does not work, you will need to file a civil lawsuit.

- Fortunately, in most jurisdictions, you can take the landlord to small claims court as long as the size of the dispute is less than $10,000.[8] The good news is that, in most jurisdictions, you don't need an attorney to go to small claims court; in fact, in some jurisdictions, you are not allowed to have one. The better news is that, if you are not allowed to have an attorney, then the landlord isn't allowed to have one either. That means you won't be trying to match legal expertise with a professional. It also means the landlord must personally show up (because if he/she doesn't show up, you win by default)—and that's great for you because it creates a hassle for the landlord, and he/she must defend his/her own bad behavior in front of a judge, which might make him/her more willing to settle your issue without going to court at all.

- A note of caution about small claims courts: They don't like to offer messy solutions. Should you win, the court is unlikely to get involved with ordering the landlord to take a bunch of specific actions to alleviate any problems. You will simply be given permission to break the contract and leave, and/or be awarded an amount of money, called *damages*—nothing else.

The second category of situation is when you want to leave before the end of the lease, but your leaving is not the landlord's fault. Maybe you got a new job in another city. Maybe you decided to move in with your significant other. Maybe your roommate is driving you nuts. In that case:

- Start by reading your lease and seeing what the early move-out penalties are. If they are acceptable, just notify the landlord and be done with it. However, pay particular attention to the advice in the previous section about getting your deposit back, because landlords are not known for their generosity in early move-out situations.

- Let's pretend you would like to leave with less financial cost than the formal terms embodied in your lease. Do your homework, and you may be able to reduce your pain:

  » Is the rental market loose or tight? Is there a waiting list for this particular complex, or are there multiple units (with your unit's particular number of bedrooms) that are already available? You want to discover whether the landlord will face a short or long challenge in securing a new tenant.

  » Examine the lease to see whether you are allowed to sublet the apartment for some (or all) of the time remaining on the lease. That way, you may be able to move out without actually breaking the lease.

  » Check the local laws. Many cities and towns have a tenant's rights ordinance. Sometimes, they require the landlord to try to re-lease the apartment and only charge you for the time the apartment is actually vacant. If this is the case in your locality, then even if you are not allowed to sublet (or just don't want to), you can minimize your financial hit if you find someone else to rent the apartment.

- Armed with this knowledge, it's time to be especially courteous to your landlord. Approach him/her as soon as possible, explain your situation, and ask if something can be done to work things out on better terms. It doesn't always work, but sometimes it can—and there's usually enough savings involved to make it worth your trouble to ask.

~

Later in life, you'll want to look back on your first post-college apartment with fond memories, unclouded by an overwhelming sense of "except for that part where..." Avoiding some of the biggest problems can help ensure that your only memories will be good ones.

ENDNOTES

[1] Megan Bullock, "How Much Should I Spend on Rent?" Apartments.com, February 22, 2019, www.apartments.com/blog/how-much-should-i-spend-on-rent. Accessed November 29, 2019.

[2] Libertina Brandt, "Here's how much it costs to rent a one-bedroom apartment in 15 major US cities," Business Insider, July 24, 2019, www.businessinsider.com/cost-of-one-bedroom-apartment-rent-major-us-cities-2019–6. Accessed November 13, 2019.

[3] Rachel Layne, "U.S. housing rents hit record-high average of $1,405 per month," CBS News, July 6, 2018, www.cbsnews.com/news/u-s-urban-rents-hit-all-time-high-at-average-1405-report

[4] "Can I get in trouble if my roommate sells drugs, does drugs or keeps drugs in the house for personal use?" Graham Donath Law Offices, December 23, 2016, www.gddlaw.com/2016/12/23/can-get-trouble-roommate-sells-drugs-drugs-keeps-drugs-house-personal-use. Accessed November 30, 2019.

[5] Ki Akhbari, "Accessory to a Crime," LegalMatch, March 5, 2018, https://www.legalmatch.com/law-library/article/accessory-to-a-felony.html. Accessed November 30, 2019.

[6] Lou Chibbaro Jr., "Study reveals LGBTQ rental housing discrimination," Washington Blade, July 3, 2017, www.washingtonblade.com/2017/07/03/LGBTQ-rental-housing-discrimination. Accessed December 10, 2019.

7 Movement Advancement Project, "Equality Maps: State Non-Discrimination Laws," n.d., www.LGBTQmap.org/equality-maps/non_discrimination_laws. Accessed December 10, 2019.

8 "Small Claims Cases," FindLaw, n.d., litigation.findlaw.com/going-to-court/small-claims-cases.html. Accessed December 1, 2019

Your First Day on the Job

There you are, on the first day of your first full-time job. The human resources department has you fill out form after form that you've never seen before, from employment contracts and confidentiality agreements to tax forms and your selection of healthcare options and retirement plans. You feel stupid asking too many questions—and when you do, the human resource administrator probably just tells you that the company requires them as a condition of your employment and/or that he/she is not allowed to guide you on how to fill them out.

In the worst-case scenario, the HR department will not release you to start your job until you finish filling out the forms, and your new boss is expecting you at a particular time for a meeting. In that case, you could be left simply guessing at the best answers—even though any one of several mistakes could cost you a thousand dollars or more in just your first year on the job.

This chapter looks at the typical (and some not so typical) decisions new employees are usually asked to make when they arrive at a new job and begin filling out those endless forms. It's designed to help you know what the right choices are in advance, so you won't be forced into just making guesses in the heat of the moment.

The forms generally fall into in four categories: those required by the government, those that enable the company to administer itself, confidentiality and noncompete forms, and selections around your employee benefits.

GOVERNMENT FORMS

• • •

Your federal, state, and local governments have a critical interest in ensuring that you have the legal right to work in their jurisdiction and that you will pay any taxes you owe. Therefore, all employers will require you to fill out several government forms before you begin work.

You almost certainly have a Social Security Number (SSN) already, but if you don't, you will be required to apply for one right away (usually in person at a Social Security Administration office) by filling out Form SS-5. When doing so, you must provide at least two documents to prove your age, identity, and either your U.S. citizenship or your right to work as a non-citizen via your current, lawful, work-authorized immigration status.[1] Your card with your SSN should arrive in about two weeks.

With your SSN in hand, the first government form you are required to fill out is Form I-9. It is required by the U.S. Customs and Immigration Service to attest you are either a U.S. citizen or that you otherwise have legal permission to hold a job in the U.S. The form is mostly filled out by the employer, but you must present to the employer certain form(s) of documentation, comprised of *either*:

- A U.S. passport (or a foreign passport that contains a visa permitting you to work); or

- Two other forms of identification comprised of (1) a valid U.S. driver's license or other government- or school-issued ID card containing your photograph, or a Canadian driver's license, *and* (2) a social security card, U.S. birth certificate, U.S. citizen ID card, or other government authorization for you to work in this country.[2]

Of note, if you don't have the required ID with you on your first day of employment, you can still legally work that day, as the company has up to three days to complete the Form I-9.[3] However, your company may not allow you to work until you have provided all the necessary ID, as matter of its own policy.

The next form is a W-4. This form comes from the Internal Revenue Service (IRS), and it discloses to the employer how much federal income tax you want withheld from your earnings each payday.

- By way of explanation, you officially pay your income taxes once a year, when you fill out an annual tax form—the dreaded Form 1040, or its equivalent—and submit it by April 15 of the year following the one for which you are paying taxes.

- However, to ensure that people will not fail to pay their income taxes in the necessary amount when they come due, the government demands to collect most of the taxes you will eventually owe in advance, at the time you actually receive your income. Specifically, the government requires you to pay 80% or more of the taxes you will eventually owe earlier than fifteen days from the end of the year in which you earned the income. (Otherwise, you may be fined.)

- To accomplish this, employees specify how much tax should be withheld from each paycheck and turned over to the government at approximately the same time the employee receives his/her paycheck. When the employee eventually fills out his/her tax return (prior to the following April 15), he/she then reconciles what has been withheld against what he/she actually owes, and either makes a final payment or receives a refund.

- Why might different employees want different amounts withheld, even if they earn the same salaries? Why is there not a single, unchangeable amount that is withheld from everyone who makes $50,000 a year and a different amount withheld from everyone who makes $75,000 a year? The answer is *deductions*. There are some expenses (such as mortgage interest payments, real estate taxes, charitable contributions, and certain taxes paid to state governments) that the government allows taxpayers to deduct from their *gross income* before they calculate how much income tax they owe; then, taxpayers pays taxes only on the reduced amount, called the *adjusted gross income*. If two taxpayers with the same salary have different deductions, they can owe different amounts of income tax.

- A long time ago, taxpayers who even had a small amount of deductions would spend hours filling out tax forms to save a little money. The government then decided to make life for most taxpayers easier. It created the *standard deduction*, which essentially says, "In 2019, if you are single and your deductions total less than $12,200, or if you are married and your joint deductions total less than $24,400, don't bother with the details. Just claim the standard deduction and be done with it. We don't care if the real amount would have been less." Of course, if all of a given taxpayer's deductions would add up to more than the standard deduction, the taxpayer can claim the higher benefit, but he/she must go through the paperwork to *itemize their deductions*.

Okay, back to the Form W-4. Because individuals might ultimately owe different taxes, the government allows each taxpayer to individually determine how much tax should be withheld from each paycheck. This is done through Form W-4, which you can download from the internet[4] before your first day on the job in order to take as much time as you would like to review it in as much detail as you would like.

During your first year out of college, you will probably have only one job, you will probably not make much money from investments, and you will probably not have enough deductions to make it worth itemizing. You will likely use the standard deduction—and that makes filling out your Form W-4 easy. Section 1 is just name and address stuff. You get to skip Section 2. For Section 3, you probably don't have dependents yet, and if you don't then the resulting entry is simply zero. And you can skip Step 4 altogether, because you will be using the standard deduction. You are done!

However, if you anticipate you will have sufficient deductions to justify itemizing deductions, you can adjust your withholding to accommodate this via Section 4, line (b). And if you own property (such as rental housing) or you inherited stocks and bonds from a relative, you might have other income that must be taxed as well—again, throughout the year. You can make tax payments on these other sources of income through *quarterly estimated tax payments*, or you can withhold extra money from your paycheck to cover the taxes owed on these other sources of income. You do that by filling in Step 4, question (c) of the Form W-4 with the additional amount you want withheld from each paycheck. In both cases, it is better to calculate the changes in withholding you want to make before showing up at work the first day.

Importantly, you are permitted to file a new Form W-4 form whenever you feel the need. So, if your situation changes, and you decide to itemize deductions or you suddenly come into an extra source of income, you can change your Form W-4 immediately. There appear to be no limits on how often you can change it (subject only to the irritation of the HR people in your company), and you do not have to provide a reason for filing a new Form W-4.[5]

The final set of government forms to be completed on your first day are very similar to the federal Form W-4, but they are required by your state and local governments if those entities also impose income taxes, which 43 states and many localities do.[6]

JUST SO YOU KNOW
A Note About Income Tax Withholding

As you've undoubtedly experienced already at certain points in your life, sometimes things in the "real world" don't go as smoothly as they should, and sometimes people don't behave in ways that conform to societal norms. Throughout this book I will occasionally insert sidebars like this one, using the headline "Just So You Know," to make you aware of such situations and the behaviors you may encounter when facing them. This information should not be mistaken (and cannot be construed) as constituting a recommendation for how you should behave—it is included only because I believe it is in your best interest to be fully informed.

Let's start with a fairly common "real world" situation: income tax withholding, where some taxpayers take a rather unconventional approach:

- Notice that your final "true up" of income taxes for a particular year (e.g., 2020) does not occur until four months after the year is over (i.e., in April 2021).

- If taxes are withheld from your pay on January 31, 2020, then the government holds onto that money for nearly fifteen months longer than if you were to withhold no taxes during the year and then pay all your taxes at the last minute on April 15, 2021, and even in a less extreme case, a full eleven months longer than if you were to withhold no taxes during the year and then pay all your taxes at the end of the 2020 tax year on December 31, 2020.

- Therefore, at the beginning of each new year, some people deliberately claim more deductions than they will really have (using Step 4, line [b] on Form W-4), thereby deliberately under-withholding for their taxes throughout the year. Then, they file a new W-4 prior to their December paychecks that withholds an amount equal to the whole year's missing tax payments. This enables them to effectively borrow money from the government for the interim months, without paying any interest.

- This approach involves some risk—such as miscalculating, or not being able to afford the dramatic decrease in your take-home pay that you would experience in December—so I do not recommend this at this stage of your life.

- However, you should know that the approach exists, and it is utilized to varying degrees by many taxpayers.

ROUTINE COMPANY ADMINISTRATIVE FORMS

• • •

There are likely to be a handful of forms your company will ask you to fill out that simply facilitate the day-to-day administration of the company.

DIRECT DEPOSIT FORM

82% of all employees in the U.S. currently elect to have their pay deposited directly into a bank account rather than receive a physical check. The form will ask you for your name and employee number, your bank's name and its ABA routing number (which you can obtain from the bank ahead of time if you do not already know how to find it), the type of account (e.g., checking or savings), and your specific bank account number.

EMERGENCY CONTACT FORM

This usually contains information regarding two to three relatives or close friends. It typically asks for their name, relationship to you, physical address, home and work phone numbers, and potentially email address and mobile number.

EMPLOYEE HANDBOOK ACKNOWLEDGMENT FORM

The Employee Handbook usually contains a list of company policies, especially any that you can be fired for violating (e.g., no stealing from the company) along with a list of contacts for such matters as HR administration and confidential reporting of bad behavior by your coworkers (such as sexual harassment). The purpose of the acknowledgment form is to prevent you from claiming you were not aware of the policies or did not have access to a channel of communication.

COMPANY POLICY ACKNOWLEDGEMENT FORM

Sometimes you will be asked to sign a copy of a specific company policy (such as a sexual harassment policy). If so, read it carefully. Asking for your signature is potentially a red flag that something has transpired in the company at some point in the past that has caused its attorneys to ask that particular precautions be taken. Unless the policy asks you to commit to something that is uncomfortable to you, it's probably okay to sign the form—just know there will be a particular sensitivity on the part of the company regarding any perceived transgressions in this area.

UNION MEMBERSHIP FORM

Depending on the company and the specific job you are starting, you may be asked to join a union, which may involve signing a form. As with the other forms, read it carefully in case there are any unusual provisions that might make you uncomfortable.

CONFIDENTIALITY AND NON-COMPETE AGREEMENTS

• • •

Some employers, particularly in high-tech industries, feel the need to restrict the potential outflow of information from their companies when employees leave. These companies often require new employees to sign contracts as a condition of employment. The employer, if it is acting ethically, should inform you ahead of time that they require such agreements, and they should be willing to share a copy of the contract before you commit to joining that company. There are three major categories of such agreements, and you may be asked to sign all three.

INTELLECTUAL PROPERTY AGREEMENTS

These agreements stipulate that anything you invent or create while you are employed by the company belongs to the company.

- At one end of the spectrum, these can be perfectly reasonable. After all, if you are being paid to conduct experiments or invent new things or design artwork (such as patterns for clothing), then your work product is the result of the deal you made with the employer—"You pay me, and I will create for you."

- At the other end of the spectrum are agreements that claim any creative thought you have, whether or not it is directly connected with the content of your job, belongs to the company. For example, if you were a customer service representative for a telephone company, and you developed a cartoon character that everyone seems to like and want to use, it is hardly fair for the company to claim ownership. Beware of such agreements.

- If at all possible, read the agreement and make sure you are comfortable with its scope before you arrive for your first day on the job. Also, to the degree that you have already invented things or have creative concepts that you have committed to paper, add a clause or addendum to the agreement that specifically excludes these from being covered.

JUST SO YOU KNOW
You May or May Not Need to Worry About
That Intellectual Property Agreement

It is very hard for a company to prove when a former employee created something, if the creation does not show up in the real world for some time after the person's employment terminated. Most companies do not even try. Therefore, if you are employed outside of the high-tech or entertainment industries, if your job specification did not include invention or creation duties, and if your invention or creation does not relate directly to the job you held or the product(s) of the company you worked for, you probably have little to fear from an Intellectual Property Agreement. However, each time your response regarding one of those "ifs" is "Well, actually...," you should be more concerned.

CONFIDENTIALITY AND NON-DISCLOSURE AGREEMENTS

These agreements, when used in an employment context, require you to not disclose specific sets of information to any third party for a specified period of time.

- There are usually two exclusions to this rule: (1) if the information becomes public through no fault of yours or (2) if a court orders you to disclose the information.

- To see whether the specific form your employer wants you to sign is fair, look carefully at the scope of the information that is considered confidential and non-disclosable. If the scope is limited to information that clearly pertains to the company being able to compete more effectively, then the agreement is probably reasonable. However, if the scope extends into any personnel matters or settlements of grievances against the company (such as for work-related injuries or sexual harassment claims), then you should be suspicious and perhaps even discuss the agreement with an attorney before signing.

NON-COMPETE AGREEMENTS

Sometimes a company believes (rightly or wrongly) that your work for the company trains you in the industry, making you more valuable, and that another company can then gain a competitive advantage by unfairly luring you away with more money. At other times, it might believe that if you join another company in the same industry, you cannot help but use the information learned while working for it to help your new company succeed against your former company. In both cases, the company would want you to sign a non-compete agreement. In such a contract, you agree to not work for another company (either specified by name or any company within the same industry within some specified geographic zone) for a specific length of time, regardless of why you leave the company.

- Regardless of the reason for the agreement (or its reasonableness from the company's standpoint), you should understand that such an agreement always has the effect of lowering your earnings potential. It can stop others in the industry from approaching you with a better job offer. It can place you on the do-not-call list for executive search firms. It can force you to choose between having to move a long distance to obtain a better job in your chosen industry or having to leave your chosen industry if you don't want to, or cannot, move.

- Therefore, you should avoid such contracts if you can, and if not, you should actively negotiate to narrow the industry definition, the geographic definition, the forbidden job specifications definition, and the time limits associated with any agreement you feel compelled to sign.

- The law can help you in some circumstances. While the majority of states recognize and enforce various forms of non-compete agreements, a few states (such as California, Montana, North Dakota, and Oklahoma) forbid them for employees. Moreover, should you end up in a fight with a former employer, most states dislike these agreements and tend to interpret them in favor of the employee, because the employee has the weaker bargaining position at the time he/she joins a company, and courts do not want to take away an employee's livelihood.[7] Most states will only enforce such agreements if the actual agreement is considered reasonable, where being reasonable is judged by whether the restriction is no greater than necessary to protect the company's legitimate business interests.[8]

- Further, if you can show the company breached its contract with you (such as not paying salary or benefits to which you were entitled) or fired you for a reason that is unfair, then you can potentially get out of the non-compete agreement.[9]

JUST SO YOU KNOW
The Primary Strategy Behind Non-Compete Agreements

While I believe everything we just told you about non-compete agreements is correct, the information above omits the primary strategy on the part of your employer. Your non-compete agreement is not really aimed at you—it is primarily intended to discourage other companies from talking to you.

If you are a low-level employee, it is rare for an employer to actually go through the litigation necessary to enforce a non-compete agreement, as you are unlikely to have enough money in your savings for it to be worthwhile for the company to sue you. Rather, the company hopes it can intimidate other companies by the implied threat that they will also be the target of lawsuits if they aid and abet you in violating your agreement.

If you disclose to a potential employer that your employment with them may violate a non-compete agreement, the intimidation may very well work. And the alternative of lying about whether you are covered by one is quite problematic from several standpoints.

Therefore, your best defense against such agreements is to limit their scope in the first place.

EMPLOYEE BENEFITS FORMS
. . .

These are the forms that can help you or cost you over a thousand dollars if you make the wrong choices. Almost every company offers three categories of employee benefits that require you to make decisions:

(1) retirement plans, (2) healthcare insurance, and (3) life and disability insurance. In addition, these three categories often require you to pay at least portion of the cost of providing the benefit. Let's examine each of the three categories to help you make the wisest choices. (By the way, there are many other employee benefits your employer may provide, such as vacations, public holidays, and paid sick leave, that do not involve first-day-on-the-job decisions and in most cases are straightforward enough that I will not address them here.)

RETIREMENT PLANS

A retirement plan is an arrangement under which an employer manages a system in which money is set aside (either by the employer, the employee, or both) during the years an employee works at the company, for the purpose of providing an income to the employee after he/she retires from working full time. These plans are completely separate from Social Security, which is a government program that requires employees to make payments into the program (in the form of separate taxes) while they are working, and then provides income to those people when they retire. In total, a person's retirement is often supported by a retirement plan, Social Security payments, and whatever other savings or investments he/she has at the time of retirement.

Most large- and medium-sized U.S. companies offer some form of retirement plan, while most small employers do not. This is reflected in the fact that only about 14% of all U.S. companies offer retirement plans, but 79% of all employees in the U.S. work for companies that offer such plans.[10]

Retirement plans come in two forms: (1) defined benefit plans and (2) defined contribution plans.

In *defined benefit* plans, the employer promises the employee that the employee will be entitled to a certain monthly payment every month after he/she retires until he/she dies. We will not explore these plans here, because they are becoming quite rare—only 16% of Fortune 500 companies (i.e., the five hundred largest companies in the United States) still offered such plans to new employees as of 2017, down from 59% in 1998,[11] and even smaller percentages of smaller companies offer them. They are becoming rare because the company bears the financial risk associated with the guaranteed payments to retirees, and that can be quite a burden if the company shrinks and the smaller company has to continue covering the retirement payments associated with the formerly-larger company.

The second form of retirement plans, *defined contribution* plans, are the dominant form of retirement plans in the United States—there are more than 650,000 such plans, covering over 100 million people.[12] The most common form of defined contribution plan is the so-called *401(k) plan*, which is the type of plan typically offered by for-profit companies. Another very similar type of plan, called a 403(b), is the type of plan typically offered by schools and other certain kinds of nonprofit institutions. The vast majority of the 79% of U.S. employees referred to above are covered by these types of plans.

The defining characteristic of defined contribution plans is that the employee or employer (or both) contribute specified monies into the plan. Those monies are invested into any of a large number of potential types of investments, according to the direction of the employee (see Chapter 7 for a fuller explanation of this feature), However, the employee, not the employer, bears the risks and rewards of those investments. Thus, only the front end (i.e., the ingoing the contribution) is defined. The back end (how much you will have at retirement) is undefined.

Here is the most important choice about your participation in a 401(k) plan (or 403(b) plan if that is what is offered in your case): *It is imperative that you choose to participate.* That may sound obvious, but when employees are given the option of participating or not (as opposed to being automatically enrolled by their employer), a surprisingly large portion—some 60%—do not participate.[13]

Why is it so imperative? There are two reasons:

- First, you need to save for retirement, and as I explain in Chapter 6, saving through a 401(k) program can result in your having 40% more money at retirement than saving the same amount from your take-home pay.

- Second, not participating often means you are rejecting free money! 51% of employers who offer 401(k) plans to their employees match at least a portion of the employee's contributions to his/her 401(k) plan. The formulas they use vary (e.g., dollar-for-dollar, up to 6% of the employee's salary, or 50% of the first $1,000 contributed). The median company matches 3% of the employee's salary to the employee's contribution.[14]

How big a deal is this? Well, if you make $51,000 (the median starting salary for new college graduates in 2019[15]), then 3% is $1,530. Moreover, if that $1,530 stays in your retirement account until age 65 and earns a historical average rate of return, it could be worth $28,060 at that time. And that is what you would give up for *every year* that you do not participate! (See Chapter 6 for details.)

Any matching by the company represents free money to you because (1) it is money the employer will not pay you if you do not participate, (2) any contribution is not taxed until you start to make withdrawals from the 401(k) after retirement, and (3) as I describe in Chapter 6, every dollar you save in your early twenties can become $18 by the time you retire.

When you sign up for a 401(k), you will be asked how much you want to save from every paycheck (either in dollar terms or as a percentage of your salary). You can usually also specify whether you want the same amount or a different amount taken from any commissions or bonus payments. And in most plans, you can change these rules throughout the year. How much should you save? That topic is addressed in Chapters 6 and 7. The next decision you will be asked to make concerns how the money in your 401(k) account should be invested, and that, too, is addressed in Chapters 6 and 7.

HEALTHCARE
Until this point in your life, you have probably been included on your parents' health plan or taken care of by your college's health service. Now that you have a job, you will be independent, and for the first time you must make your own choices.

Under the Affordable Care Act (a federal law), all employers with more than fifty employees are required to provide healthcare coverage to all full-time employees.[16] As of the writing of this book, that requirement is still in place, although there have been multiple legislative and litigative attempts to eliminate it.

Further, it is estimated that at least 50% of firms under fifty employees also provide health plans.[17]

Therefore, it is highly likely your new employer will offer health plans. However, they usually offer a variety of plans, and you must choose which one is best for you. Further, almost all health plans require the employee to bear a large portion of the total cost. On average, that will be 29% of the total cost. Even for an employee who is single, the annual out-of-pocket cost averaged over $2,000 in 2019.[18] Given the amounts at stake and the high consequences of wrong choices (such as having inadequate coverage, paying more for coverage by out-of-network doctors, or having funds in a healthcare savings account that are stranded at the end of a year), it is worth your time and effort to make the best choices for yourself.

To understand how healthcare plans function, and therefore which one would be best for you, you must understand the idea of healthcare networks, at least in simplified form. Here are the basics:

- Years ago, almost every doctor (or small group of doctors) was entirely independent of each other and independent of the health insurance companies. A patient would visit the doctor, and then submit a claim (or a receipt) to the insurance company, who would pay the doctor (or reimburse the patient) for that particular visit at whatever rate the doctor charged (so long as it was not outrageous).

- Every doctor (or group of doctors) was forced to seek patients, and some doctors might be very busy while others did not have enough work. Or, a single doctor might be too busy at times and not busy enough at other times. So, health insurance companies invented the idea of managed care, which basically used analytics to smooth out the system, save money, and thereby enable them to reduce rates. In effect, they said to thousands of doctors, "We will guarantee to send you at least X number of patients each month, but in return you will give us a discount of Y% from your normal prices." Those doctors who agreed were then in the health insurance company's network of doctors. Now, for the most part, the doctors were not forced to grant that particular insurance company exclusive access to their services, because doctors could be in multiple networks, but soon there were more networks than any one doctor or practice could handle. So, every doctor or group of doctors were in some networks but not others.

- On the insurance company side, the statisticians went a step further than just negotiating discounts for bundles of individual services from doctors. They learned to statistically predict the numbers of each kind of procedure that a large population of people would need (in aggregate). That allowed them to better match supply and demand and therefore save money and reduce prices even further, but only if the population would choose to have all (or close to all) of the predicted procedures performed by the doctors who were in their network.

- The result was the creation of three main types of health insurance products on the market today, with a few variations on each major theme:

  » There is the old-fashioned indemnity plan. It allows you (the insured) to go to any doctor you want at any time. It is quite expensive and typically offered only in very high-paying professions.

  » There are the preferred provider organization (PPO) plans. These allow you to choose doctors who are either in the network or not, but if you choose to go to a doctor who is out-of-network, you will pay a much higher portion of the costs (referred to as your copay) than if you had chosen a doctor who was in-network.

  » Then there is the health maintenance organization (HMO), which tends to be less costly than a PPO. Here, you must use an in-network doctor (unless it is an emergency), or the HMO will not cover any of the cost of the doctor. In addition, in an HMO, unlike a PPO, in most cases, you must get a referral from one of the HMO's doctors before you can see a specialist or have a procedure (such as surgery) performed. This is called *pre-authorization*. It is designed to prevent supposedly unnecessary procedures or visits to expensive specialists when such expertise is not really required. This, of course, lowers the demand for such expensive resources, and results in lower costs and smaller health insurance premiums. However, it is often the source of frustration on the part of the people being insured, because there can be strong disagreements about whether a specialist is needed or whether a procedure is a good idea.

So, what are the steps to wisely choosing your healthcare plan?

STEP 1: Decide who you want to have covered by your plan.

- Is it just you, because you are single? Or just you, because your spouse has coverage through his/her employer?

- Or, do you need coverage for an entire family?

STEP 2: Decide whether you care (and if so, how strongly) about having access to specific doctors, and therefore whether you prefer a PPO or an HMO.

- If you are new to a city and you don't know any doctors, you may not care. In this case, an HMO could save you money, because you don't mind being restricted to a specific list of doctors.

- However, if you already have doctor relationships that are important to you, then you will need to see which networks they belong to and use that information to decide which options to consider.

- If all your doctors belong to one insurance company's network, and you do not use specialists very often, you might favor that company's HMO (because it will be the least expensive option). If, on the other hand, some of your doctors are in certain networks but not others, while other of your doctors are in the opposite network, or if you use a lot of specialists (and therefore do not want to go through the hassle of getting a referral every time), you will most likely want to look exclusively at PPO options (but decide which insurance company to choose based on the details of which one includes more of your doctors, so that fewer will be out of network).

STEP 3: Decide whether you want a standard plan or a high-deductible health plan (HDHP).

- Despite the fact that you must pay monthly premiums for both HMOs and PPOs, both of these plans force you to pay a certain amount out of your own pocket (called a deductible) for doctors and prescriptions each year before their coverage steps in. (By the way, even after coverage steps in, it does not cover all the costs of a visit or a prescription drug. You must pay part of each transaction. That is referred to as your copay. We will discuss it below.)

- Both HMOs and PPOs come in two flavors: a standard plan and a HDHP. They are exactly what they sound like. Between them, they offer you a tradeoff.

- On one hand, you will pay lower monthly premiums under the HDHP, but you have to cover more doctor visits before the coverage starts. So, if you are the type who never gets sick and therefore does not visit doctors very often or use very many expensive prescriptions, the savings on the monthly premiums may more than offset the extra cost of not being reimbursed for as many doctor visits (because you won't have those visits).

- On the other hand, if you visit doctors often, you may welcome the coverage starting after the lower deductible, in which case you would prefer a standard plan.

- Therefore, estimate how many doctor visits you will make, how many prescriptions you will need, and calculate the costs under both a standard plan and an HDHP. It will probably be obvious which you should choose.

STEP 4: Decide whether you are interested in a Healthcare Savings Account (HSA) or Healthcare Financial Savings Account (FSA).

- If you are leaning toward an HDHP (and only in that case, as HSAs and FSAs are not permitted unless you have an HDHP),[19] ask your company if it offers the option of either an HSA or Healthcare FSA. We will focus on the HSA first, and then touch on the differences with a Healthcare FSA.

- In an HSA, money is set aside each month into a savings account for medical expenses, including those expenses that come before your deductible is satisfied as well as copays once your deductible is satisfied. Happily, the money you put into the HSA is not subject to income tax. So, if your salary is $50,000, and you put $2,000 into an HSA, you will pay income tax on only $48,000 of income. Further, you do not pay income taxes when you use the money (as long as the medical expenses are qualified, which most are), so the amount escapes income tax permanently. Your employer can also make contributions to your HSA that are income-tax free.

» On the one level, HSAs are terrific, because they convert expenses that you would normally pay with after-tax earnings into expenses you pay with before-tax earnings. For someone making $50,000 a year, that can be the equivalent of a 22% discount. That said, there are two potential drawbacks to the HSA strategy. First, if you do not use all of your deposits into the HSA within the year, you do not get to withdraw them at the end of the year without paying taxes on them. To keep the tax benefit, the money must stay in and roll over to the next year. Second, there is quite often a gap between how much someone contributes to an HSA and the size of the deductible in an HDHP. If you get surprised by unexpected medical bills, you may have to come up with money to fund the gap from other sources, and end up paying out more in total than if you had chosen the standard plan to begin with.

» In general, though, if you believe an HDHP is the right choice for you, opening and funding an HSA is almost always better than having an HDHP without an HSA.

• As to a Healthcare FSA, the account is similar in many ways to an HSA. However, you cannot roll over any more than $500 from year to year. The rest is paid out and taxed each year. Further, whereas an HSA is your money and can be taken with you if you change employers, any money in an FSA reverts to the employer if you leave employment at that company.[20]

STEP 5: Compare plans across healthcare insurance companies based on key qualitative features.

• Now that you know the type of plan you want (e.g., a standard PPO plan), it is time to compare the various options. This can be very tedious.

• To begin, obtain the list of companies and plans that your employer allows. That alone may make the choice for you, if your employer offers only one alternative in your chosen plan type.

- If you have choices, narrow the list of health insurance companies you are willing to consider. If you care about your existing doctor relationships, remove any companies who consider all or most of your doctors to be out of their network.

- Next, remove any companies that have a bad reputation in your area for being difficult about referrals or preapprovals before comparing the remaining companies and plans.

STEP 6: Compare your remaining options based on a financial comparison, as follows:

- First, compare the plans' out-of-pocket maximums. These represent the worst-case scenario. What is the maximum you would have to pay out of your own pocket if your medical costs this year were huge? If you find that any of the plans leave you so vulnerable that you cannot tolerate the risk, eliminate them from consideration.

- Next, compare in-network copays versus deductibles. If one plan has a lower copay percentage for physician visits and prescriptions, while the other has a lower annual deductible, subtract the lower deductible from the higher one. Then, subtract the lower copay amount from the higher one. By dividing the difference in the deductible by the difference in the copay amounts, you can calculate how many visits or prescriptions it would take before the lower deductible/higher copay plan became more expensive than the higher deductible/lower copay plan. Obviously, if one plan had both a lower deductible and a lower copay, then that would be the less expensive plan.

- If you have no choice but to rely on out-of-network doctors, you can repeat the above calculations using weighted averages of the in-network copays and out-of-network copays, where the weightings are based on the portion of your doctor visits that would be with doctors who are out-of-network for each plan individually.

- Finally, perform a sanity check to ensure the plan that looks best so far does not have problematic copays for the remaining items, such as surgeries and hospitalizations.

- Notice that I am focusing this cost analysis on the normal, everyday expectations for medical needs, because the large majority of persons in their early twenties rarely require hospitalizations etc. If you believe there is a significant chance you might need more intensive care, then you should adjust your comparisons accordingly.

At this point, it is probably obvious that you will not be able to make a wise choice of healthcare plan while sitting in the HR office on your first day on the job. The right choice can take hours. In fact, many people spend hours on this subject every year, because you have to renew your choice of plan every year, and each plan seems to change its parameters every year.

Therefore, before your first day of work, find out whether the company (or more specifically the HR person or department) expects you to choose your healthcare benefit on your first day or whether they will allow you a few days to decide. If the former, insist that they forward you all of the information materials at least two weeks before your start date, so you can conduct the analysis, make your choices, and fill out the forms in advance. Don't worry, you won't be the first new-hire to make this request. In fact, anyone who joins this company from another company probably asks for the same materials in advance, because anyone who has ever been through this process even once knows better than to try figuring it out while sitting in the HR office.

LIFE AND DISABILITY INSURANCE
· · ·

Another benefit that many companies offer is various forms of insurance, either paid for by the company or available at rates that are cheaper than what you could get if you were to shop for a policy on the open market. Two are most important: life insurance and disability insurance.

- The majority of companies offer life insurance coverage. They usually pay for a certain basic level of coverage (e.g., equal to one or two years of your salary) and allow you to pay for additional coverage if you'd like to have more. The coverage is usually inexpensive. You should be aware of two points, though:

» First, the policies are almost always so-called term policies, meaning they only cover you while the premiums are being paid. That means if you leave your job, the coverage will likely stop at the end of the month in which you terminate—both the employer-paid coverage and the coverage you pay for—because there is suddenly no mechanism to deduct the premium from your salary. (There are certain cases in which the life insurance company may allow you to continue your coverage even after you leave the company, by paying all the premiums yourself directly to the life insurance company, but those cases are rare and may involve other issues such as paying a higher premium for the same coverage).

» Second, you may not need coverage beyond what the company pays for. Certainly, if you are married, and particularly if you have children, you need more coverage to protect their finances in the event of your death. But if you are single and do not have children, then you probably have no one whose needs would exceed the amount covered by the employer.

• The second category of insurance coverage is disability insurance. This insurance pays you a specified amount per month (e.g., a certain percentage of your regular salary, up to a certain limit per month) for short or long periods of time (potentially your entire life) if you are injured or become otherwise disabled (e.g., through disease) and cannot work. Many employers provide both short term disability coverage and long-term disability coverage, and many employers pay all or part of the premiums for such coverage—but even if you have to contribute part of the premium, this coverage is usually worthwhile. It is cheap, and if you ever need it, you will be really glad you have it.

» Of note, there are many variations from policy to policy in the rules around the coverage (e.g., what kinds of disabilities are covered? when do the payments start? how large are the payments?). You can look into these in as much detail as you want, but frankly, the HR professionals in your company have probably already spent a lot of time trying to make sure the coverage is good, so you can usually assume they have done their job well and accept whatever the coverage may be.

~

Every day, thousands of new employees blithely fill out the forms thrust in front of them by the human resources department of their new employer. Many do not realize the money they have at stake, money that is hidden in the details of administrative forms, retirement plans, and healthcare plans. Now, you do understand what's at stake, and you have several key tools to help you make wise choices.

ENDNOTES

[1] "Application for a Social Security Card," Social Security Administration, n.d., https://www.ssa.gov/forms/ss-5.pdf. Accessed December 22, 2019.

[2] "I-9, Employment Eligibility Verification," U.S. Citizenship and Immigration Services, n.d., https://www.uscis.gov/i-9. Accessed December 22, 2019.

[3] "Completing Section 2, Employment Review and Attestation," U.S. Citizenship and Immigration Services, n.d., www.uscis.gov/i-9-central/complete-correct-form-i-9/completing-section-2-employer-review-and-attestation. Accessed December 30, 2019.

[4] "W-4, Employee's Withholding Certificate, 2020," Internal Revenue Service, n.d., www.irs.gov/pub/irs-pdf/fw4.pdf. Accessed December 22, 2019.

[5] Rachel Blakely-Gray, "Can Employees Change W-4 Forms?" Payroll Blog: Payroll Training, Tips, and News, October 8, 2018, www.patriotsoftware.com/payroll/training/blog/can-employees-change-w-4-forms/. Accessed December 22, 2019.

[6] "State Income Tax," Wikipedia, November 27, 2019, en.wikipedia.org/wiki/State_income_tax. Accessed December 22, 2019.

[7] Catherine Pastrikos Kelly, "Non-Compete Agreements: What Every Company and Employee Should Know," American Bar Association, July 26, 2016, www.americanbar.org/groups/litigation/committees/business-torts-unfair-competition/practice/2016/noncompete-agreements. Accessed December 23, 2019.

[8] "Non-compete clause," Wikipedia, October 26, 2019, en.wikipedia.org/wiki/Non-compete_clause#United_States. Accessed December 23, 2019.

[9] Luke Arthur, "Is a Non-Compete Agreement Valid If You Are Fired?" Career Trend, August 14, 2019, careertrend.com/is-a-non-compete-agreement-valid-if-you-are-fired-13658490.html. Accessed December 23, 2019.

[10] Maurie Backman, "Does the Average American Have a 401(k)?" The Motley Fool, June 19, 2017, www.fool.com/retirement/2017/06/19/does-the-average-american-have-a-401k.aspx. Accessed December 22, 2019.

[11] Gabrielle Olya, "14 Companies That Still Offer Pensions," Yahoo Finance, June 6, 2019, finance.yahoo.com/news/14-companies-still-offer-pensions-100000381.html?guccounter=1&guce_referrer=aHR0cHM6Ly93d3cuZ29vZ2xlLmNvbS8&guce_referrer_sig=AQAAAL40EuxvVlDtg7sjRSeW0x8TiK111VThWjg_glyenIIwPvB8Fu-9wy781gArMIcbzF64dF9d38UT-FAgLKWKjywBVbkWRZkWZLJhSfkb7smBkpl05ZhvHgvwsmdA4XYXgFG4I7rjzUcPJJKIkUrJosptPRrtfrX2B87eTvtN5vg3h. Accessed December 22, 2019.

[12] "401(k) Fast Facts," American Benefits Councils, January 2019, www.americanbenefitscouncil.org/pub/e613e1b6-f57b-1368-c1fb-966598903769. Accessed December 22, 2019.

[13] Backman, "Does the Average American Have a 401(k)?" www.fool.com/retirement/2017/06/19/does-the-average-american-have-a-401k.aspx. Accessed December 22, 2019.

[14] G. E. Miller, "Does Your 401(k) Match Up Against the Averages?" 20Something Finance, August 13, 2019, 20somethingfinance.com/401k-match. Accessed December 22, 2019.

[15] Stephen Miller, "Average Starting Salary for Recent College Grads Hovers Near $51,000," SHRM, August 22, 2019, www.shrm.org/resourcesandtools/hr-topics/compensation/pages/average-starting-salary-for-recent-college-grads.aspx. Accessed December 23, 2019.

[16] Source: www.nolo.com/legal-encyclopedia/what-employers-healthcare-insurance-requirements-under-obamacare-2015.html Accessed December 23, 2019

[17] Stephen Fishman, "What Are Employers' Healthcare Insurance Requirements Under the Affordable Care Act?" Nolo, n.d., www.ehealthinsurance.com/resources/small-business/small-business-health-insurance-rules-in-2019. Accessed December 23, 2019.

[18] Anna Wilde Mathews, "Cost of Employer-Provided Health Coverage Passes $20,000 a Year," *Wall Street Journal*, September 25, 2019, https://www.wsj.com/articles/cost-of-employer-provided-health-coverage-passes-20–000-a-year-11569429000. Accessed December 23, 2019.

[19] "Publication 969 (2018), Health Savings Accounts and Other Tax-Favored Health Plans," Internal Revenue Service, n.d., www.irs.gov/publications/p969. Accessed December 30, 2019.

[20] Mayo Clinic Staff, "Healthy Lifestyle: Consumer Health," March 16, 2019, www.mayoclinic.org/healthy-lifestyle/consumer-health/in-depth/health-savings-accounts/art-20044058. Accessed December 22, 2019.

CHAPTER 4

Establishing and Living Within a Personal Budget

I n a recent poll reported in *USA Today*, only 53% of college students reported they were confident they could wisely handle their money.[1] It did not test what portion of that 53% were correct in this self-perception, but it is likely that the significant majority of recent college graduates (the other 47% plus maybe as much as a third of the 53%) need help in this regard.

At the risk of stating the obvious, the single key to handling your money is to keep expenses below your income. The only way to accomplish that is to (1) develop an accurate budget, (2) track your spending in real time so you know when to impose that discipline on yourself, and (3) have the discipline to stick within your budget.

While these points sound obvious, experience shows that most recent grads will falter on one or more of them without some guidance. This chapter will show you how to do all three successfully.

DEVELOPING AN ACCURATE BUDGET
• • •

It is difficult to get motivated to create a budget. No one thinks it's fun, and everyone has a queasy feeling that they don't know enough to make it usefully accurate. Many resort to having an "All Other" category that constitutes about a third of their entire budget.

However, there is a way to create a useful, accurate budget even from the first time you try. There are online programs that can help you do this, but I am going to describe how to create one on your own, because if you create one of your own, or just follow the logic I lay out, you will understand how all the pieces of your personal day-to-day finances work together.

It takes an afternoon. Further, it is much easier if you create your budget using an electronic spreadsheet such as Excel, so the computer will recalculate everything whenever you find some new fact or have to adjust some plan. However, even if you just use pencil and paper, you can master this.

THE BASIC IDEA

A budget is a cross between a forecast and a command. It begins with your income, and then subtracts your expenses. That results in you either having money left over or having a shortfall. Then, you apply any leftover money to pay down debts, place money into savings, or simply to increase your bank balance. If there is a shortfall, your bank balance goes down (and you don't have the money to reduce your debts or place money into savings). If the bank balance (as forecasted by your budget) goes down too far, you must either borrow money or make some tough decisions either to increase your income (e.g., via a second job) or reduce your expenses.

THE MECHANICS OF DEVELOPING A BUDGET

There are eight essential steps in developing a budget. I'll cover each one, some in more detail than others. Fair warning: some of the details will be tedious—but hang in there, because if you develop a good, thorough, practical, realistic budget, you'll set yourself up for a much more enjoyable, and much less stressful, existence.

STEP 1: Set up your template.

- In this step, you will create a template for conducting your calculations. Don't worry yet about filling in the amounts. That will come later.

- You will need to set up a matrix with one column for labels plus 12 columns (one each for the next 12 months). You need to budget out a full 12 months, because many first-time budgeters fail to set aside funds each month to cover seasonal items (e.g., Christmas shopping, or April 15 tax payments). Then, at the last minute, they don't have the money to cover these items, so they rely on credit card debt. As I will demonstrate in Chapter 5, that can be the equivalent of paying 50% extra for every item you buy.

- Your matrix will contain many rows. The rows are divided into six sections: Income, Monthly Expenses, Irregular Expenses, Debt Repayment, Cash in the Bank/Loans Outstanding, and finally After-Tax Savings. There will also be a few individual lines between some of the sections.

- In the Income section, create rows for Salary, Gifts and Other Income, as well as a row for Total Income, which totals the previous three rows.

- In the Monthly Expenses section, create a separate row for each category of expenses that you incur in most or all months. You should have a separate row for any expense that is regularly more than about 5% of the total. While you should tailor the list to your needs, here are some categories others have found useful: rent or mortgage, utilities, internet, cell phone, groceries, transportation (including gas expenses), insurance you must pay monthly (such as car insurance), clothing, subscriptions (including apps, TV, gym), eating out, entertainment, travel, pets, and miscellaneous. You will also need a monthly category for interest on your credit cards, as I will explain later (however, you will not need a category for credit card payments as part of your budget). Finally, you will need a category called Mystery Payments Made in Cash, to account for those items that drain your wallet but you cannot remember what they are. Build in a line for Total Monthly Expenses that you will use to sum up all the expenses in this section.

- In the Irregular Expenses section, set up separate lines for income tax payments, other tax payments (such as car registration), Christmas gifts (that you will purchase for others), any other large gifts you plan to purchase (e.g., birthday gifts for your loved ones), large one-time items (e.g., furniture, or a car), tuition or membership payments that come due regularly (e.g., quarterly, every six months, or annually), and vacations. There should not be a miscellaneous category in the Irregular Expenses section, because by definition every expense you put into this section is significant enough that you should account for it separately. Build in a line called Total Irregular Expenses that you will use to sum up all the expenses in this section.

- At this point in your template, build in a line and label it Monthly Profit or Loss. It will eventually be calculated from the above sections.

- In the Debt Repayment section, you should include balance reduction payments on credit cards (which I'll explain later), payments on student loans, and payments on other loans. Again, you will create a Total Debt Repayment line that sums up the various payments.

- Next comes a one-line section titled Contributions to After-Tax Savings. (Once you read about savings in Chapter 6, you may also choose to create subcategories for the four types of savings described in that chapter.)

- Add another one-line section for Additional Borrowings, in case you choose to (or are forced to) borrow money at any point in your budget.

- The Cash In The Bank/Loans Outstanding section has the following lines: Bank Balance at the Beginning of the Month, and Bank Balance at the End of the Month.

STEP 2: Gather the information that will inform your budget estimates around your expenses.

- If your living situation over the next 12 months will be similar to what it has been for the last few months, you can use historical information to develop the expense portions of your budget. If not, you will have to build a temporary budget based on some common percentages of income that I will provide you, and then rebuild a more accurate budget once you have a couple of months' experience in your new living situation.

- If your living situation is a continuation of the recent past:

  » Gather all the available information on what you have been spending in each expense category. You will need three months of statements for each credit card you have (including online accounts such as Apple Pay) and three months of statements from your bank accounts. Further, if your parents have been covering any of your expenses through direct payments from their accounts, you will need information on those expenditures as well.

  » Next, slot every dollar you spent over the past three months into a spending category. In some categories, there will be expenses every month. At other times you will discover a significant expense in only one month. You may need to create new categories if you find no obvious home for certain expenses, but be sure to account for every dollar you spent—the worst mistake you can make is to omit significant amounts of spending, because that will lead to you fooling yourself later into thinking you have a comprehensive budget in place, only to discover that you are unprepared for these additional expenses you will incur.

  » Specific line items from your credit card and specific checks or bill payments from your checking account (except for the above-mentioned payments of credit card bills) will be easy to allocate to various expense categories. More difficult will be payments made in cash. To account for cash payments, calculate the total amount of cash you withdrew from ATMs, etc. Then, unless you have built up a large reserve of cash in your wallet or purse, assume that you spent that entire amount. Take your best guess as to which categories you spent the cash on, but be sure the total of your guesses equals the amount of cash you withdrew.

  » Finally, note offline (i.e., not in any category in your budget) any payments you have made in the last three months from your checking account to credit card companies.

- If your living situation will be entirely new:

  » You will need to take educated guesses, and then revise the budget as time goes on. A number of websites provide approximate percentage breakdowns of how young adults spend their money. Here is one such breakdown: housing, 25%–35%; utilities, 5%–10%; food, 10%–15%; transportation, 10%–15%; health, 5%–10%; insurance (including auto, renters, and life), 10%–25%; personal, 10%–15%; recreation, 5%–10%; and savings/debt reduction, 10%–15%.[2]

STEP 3: Use the information in each category to make your initial estimates for future spending in each expense category for each of the next 12 months.

- The process will be relatively straightforward for most categories. Sometimes there will have been relatively constant spending in each of the three months. Sometimes there will have been different amounts spent each month, but it will be obvious you should average them. Sometimes there will have been spending you know will not repeat itself over the next 12 months (e.g., when you bought a bed). Sometimes there will have been spending that will repeat, but these expenditures will be unique to that particular month (e.g., a car registration payment), and you should simply reflect a similar amount in only that month over the next 12 months. This is also the best time to fill in initial estimates of similar month-specific expenses in the rest of the 12-month period (e.g., for Christmas gifts or a vacation).

STEP 4: Fill in your income categories for each of the next 12 months.

- Fill in rows for salary, commissions (if any), any large gifts you might receive (such as monetary support from your parents), and any miscellaneous income you predict you will have from side jobs or businesses.

- As to salary, if you have already started a job, you will likely already know how much pay you will have left over each month after your employer deducts for federal and state income taxes, social security, etc. You will also have decided on how much will be deducted for your 401(k) account. The remaining amount is known as your take-home pay, and that is the amount you should enter into the monthly columns. If you have a job lined up but have not started, brace yourself. The portion of the salary you are paid that actually finds itself as take-home pay is probably smaller than you imagine, even if you have previously received salary payments for summer jobs. There are various sources on the internet that can help you estimate what your actual take-home pay will be.

- Many recent college graduates accept jobs that consist of selling, which often pay commissions in one form or another. In this first budget, you will know the timing of such commission payments (e.g., monthly, quarterly, semiannually, or annually), but you will not know the amounts. I suggest you be very conservative in guessing what your commissions will be for the first year. Even if your employer has provided you with information on what the average person makes in commission during his/her first year, I suggest you budget based on only a fraction of that average (e.g., one-half to two-thirds). When it comes to finances, it is always better to receive a positive surprise at the end of the year than a negative one.

- As to gifts from your parents, if you will receive regular support payments, it is not impolite to inquire from your parents as to what payments you might expect. Simply explain you are trying to create a sustainable budget. They will not be offended—if anything, they will likely be pleased at your show of fiscal responsibility. However, do not push. Depending on their own financial situation, they may not know how much support they can give beyond the next month or two.

STEP 5: Fill in the Debt Repayments section (except your credit card balances).

- You should be quite accurate with respect to the required payments for student loans and other fixed debts, such as an automobile loan. Do not estimate changes to your credit card balances. I will cover this subject in Step 7.

STEP 6: Logically connect the sections of the template categories as if you did not have any credit cards.

- Calculate the Monthly Profit or Loss by adding all your Income and subtracting Total Monthly Expenses and Irregular Expenses. That line shows you whether you improved your financial position during the month (i.e., had a profit) or made it worse (i.e., had a loss).

- Next comes Debt Repayment. You already filled in these figures (except for the credit card line, of course).

- Leave the Contributions to After-Tax Savings and Additional Borrowings lines blank for the moment.

- Finally, you will connect the section called Cash in the Bank/Loans Outstanding. This section explains where you put the money you made or where you either drew down your bank account or borrowed money to make up for the loss you incurred.

- The section starts with the line labeled as Beginning Bank Balance. In the first month, enter the figure that is your actual bank balance today. Then connect the Ending Bank Balance line by starting with the Beginning Bank Balance Line, subtracting the Total Debt Repayment line, subtracting the Contributions to After-Tax Savings line, and adding the Additional Borrowings line.

- Finally, for every month *after* the first month, program the Beginning Bank Balance to equal the prior month's Ending Bank Balance.

- At this point, pause a moment to review your work and review the numbers. You should be able to see how your financial picture works. Just as I promised at the outset of this chapter, it starts with your income, and then subtracts your expenses. That results in you having money left over or having a shortfall. Then you can see the leftover money being applied to pay down debts, go into savings, or result in a larger bank balance. If it results in a shortfall, you can see your bank balance go down. If the bank balance goes down too far, the only ways to bring it back are either to borrow money or to adjust the income and expense items above. That is budgeting!

STEP 7: Conduct the credit card calculations.

- Credit cards make budgeting more complicated because they combine (1) a method (other than your checking account) to *temporarily* pay for expenses with (2) a very flexible loan mechanism in which your loan balance can go up, stay the same, or decrease each month, based on your personal choices. This combination can disguise your finances and make it appear that your budget is in balance when it is not.

- Let's use an example to show how money flows through a credit card account (and how it shows up in the budget), and then we will discuss how to budget when you make use of credit cards:

  » Let's say that on March 1, Krista has $2,000 in her checking account and a $1,000 balance on her credit card. During the month, she uses the credit card to purchase groceries that cost $500. On March 25, she receives a statement from her credit card company with the following information: (1) she has purchased $500 worth of items, (2) she has been charged $15.83 interest, (3) her new balance is $1,515.83, and (4) her minimum payment is $75.79.

  » Let's assume Krista makes a payment of $400 on the credit card before the end of March. Note that the credit card company will apply $15.83 to interest and $384.17 (i.e., the $400 payment minus the $15.83 interest) towards her balance, which would now become $1,131.66.

  » Here is what would happen to the various budget accounts:

    › Monthly Expenses: Groceries would be charged $500.

    › Monthly Expenses: Interest would be charged $15.83.

    › Additional Borrowings would occur in the amount of $131.66 (the net effect of charging $500 which increases the balance, incurring $15.83 interest, which also increases the balance, and making a $384.17 payment to the outstanding balance).

    › The net result of the above would be to reduce the Ending Bank Balance by $400 (the amount paid to the credit card company).

- So how do you budget for credit card–related items? First, you never enter into your budget (in one place) the entire payment you make to the credit card company. You will split the purchases (which you enter into the expense categories) from the interest the credit card company is charging you (which you enter into the Credit Card Interest line) from the *net payment* you are making toward reducing or increasing your debt balance. To make this clearer, here are the four possible situations:

  » If you have a zero balance and you intend to pay off your credit card balances every month, you can simply ignore the cards because the money to cover any purchases will flow out of your bank account (to the credit card company) each month. So, from a budgeting standpoint, it will look the same as if you paid for everything with a check.

  » If you have a balance but plan to pay off all the new purchases you make on the card each month, then in your budget model, you will again ignore the existence of the card with respect to these new expenses (groceries, cell phone, etc.) and treat them as if they are being paid by check. However, you will separately need to budget an amount (in the Credit Card Interest line) to cover the interest on your outstanding balance, again paying this amount with a check.

  » If you have a balance and intend to pay it down over the next year (recommended!), then in your budget models, account for reducing your debt by making an entry in the category Credit Card Balance Reductions.

  » If you intend to let your balances increase, you should treat all of your current expenses (including credit card interest payments) the same as they are in the preceding paragraph, but reflect the intended increase in your credit card balances each month in the Additional Borrowings line.

STEP 8: Go back and adjust your estimates.

- The first time you complete the spreadsheet, even after you have corrected all of the arithmetic and logic errors, you should expect your bank balances to go wildly negative. Everyone who is just starting their first full-time job or their first independent living experience has an unrealistic expectation about how far their money can stretch. They believe they can afford to spend whatever they want to and still be able to make their savings goals. That is when the hard part comes—namely, figuring out how to make everything balance.

TRACKING SPENDING IN REAL TIME
· · ·

No budget is worth the effort unless you also invest the effort to track how closely the reality of your finances resembles the budget. That is the only way to either (1) revise your budget to better match the realities of what you face in real life, and/or (2) change your spending habits so you can achieve the goals you laid out for yourself.

In truth, for the first few months after you create the budget, you will do both. You will find that life is legitimately different than you thought when you created the budget, so revisions are needed in your plan. But you will also find you must change your behavior patterns because you will never meet your financial goals of being self-sustaining if you do not learn to live within a revised budget.

The best way to track your spending on an everyday basis is to pay for everything you can through payment mechanisms that produce a consolidated record at the end of the month. For example, payments directly from your checking account (such as through online bill-paying services) show up in detail on your monthly checking account statement. So do purchases with debit cards. Physical checks show up on your bank statement but provide fewer details. Credit card purchases and Apple Pay accounts also produce records. The worst payment vehicle (in terms of tracking) is, of course, cash. For cash purchases, you need to note it (perhaps in your smartphone's Notes app). Each purchase over $20 needs to be recorded at the time, because you will most likely lose any receipts, and no one ever remembers at the end of the month that purchase they were sure they would remember back on the fourth of the month.

Then, once a month, it is time to collect the monthly statements and compare your actual results with the budget's forecast for that month. Create an identical template as you did for the budget and fill in actual results from your pay stub, your checking account statement (viewed online the same day as when you are conducting this tracking exercise), your credit card bills, etc. If you have captured all your spending, your ending bank balance should closely match the balance in your checking account that day. It will not match exactly, because there may be checks you have written (and therefore you include in your expenses) that have not yet made it to your bank yet. However, if the balance you show on this updated spreadsheet is vastly different from what your bank says you actually have in the account, you need to solve the mystery before you compare the updated spreadsheet to the budgeted one.

Compare the two on a line-by-line basis. Note where they deviate and whether the deviation is the result of something you cannot control (such as your take-home pay being different than you expected or your student loan payment being higher than you expected) or whether the deviation was the result of choices you made.

DISCIPLINING YOURSELF
TO STICK TO A BUDGET
• • •

Obviously, no amount of tracking helps if it is just an exercise in documenting undisciplined behavior. You must translate the lessons into practical steps. Here are six steps that some experts say can help.

STEP 1: Pay yourself the debt reduction and savings bills first.

- If you treat these as an obligation at the beginning of each month rather than as something you pay at the end of the month (and only if you have money left over), you will be more likely to succeed. Simply having less money hanging around for discretionary expenditures has the effect of reducing such expenditures.

- Should you save first or pay down debts first? Unless you can rely on your parents to provide you with a financial safety net, I recommend you first build up a safety net of savings (because in life you never know when something might go wrong). Then, I recommend allocating about 80% of this category to paying down debts—particularly credit card debts—while allocating the remaining 20% to savings. The reasoning is that the interest you pay out on debts far exceeds the likely earnings you can achieve on savings. How lopsided is it? Consider the following scenario:

» Let's assume you have a credit card balance of $1,000 and—due to some lucky event—you have a spare $1,000 in hand.

» If you invest the $1,000 in the stock market for a year and achieve the average gain, the $1,000 will grow to $1,070, minus income taxes of perhaps 22% for a net of $1,054.

» On the other hand, your credit card debt will have grown to $1,192 (assuming you were charged the average interest rate on new credit cards).

» Choosing saving over reducing debt therefore cost you $138 (i.e., $1,192 minus $1,054).

• Why don't I advocate putting 100% toward debt reduction? From a purely financial standpoint, I actually would advocate for that—but psychologically, most people find it too hard to never see their savings balance increase, and that leads them to abandon the practice of paying the savings/debt reduction bill at all.

STEP 2: Give yourself a weekly allowance for all the fun stuff.

• The problem with budgeting for a month can be that you feel rich during the first week or two, and you overspend on items such as entertainment, eating out, buying gifts, or buying toys for yourself. You tell yourself you will make up for it next week. Then, during the final week of the month, you have no funds…but you can't stand doing nothing nice for yourself, so you spend a little something. Sure enough, the combined spending over the month blows the budget.

• Avoid this scenario by taking all of the fun expense categories and breaking them into weekly budgets. Do not cheat! On average, there are 4.2 weeks in a month, not 4 weeks. Do not just divide the monthly budget by 4, or you'll wonder how you blew the budget when you were so disciplined.

STEP 3: Deliberately budget the necessities on the high end of their potential range.

- Many necessities consist of items that are not knowable in advance, such as utility bills, transportation expenses, and groceries. That means, when you are budgeting, you insert a specific dollar figure that represents an estimate.

- That's fine, but look at what you do next. You then plan to spend all the money you can afford (i.e., all the money that is left after you budget for the necessities and your debt reduction/savings) on the fun stuff. If the necessities come in higher than estimated, you blow the budget, even if you have been disciplined about staying in budget on the fun things.

- To avoid this, budget toward the top end of the potential range of expenditures for the necessities. That way, if they come in where you budgeted, you will still meet your goals. And if they come in lower, you can either reduce your debt even faster or you can afford a little extra celebration.

STEP 4: If you can't afford to buy something this month, don't go shopping for it.

- If you look for something, you will find it. And you will find some reason why it's better to buy it now instead of waiting until you can actually afford it.

- Worse yet, when cash is short, you will put it on a credit card. Not only will you have blown your budget, there is a very good chance you will have just paid a 50% premium for the item! (To see why this is true, see Chapter 7.)

STEP 5: Plan your meals and shop ahead.

- Eating out is more expensive than eating at home. If you run out of food at home or even if you just run out of your favorite foods at home, you will resort to eating out, and you'll tell yourself it's just this once until you can get to the grocery store. And just this one other time. And then…

STEP 6: Rid yourself of two common vices.

- No judgment here, just the cold, hard economic facts:
  - » If you smoke or vape, the expense is killing you financially even as the chemicals are killing you literally.
  - » And if you like mixed drinks when you go out in the evening, the expense is quietly draining your wallet.

∼

As we discussed at the outset of this chapter, no one enjoys budgeting—but make no mistake, no one enjoys the chaos that results when they get into financial trouble either. In 2016, the Federal Reserve asked a large sample of Americans how they would handle a $400 emergency. 47% said they would have to take out an emergency loan, or sell something, or that they simply would not be able to handle it at all.[3] You do not want to be among that 47%—and budgeting and discipline are your tools for avoiding that fate.

ENDNOTES

[1] Charisse Jones, "Many college students doubt they'll be able to pay off their student loans—ever," USA Today, May 29, 2019, www.usatoday.com/story/money/2019/05/29/college-students-fear-they-wont-able-pay-their-student-loans/1258761001. Accessed December 20, 2019.

[2] "Budget Basics: How to Stick to Your Budget," Every Dollar, n.d., www.everydollar.com/blog/steps-to-help-you-stick-to-your-budget. Accessed December 22, 2019.

[3] Neal Gabler, "The Secret Shame of Middle-Class Americans," The Atlantic, May 2016, www.theatlantic.com/magazine/archive/2016/05/my-secret-shame/476415. Accessed December 22, 2019.

PART II

Your First Year Out of College

CHAPTER 5

Establishing and Managing Your Credit

Seventy percent of college students graduate with student loan debts. In 2016, the average student loan debt upon graduation was $37,162. In addition, a 2019 poll found 36% of college students already carried credit card debt of more than $1,000 upon graduation. Most college students have at least some experience using a credit card that is associated with their parents' account.

But now you must manage credit on your own, and the consequences of good or bad management are far-reaching. For starters, the average 25-year-old has already accumulated $2,675 of credit card debt, which is on its way to becoming $4,216 by age 30.[1]

Relatedly, your credit rating affects your ability to borrow money and the interest rate you will be charged. It can raise the price you must pay for cell phones and insurance. It can affect whether a landlord will lease you an apartment. And nearly half of all employers run credit checks on job candidates, because they believe it reduces the likelihood of theft and embezzlement and helps prevent negligent hiring.

Clearly, this is not a subject that goes away if you ignore it. You almost certainly already have a credit rating, and if not, you will have one very soon.

Whether you know it or not, it's out there, in the background, helping or hurting you every day.

To manage your credit well, you need to understand:

- How to establish a track record so you can be said to have good credit
- Credit scores
- How to repair your credit score in 30 days
- Common credit traps to avoid
- Personal bankruptcy

The only major credit subject we will not discuss here is mortgages, which is discussed separately in Chapter 14.

ESTABLISHING A TRACK RECORD
· · ·

You will want to begin establishing a credit record as soon as possible if you have not already done so. But it can be frustrating, because of the chicken-and-egg problem. How can you build a record of behaving responsibly in handling credit, if no one will grant you credit until you already have a track record? There are a couple of ways:

- First, you can become an authorized user on someone else's credit card account. The activity then begins to build your credit record. Before you do this though, find out if that particular credit card company reports credit card usage for all authorized users. Otherwise, your activity will not have any impact.

- Second, even as a recent college graduate, you can usually obtain a starter credit card. For example, many companies issue so-called student credit cards, even while the cardholder is still in school. Their research tells them that people stay loyal to their first card, so their intent is to help you get started, and then raise your limit once you are employed. The credit limit starts off low, but it is enough to enable you to establish a pattern of reliably charging and paying, which drives your credit score (as described below). Another type of starter card is a so-called secure credit card. This card does not actually involve the issuer taking risk. Rather, the card requires you to deposit an amount that is equal to the credit limit on the card (e.g., a $500 deposit for $500 of credit). However, like the prior card type, this card enables you to establish a pattern of reliability.

Whichever way you obtain a card, use it to no more than 25% of the credit limit, and be sure to pay off the balance completely, each and every month, for at least the first few months. This will help you quickly build a track record of reliability.

Of note, one thing you should not do is take out a loan for the purpose of building your credit record. If you do not need the money, the interest payments make this approach more expensive than it is worth. Further, when your credit score is being calculated, installment loans (i.e., a typical form of loan) do not count as heavily as revolving credit (i.e., having a credit line you can draw on as you need it, as is the case of a credit card), so payments on installment loans have less effect on boosting your credit score per dollar of borrowing than simply taking out one of the above credit cards and paying them off each month.[2]

ALL ABOUT CREDIT SCORES
. . .

Once you have established a credit track record, companies make decisions about whether to grant you a loan based on a combination of two factors: (1) whether they believe you can afford to pay back the loan and (2) how reliable you are likely to be at making payments when you are supposed to. These are not the same thing—there are many people who are wealthy or have high incomes but who are simply not very reliable.

While each company is free to make its own determination as what it considers to be the most you can handle, many of them rely on an informal rule known as "28/36." It simply states that households should spend a maximum of 28% of their gross income on home-related expenses (i.e., rent or mortgage payments, homeowners insurance, property taxes, and condo or homeowners association fees) and a maximum of 36% on all debt and/or rent payments (i.e., housing expenses plus other debts, such as car loans and credit cards).[3] Companies often ask potential borrowers about their income and debts on the loan application. Otherwise, they can obtain the information by checking with the three major credit bureaus, also called credit-reporting agencies, which are companies that maintain this kind of data on most Americans, based on data supplied by most large financial institutions across the country. The three main credit-reporting agencies are Experian, Equifax, and TransUnion.

Your reliability is judged by your *credit score*, which is a number between 300 and 850 that is calculated using a variety of factors, again drawing on data from the credit-reporting agencies.

- Technically, you have two credit scores, because there are two vendors who calculate them for all the financial institutions, FICO and VantageScore. However, broadly speaking, these use similar algorithms, so the scores are close. Further, their interpretation of the meaning of a particular score is generally consistent. Here, I will describe the FICO system, which has been around longer.

  » In FICO, about 21% of people have a score between 800 and 850, and that is termed Exceptional. These people are at the top of the list for the best rates from lenders. (However, they must still meet the affordability tests I referred to in the previous paragraph, of course.)

  » About 25% receive a score between 740 and 799. These are termed Very Good and are likely to be granted better than average rates from lenders.

  » Another 21% are termed Good. They have scores between 670 and 739. They are considered average, and, in fact, about 8% of these people turn out to experience a serious delinquency at some point in the future.

  » Applicants with scores between 580 and 669 (17% of people) are termed Fair, but in fact they are considered sub-prime (i.e., less than average) borrowers, which means they will have a harder time getting credit and will likely have to pay higher interest rates.

» The final 16% of people are rated Very Poor. Note the categories jump directly from Fair to Very Poor, suggesting what the system really thinks of those rated Fair. These are persons who score between 300 and 579. They are likely to be declined, charged very high rates of interest or fees, or required to make security deposits before a loan will be granted.[4]

- While each company keeps secret the specific algorithms used to calculate its credit scores, the categories of factors that go into calculating the score, and the weights given to each factor, are well known:

  » The highest-weighted factor is your payment history (i.e., have you been reliable in the past?). This accounts for 35% of your score.

  » Next, weighted at 30%, is your credit utilization ratio, which is a measure of how much you have actually borrowed versus the maximum you have been authorized to borrow. Lenders are frightened of people who max out their credit cards. Lenders like people who utilize only about 25% of the credit lines they have available.

  » The third factor, weighted at 15%, is the length of your credit history. The longer the better. That is why the previous section of this chapter was necessary—you need to build up a strong early credit history to overcome a lender's bias against being the first to lend you money.

  » The final two factors, each weighted at 10%, are new credit and type of credit. These factors enable lenders to distinguish between whether the new application seems safe or an act of desperation—and whether you seem to have made a lot of applications to different institutions at the same time (which is, not surprisingly, a red flag for lenders).

- Now for the most interesting part. You would think that your credit score would be calculated periodically, and you are stuck with that score for some length of time until the score gets recalculated. Not true—here's what actually happens:

  » Your score is recalculated every time you apply for credit, or when a potential lender officially checks your credit (called a hard inquiry).

» On one hand, it allows lenders to factor in the impact of making multiple loan applications all over town.

» On the other hand, if you are *not* making multiple applications, it enables you to rapidly improve your credit score, because credit scores are calculated off your *current* credit record each time.

» Said another way, credit scores have no memory.[5]

• As your credit score builds over time, use it to switch your primary card or cards to new cards with lower interest rates (perhaps upgrading one card every six months—don't add several cards, and certainly don't add them too quickly, as that itself will hurt your credit score). Many preferred (and lower interest rate) cards allow you to transfer balances. By switching your balances to these cards, more of the same monthly payment you have been making will go toward reducing your balances, which will both save you money and lower that credit utilization ratio, thereby improving your credit score over time.

HOW TO IMPROVE
YOUR CREDIT SCORE IN 30 DAYS
• • •

If you are considering a loan application and have any concerns about what your credit score might be, there are ways to improve your score quite quickly. Begin by obtaining your credit score, as well as a copy of your full credit report, from each of the three major credit-reporting agencies (Experian, Equifax, and TransUnion). You are entitled by law to do this for free, once a year, at AnnualCreditReport.com.[6] Then, if you are not satisfied with your score, you can take any (or all) of the following steps to improve your situation:

• First, you can pay down any credit card lines that are utilized more than 25% (remember, utilization of revolving credit lines has the second largest impact on your credit score). People with scores above 780 typically use only 15% to 25% of their available lines, whereas people with scores around 680 typically use 40% to 50% of their lines.

Note, however, to restrict your paydowns to your credit card balances—you don't boost your credit score very much by paying down installment loans.

- Next, look at your full credit reports to see if there are any recent late payments reported on them. A single 30-day late payment can subtract 60 to 80 points from a mid-range credit score. If your payment was not actually late, call the creditor and ask to speak to the dispute resolution department. Or, to get a legitimate late payment removed from your report, ask the creditor for a *goodwill adjustment* (i.e., an adjustment in which they remove the item from the report just to make you happy, so that you will use their card more). They might well agree, particularly if you do not have a pattern of previous late payments. If they resist, you may be able to negotiate the removal in return for signing up for automatic payments.

- If there is an item on your report that shows you have an account in collection, you will definitely want to get that removed. However, don't just pay off the amount and stop there; a paid collection alone does not help your score! Rather, negotiate a *pay-for-delete agreement*. And be sure to get the agreement in writing. Only then should you make a payment, and you should still expect some administrative hassle in getting the item removed.

- Call the issuers of the credit cards where you have the best track record, and see if they can raise your credit limit through a "soft pull" of your credit. (You do not want a "hard pull," since this would appear in the scoring algorithm as if you were applying for credit across multiple lenders, as we discussed in the previous section.) If this succeeds, it will automatically lower your credit line utilization, as discussed above.

- Finally, if you have any unused credit cards, go buy something relatively small using those cards, and then immediately go online and pay off the balances before the monthly statement comes. The algorithm sees this as you behaving reliably, which adds to your score.[7]

Take these steps and, just one month later, you'll be ready to make your improved application for a loan.

COMMON CREDIT TRAPS TO AVOID

• • •

Most people find financial issues boring and confusing. They try to avoid thinking about the subject. While that is certainly understandable, it also affords companies an opportunity to exploit that inattention via some practices that may look as if they're consumer friendly but are actually designed to cost borrowers heavily.

TRAP 1: The Minimum Payment Trap

- Each month, your credit card statement shows the total amount you owe (i.e., the outstanding balance) as well as the minimum required monthly payment. Credit card companies use various methods to calculate the minimum required payment. Some of them place it in the range of a fixed 2% to 5% of the outstanding balance. Others take that number and add to it any fees that were charged that month. Still others take the interest that was charged for the month and add a fixed percentage of the outstanding balance (e.g., 1%) to the interest charges.[8]

- The trap is that the minimum required payment almost always results in the customer only paying off the balance over a very long period of time, thereby causing the customer to incur substantial interest charges.

- How bad can this be? Let's look at an outstanding balance of $1,000 on a credit card that carries an interest rate of 19.21% (the average rate charged on new credit cards in 2018):

  » If, under the first method outlined above, the credit card company sets the minimum at 5% of the outstanding balance, the customer will take about 13 years to pay down the balance to $10, and will have incurred over $466 in interest payments on top of the $1,000 balance.

  » If the credit card company only requires payments to equal 2% of the balance, after 30 years the customer will have paid over $3,800 in interest payments and still owe more than $200 on the card! (The other outcomes are similar).

- You, rather than the credit card company, should calculate how fast to pay down a balance. Make it as fast as you can, because credit card companies generally charge much higher rates than any other debt you will incur.

TRAP 2: The Zero Interest for Many Months Trap

- Many retailers of large items, such as furniture, offer a plan in which they promise you will pay no interest for some period (sometimes as long as sixty months) if you pay in full within the specified time period. That is accurate, and it's great *if you successfully pay off every dollar within the specified period.* However, if you fail to achieve that, even by a little, the whole debt can come back to haunt you. Specifically:

  » The interest is treated as *deferred,* not nonexistent, for that period.[9] So if you buy some furniture for $1,000 under a five-year deal where you pay $16.67 a month (i.e., $1,000 divided by 60 monthly payments), what is really happening in the background is that, the first month, the furniture company (or, in fact, its financial partner) is calculating the interest on $1,000.

  » These companies charge extremely high rates, close to 30% in many cases. So, one month of deferred interest would be $25. The next month, if you made your $16.67 payment the first month, you still owe a balance of $983.33, so they deferred another $24.58 of interest. And so on.

  » If you fail to meet the terms of the contract (i.e., fail by even a small amount to fully pay off the loan in time), they come back and charge you for all the deferred interest, which would be roughly $750.

- Do not sign up for this deal unless you are confident you can successfully see it all the way through. Then, pay off any remaining balance about three months before the last payment comes due, just to make sure there are no timing mistakes.

TRAP 3: The No Annual Fee (But Higher Interest Rate) Trap

- No one likes to pay an annual fee on a card. Therefore, many card companies approach existing customers (or even new ones, using patterns learned from the credit-reporting agencies) with the option of a different card, one that has no annual fee. It simply carries a higher interest rate.

- However, the customers the company approaches are not random customers. They have a history of carrying large balances on their cards. So, for example, in return for eliminating a $30 annual fee, the customer pays 5% more on a $3,000 balance, or $150 more in interest payments.

TRAP 4: The "Interest From Date-of-Purchase" Trap

- When you purchase items with a credit card that has a zero balance, you only owe the credit card company the cost of the actual items you've purchased. You do not owe any interest on the money you technically borrowed from the credit card company until (1) the credit card company sends you the bill and (2) you have used up the time period in which you have to pay the bill. This can be as long as two months, if you purchase the item the day after the credit card company has sent its most recent bill (because it doesn't bill you for another month, and then you have a month to pay the bill).

- However, as soon as you carry any balance, many credit cards begin to charge you interest on a particular purchase (which *it* thinks of as you borrowing more money) from the day you actually make the purchase. At 19.2% per year, two months of interest adds $32 of additional cost to every $1,000 you spend *before* you really have a chance to pay!

- It is much better to buy items on cards on which you are not already carrying a balance, which is one reason why you may want more than one credit card, so you can differentiate between items you will pay off each month and those you will pay off only over time.

TRAP 5: The Permanent Payday Lender Trap

- There may be an unusual occasion wherein you desperately need cash before your next paycheck, and under those circumstances, a payday loan may be necessary. However, if you fail to pay off the loan entirely with your first paycheck, you will be on your way to a very costly trap.

- Consider the following analogy:

  » You need to take a trip in a car. That trip is only one mile long. A taxi is a better choice than a rental car. It may charge you a $2.00 flag-drop fee, followed by a mileage rate of 20 cents per one-tenth of a mile. So, the trip costs you $4.00 rather than the $50-per-day cost of a rental car. But what if the trip were 250 miles long? The taxi would cost you $502, which is considerably more than the rental car.

  » As they say on TV, "But wait! There's more!" Imagine now that the particular taxi you choose uses a different rule—it stops after every mile and starts a new trip. That particular taxi trip would cost you $1,000, because it would charge you $4.00 each for 250 separate trips. That is horribly worse than the rental car.

- Payday loans are analogous to that second type of taxi trip. There is a fixed cost to setting up a loan, regardless of its size. Then there are interest charges on the money (analogous to the mileage rate). But the payday taxi is set up for short periods (analogous to short distances) only. Every couple of weeks, the loan gets rolled over into a new loan, complete with an extra setup fee.

- Consumer advocates hate payday lenders, because the effective interest rates (i.e., interest and fees divided by the loan amount) can run to 300% to 500% per year,[10] and the payday lenders know that the majority of customers will need to roll over the loan time and time again.

- From your standpoint, like a taxi, the high cost per mile might be worth it in a pinch—but you need to ensure you never take a long trip.

PERSONAL BANKRUPTCY
• • •

Chances of personal bankruptcy increase with age, at least until age 40. According to a 2017 study, only 5% of persons who filed for bankruptcy were 24 years old or younger, and only 12% were between 25 and 29 years old.[11]

That said, many young people consider bankruptcy when times are difficult, so it is important to understand the issues and consequences before you make any decisions. Here are the most important things to know:

- The purpose of bankruptcy is to allow a person to get out from under an unsustainable level of debt and fixed payments, and hit the Reset button on their lives. However, the Reset button comes at a steep price, so it is certainly not something most people would prefer.

- Filing for bankruptcy protection is a legal process that is conducted through a special branch of the federal court system. The laws governing the process for personal bankruptcies come in two chapters of the bankruptcy code: Chapter 7 and Chapter 13. By about a two-to-one margin, most people file for Chapter 7 bankruptcy, which wipes out unsecured debt (like credit card or medical bills) but not secured debts (i.e., items such as mortgages, student loans, taxes, and child support). Under Chapter 13, which is for people who think they will be able to repay their lenders and want to hold onto their home and other belongings, filers agree to repay creditors over a 3- to 5-year period.

- To qualify for either process, a person must pass a *means test* that weighs your income against your ability to pay creditors. The thresholds are different for the two chapters. Generally, it is safe to say most families earning under $100,000 will pass the test if they are truly under stress.[12]

- The cost to declare bankruptcy varies based on a number of factors, but the attorney fees constitute the largest portion. Nationally, a Chapter 7 bankruptcy seems to cost between $1,500 to $3,000, and the cost of a Chapter 13 bankruptcy seems to run between $3,000 and $4,000.[13] You should expect to have to pay most of that at the outset of the process, as bankruptcy attorneys long ago learned that clients who declare bankruptcy often have problems making payments.

- Once you file, an automatic stay requires the affected creditors to immediately cease collection efforts. (Under Chapter 7, you will still need to pay on mortgages and other secured debts.) A trustee will be quickly appointed by the court, and that trustee will assess your finances and issue his/her plan. Creditors then have about 60 days to object to the plan, after which your debts will be discharged according to the trustee's plan. However, only debts that you submit to the process will be affected. And any debt you incur after the process starts will not be covered. In total, the process takes about four months.

• Now for the bad news: A bankruptcy filing will definitely hurt your ability to get credit going forward, for a long time. A Chapter 13 bankruptcy stays on your credit report for seven years, while a Chapter 7 bankruptcy stays on your credit record for ten years. Previous good credit scores will likely drop while previous bad scores will change little.[14]

~

Credit is essential for modern life. However, even if you have no credit history, you can establish one relatively quickly. Then, by actively following your credit score and taking a number of modest steps, you can maintain and improve your access to credit over time.

ENDNOTES

[1] Matt Tatham, "Americans in Their 50s Have the Highest Average Credit Card Debt," Experian, November 5, 2019, www.experian.com/blogs/ask-experian/research/credit-card-debt-by-age/. Accessed December 12, 2019.

[2] Natalie Issa, "How to Start Building Once You Turn 18," Credit.com, April 18, 2019, blog.credit.com/2019/04/how-to-start-building-credit-once-you-turn-18–139817/. Accessed December 11, 2019.

[3] Elvis Picardo, "What Is a Reasonable Amount of Debt," Investopedia, May 24, 2018, www.investopedia.com/ask/answers/12/reasonable-amount-of-debt.asp. Accessed December 11, 2019.

[4] "Score Advice: What Is a Good Credit Score?" Experian, n.d., www.experian.com/blogs/ask-experian/credit-education/score-basics/what-is-a-good-credit-score. Accessed December 11, 2019.

[5] Chad Langager, "How Is My Credit Score Calculated?" Investopedia, April 6, 2019, www.investopedia.com/ask/answers/05/creditscorecalculation.asp. Accessed December 11, 2019.

[6] "How to check your credit score," Wells Fargo, n.d., www.wellsfargo.com/financial-education/credit-management/check-credit-score. Accessed December 11, 2019.

[7] "How to Improve Credit Score in 30 Days," Go Clean Credit, n.d., https://www.gocleancredit.com/how-to-improve-credit-score-in-30-days/. Accessed December 11, 2019.

[8] Latoya Irby, "Credit Card Minimum Payment Calculation," The Balance, January 27, 2019, www.thebalance.com/credit-card-minimum-payment-calculation-960238. Accessed December 10, 2019.

[9] "I got a credit card promising no interest for a purchase if I pay in full within 12 months. How does this work?" Consumer Financial Protection Bureau, April 28, 2017, www.consumerfinance.gov/ask-cfpb/i-got-a-credit-card-promising-no-interest-for-a-purchase-if-i-pay-in-full-within-12-months-how-does-this-work-en-40/. Accessed December 10, 2019.

[10] Bill Fay, "Payday Lenders and Loans," Debt.org, n.d., www.debt.org/credit/payday-lenders/. Accessed December 12, 2019.

[11] Jonathan Fisher, "Who Files for Personal Bankruptcy in the United States," Census.gov, September 2017, www2.census.gov/ces/wp/2017/CES-WP-17–54.pdf. Accessed December 11, 2019.

[12] Associated Press, "Personal bankruptcy: What you should know," NBC News, November 12, 2008, www.nbcnews.com/id/27684203/ns/business-personal_finance/t/personal-bankruptcy-what-you-should-know/#.XfFrA2Am4eE. Accessed December 11, 2019.

[13] John O'Connor, "How Much Does It Cost to File Bankruptcy?" National Bankruptcy Forum, December 15, 2017, www.natlbankruptcy.com/how-much-does-it-cost-to-file-bankruptcy-2/. Accessed December 11, 2019.

[14] Associated Press, "Personal bankruptcy: What you should know," NBC News, November 12, 2008, www.nbcnews.com/id/27684203/ns/business-personal_finance/t/personal-bankruptcy-what-you-should-know/#.XfFrA2Am4eE. Accessed December 11, 2019.

CHAPTER 6

You Need to Start Saving Right Away

Probably the last thing you want to think about when you graduate from college is saving money and planning for retirement. But you need to save for simple things, such as a car or furniture. And you need a safety net, because new college graduates end up between jobs quite often in their first few years, as we will see in Chapter 9.

And then there is the issue of retirement, something that sounds irrelevant to you today. However, there is an old adage in the financial planning business that the money you save in your first ten years out of school matters more than any other money you will ever save. Why? Because of a phenomenon known as *compound interest*. Imagine two people graduating from college at the same time. One saves $1,000 a year for the first ten years after he/she graduates but never saves another dime after that. The second doesn't save anything for the first ten years, but then he/she saves $1,000 a year every year until he/she retires forty-five years later. Who has more money at the time of their retirement? The answer (given historical rates of return in the stock market) is the first person—by almost $42,000! That is almost $1,000 extra for retirement for every year he/she worked—and that is why you need to understand these issues now.

In this chapter I provide you with a framework that will guide you on how much to save and how to accomplish that amount of savings. In the next chapter, I will provide you with a guide for where to invest your long-term savings for retirement, including giving you an understanding of how finance actually works so you can objectively evaluate any advice you get from investment professionals, who may be biased in their recommendations based on what's best for themselves.

This chapter discusses:

- How much of your income should you save each month?
- What's the deal with before-tax savings versus after-tax savings?

HOW MUCH TO SAVE
• • •

To state the obvious, you save in order to have the money necessary to buy non-recurring items when you need them. There are five categories of non-recurring items, and you need to be saving (in different amounts) for four of them.

RECURRING, BUT NOT MONTHLY, ITEMS
You need to set aside money for the items that come up every three months, six months, or annually, rather than monthly. For example, if you own a car, the taxes on the car are charged annually in most jurisdictions. If you own a house, property taxes are due annually (although the company that holds your mortgage may take care of this for you by including it in your monthly payment), and homeowner association dues are generally collected quarterly. Clothing expenses are usually seasonal. If you or your spouse is still in school, tuition is usually charged once or twice a year.

Why save up for these items, instead of just handling them as they come up? Because if you are like the vast majority of people, what will happen is that in the months these come due, you will decide to pay them by contributing less money toward your other savings goals—but just for this month. And then you will do it again the next time one of these payments comes due. And so on. The result will be that you contribute to longer-term savings only in the months where none of these recurring expenses comes due.

With quarterly payments, semi-annual payments, and annual payments, you'll be lucky if you reach half of your long-term savings goal for the year.

So, compile a list of all of the non-monthly expenses that will occur in the next year, add them up, and divide by 12. Then contribute one-twelfth of that amount into a separate pocket for these items and draw from that pocket when these events occur. The pocket might be a separate savings account or a money market account, but you should not try to mentally set aside funds in your checking account as savings. That never works.

SAFETY NET OR EMERGENCY FUND

You already know that life does not proceed as planned. Therefore, you need to have a safety net for when problems occur. If you're lucky, your family may be willing to serve as your safety net. If so, and if you do not mind relying on them, then you may not need a separate pool of savings for this purpose. However, you should not simply assume they will be your safety net under all circumstances without explicitly discussing that with them, as discussed previously in Chapter 1. Waiting until a crisis to discover that you and your parents have different points of view could easily add a family crisis to the financial crisis you are already facing.

Let's assume you cannot or do not want to rely on your family (except perhaps in the most extreme circumstances). How much should you have in safety net savings? If you imagine the worst situation that could possibly happen, you will calculate a necessary amount of savings that is impossible to achieve, and your discouragement will prevent you from saving anything. A better way to think of this is an idea borrowed from the insurance industry—namely, the concept of *maximum probable loss*. Under this concept, you think about the worst case that has a 10% to 15% chance of happening to you, and you develop a plan to cover that much cost.

Financial planning experts use a rule of thumb that a person under age 30 should have a safety net equal to three to eight months of their normal expenses. That is a wide range, so let's look at how they develop their formula so you can tailor it to your circumstances:

- At your age, the likelihood of a lifelong illness not covered by insurance is quite low.

- Being sued is also unlikely, and the vast majority of lawsuits against individuals of your age involve auto accidents that are covered by insurance.

- While each individual is different, and you should think about the specifics of your own situation, for most recent college graduates the maximum probable loss scenario is losing your job. (In fact, as I describe in the next chapter, the *average* college graduate changes jobs four times before turning 30, so you are likely to face this situation *several times* in the next few years.) Therefore, you need enough in safety net savings (usually kept in a separate savings account or money market fund) to carry you until you get your next job.

  » Statistically, in the summer of 2019, the average (median) duration of unemployment in the United States stood at about 21 weeks. That would suggest the average person needs an amount of money to carry them 21 weeks or even a bit longer—say, four to six months.

  » However, no one is average. The amount a person needs to build up depends on the type of job they have. If it is one where movement between jobs is rapid (e.g., working in restaurants in a resort town), then the safety net can be less. If the job is highly specialized (e.g., aerospace engineer), it may take much longer to find a new job, and the safety net needs to be bigger. If a person can reliably expect to earn part-time income (from anything from babysitting to consulting), the safety net can be smaller. Also, remember that all jobs are tougher to find during a recession, so in those times the safety net needs to be larger.

Because no one is average, financial planning experts recommend the three- to eight-month range. That's a lot of money to build up, but there are two pieces good news. First, every little bit helps—you would certainly rather be facing unemployment with only four weeks of savings than no savings. Second, the funds in other pockets can be drawn upon if necessary. For example, if you are saving for a trip but become unemployed, you can access that pocket too. And in a true emergency, you can even access your savings for retirement (discussed below), albeit with some tax consequences if you are not careful. Therefore, although you would ideally have enough savings in your emergency fund pocket alone, you actually have a pretty good safety net if the sum of all your savings pockets lies in the recommended range.

LARGE ONE-TIME ITEMS

You need to save for all the large one-time items you hope to buy—a new car, a big trip, a wedding, etc.—using a separate pocket for these savings.

Everyone hates to wait, and many people respond to the savings point by saying, "I can just buy it now using my credit card, and then pay it off each month with the money I would have saved for the same purchase. And I get to have my item now!" But without knowing it, these people have added *almost half* to the cost of the item they want to buy. How?

- Let's pretend you want to purchase an item that costs $1,000. You can follow either of two strategies.

- Under Strategy 1, you save $50 a month for 20 months and then purchase the item. Well, it probably actually takes you 24 months, because there are four months along the away when unexpected expenses prevent you from contributing and funds to this savings. Along the way, you earn a tiny amount of interest on the money you have saved ($10.29 if the bank pays 1% interest on your savings), so you really only have to save $990.

- Under Strategy 2, you purchase the item today with a credit card, and then pay off the credit card over time.

  » Do you know what interest rate your credit card charges? Most people do not. As of January 2019, the *average* interest rate charged to new credit card customers was 19.24% (so roughly half of new customers paid even more!).

  » The interest on the $1,000 increases how much the item will actually cost you. So, for example, in the first month alone, the credit card company will charge you 1.6% interest (i.e., 19.24% divided by 12) on the $1,000 you just borrowed. That adds $16 to the cost. It also means that your $50 payment only reduced your debt by $34, not $50, so the next month you pay interest on $966, not $950. The same phenomenon holds true every month (i.e., interest eating into the impact of your $50 payment on how much your debt gets reduced).

» But wait, there's more! Remember the four times when you couldn't save the $50 that month? In this strategy, missing a payment costs you a late fee. Credit card companies can charge you a fee of $25 the first time that happens, and $35 if you have been late within the last six months (as well as make reports that can harm your credit rating, as we discussed in Chapter 5). That adds back to the balance—in this case, $130 if you miss four times during this period. And of course, that additional balance adds more interest charges.

» Trace the math all the way through until you have paid off the entire debt, and you will find the total amount of money you will have paid is $1,449—*which represents nearly a 50% premium versus the base cost of that $1,000 item.*

So, if you want (or need) an item so much that you are willing to pay that much extra for it, go ahead. Otherwise, you will be far better off waiting until you have the money saved up.

Just as above, you should create a separate pocket, such as a separate savings account, to set aside these funds.

RETIREMENT

The final category of a non-recurring event you should save for is, of course, retirement. The reason you need so much for retirement is that the amount of money you can earn on your savings, even when it is well invested, is typically only about 5% per year above the rate of inflation (after you pay taxes on those earnings). If that is the case, then in order to have the same income the day after you retire as you did from your salary the day before you retired, you would need savings equal to about 20 times your final salary. That's a lot of money!

Fortunately, you don't need quite so much money set aside on the day you retire. First, your expenditures will most likely go down when you retire. Second, when you retire, you will (hopefully) be able to collect Social Security, so not all of your income will have to come from earnings on your savings. Therefore, experts talk about a target range of 15 to 20 times the amount you will need to earn from your savings.[1]

Also, the amount you will need to save every year is reduced if you start saving money early on, because that money generates interest, and then you earn money on the original amount as well as the interest, and so on. For example, every $1 you save at age 22 would be result in you having $18.34 at age 65 if you can earn a typical investment rate of return of 7% per year. So, if you save $3,000 the year you are 22, you would have $55,000 at age 65. Do the same thing every year though age 30, and you would have $578,000 at age 65—enough to replace a $38,000 salary.

We all know it is hard to start saving in the first year or two out of college. But financial experts have an adage that says if you want to reach your retirement goal, you should save between 10% and 15% of your pre-tax pay every year, beginning in your 20s. Other experts use a slightly different rule of thumb that amounts to about the same rate of savings—they suggest you should have an amount in retirement savings equal to your then-current annual salary by the time you are 30 years old.[2]

PROVIDING FOR YOUR LOVED ONES
IN CASE OF YOUR DISABILITY OR DEATH

A conscientious college graduate will recognize that disability or death constitutes a non-recurring item, and he/she may instinctively worry about the need to save against such contingencies.

However, you should not use savings to protect your loved ones here; instead, you should use insurance, most likely purchased through your employer. The amount of funds necessary to support you or your loved ones for the rest of your/their life (lives) is staggeringly large. You cannot reasonably expect to build up that amount of savings unless you happen to become the entrepreneur whose startup becomes the next big thing.

Fortunately, the odds of significant disability or death befalling you at a young age are extremely small, and because of that, there is affordable insurance available to cover you against both of those risks, probably at particularly low rates through your employer. In many cases, the premiums may even be covered by your employer.

With regard to disability insurance (i.e., coverage that replaces your paycheck if you become disabled through injury or illness), experts seem to recommend policies that would replace 60% to 70% of your paycheck for as long as you are disabled. Fortunately, given that disabilities are relative rare, such insurance usually costs between just 1% and 3% of your income, and it is often covered by your employer.

As for life insurance, how much you need varies based on whether you have a spouse, a loved one, and/or family who are financially dependent on your income. If you are single and do not support anyone, you may not need any life insurance. However, for an average family, experts start their calculations in the range of 7 to 12 times the annual income that would need to be replaced. Some amount of life insurance is usually provided by employers. If you have to purchase more, such insurance is usually not very expensive at this stage of your life—e.g., a sample individual policy providing $500,000 of coverage for a 22-year-old unmarried male non-smoker runs only about $15 per month.

A FINAL WORD ABOUT HOW MUCH TO SAVE

As mentioned above, there are some relationships among the five savings categories that can affect the total amount you save.

- First, once you have sufficient funds in retirement savings, you may no longer need a separate pocket for emergencies. Particularly if part of your retirement savings is not tied up in a pre-tax retirement account (as described below), you can dip into your long-term pocket in a short-term emergency (just be absolutely sure you repay your retirement pocket once the emergency is over). Further, during certain emergencies, there are ways to temporarily borrow even those funds that are tied up in pre-tax retirement accounts.

- Second, pay attention to avoid self-defeating strategies. If you have large amounts of credit card debt, you still need *some* level of emergency funds etc., but don't set aside too much—instead, focus primarily on paying down your credit card debt. After all, you will actually get poorer every time you place more money in an account that earns you 2% to 5% interest while you are, at the same time, paying 24% interest on credit card debt.

- Finally, if the combined amounts suggested above seem too much to handle, try sneaking up on the total level. When you first start working, save as much as you can comfortably save (e.g., 5% of your pay toward retirement, and another 3% toward your other goals). Over the next year, learn to live within the remainder of your pay. Then, when you get your first raise, immediately devote *half of the amount of the raise* to additional savings. So, if your savings rate was 8% of your income, and you get a 5% raise, you increase your savings rate to 10.5% of your new level income. That way, you get to immediately enjoy half of the raise and begin moving toward the recommended savings range before you ever get used to having the full amount of the raise in your wallet (which will tempt you to increase your current spending). If you repeat this practice for two or three years, you will soon reach the full recommended savings levels and it will have been relatively painless to do so.

BEFORE-TAX SAVINGS VERSUS AFTER-TAX SAVINGS
• • •

By far your largest amount of savings will consist of retirement savings. In the next chapter, we will discuss the types of investments (e.g., stocks, bonds) that you should make with those funds. But before we get to that subject, you should know that retirement savings can be placed into different pockets, and which pocket you choose can have as much or more effect on your retirement income as which types of investments you choose.

Recent college graduates often argue—mistakenly—that the most appropriate way to save for retirement in their very early years is simply to set aside money when they can, rather than have their employer set aside money automatically each month. They argue that this provides flexibility, so if money is particularly tight one month, they can forego saving for retirement that month and make up the deficit the following month. However, even if they have a perfect record of making up the deficit—and very few do—it turns out they pay a huge price for that flexibility, because by doing it that way, they are foregoing a major government tax subsidy of their savings and potentially rejecting free money from their employer. How can that be? Let's take a look…

A few decades ago, the U.S. government was concerned that Americans were not saving enough for their own retirements, so it created two sets of plans (described below) to give people an incentive to save, both of which featured a powerful tax break. Specifically, if you save money using these plans, the government will not tax that money until you actually take the money *out* of these plans—that is, after retirement. Here is how they work and why they are so valuable.

The first plan (or vehicle from your point of view) is an *employer-sponsored retirement plan*, which is called a 401(k) plan when the employer is a company or a 403(b) plan when the employer is a non-profit institution.

Under this type of plan, your employer sets aside a fixed amount of your income, which you choose before the beginning of each year, every month throughout the year, putting into your 401(k) account. The key is that you then do not pay income tax on that amount. So, if your pretax salary is $50,000 a year, and you set aside $500 per month (i.e., $6,000 per year), your income tax will be based on earnings of $44,000, not $50,000. Further, any earnings you make on your 401(k) funds in later years will also not be taxed at the time you earn them. Instead, after you retire, you will then pay income taxes on the money only as you withdraw it from your account. Here is why that matters:

- You might think that the taxes even out in the long run, so it makes no difference whether you pay the tax now or later. But it actually makes a huge difference in two ways.

- Let's assume two 25-year-olds each earn $50,000 a year, and each is committed to saving $6,000. Their marginal tax rate (i.e., the tax on the last $6,000 they earned) was 22% in 2109.[3]

- Person A puts $6,000 into a 401(k) program. He/she pays income taxes on $44,000. Person B pays taxes on all $50,000 of income, so he/she pays $1,320 *more* taxes than Person A (i.e., $6,000 of extra taxable income times 22%). That means Person B therefore ends up with $1,320 less in his/her pocket after paying taxes *and* putting $6,000 into savings. If Person B cannot reduce his/her lifestyle, then he/she can only afford to make a smaller contribution to savings, 22% smaller to be precise.

- Next, let's look at the effect of the 401(k) tax shelter on the earnings that accrue to the savings between the ages of 25 and 65, including the subsequent taxes when the funds are withdrawn from the 401(k).

- Person A places the $6,000 of funds in a 401(k) that annually earns 7% return until the person reaches age 65. She pays no taxes on the earnings along the way. When she turns 65, the account will have $89,847 in it. Let's pretend she withdraws it all that day, paying taxes of 22%. She is left with $70,080.

- Person B invests his $6,000 directly—i.e., not through a 401(k)—and also earns a 7% annual rate of return. However, each year, he may pay income taxes equal to 22% of those earnings (e.g., if they are in the form of interest and dividends). At age 65, he will not owe any taxes when he withdraws his money, but his account will hold only $50,311.

- The result? On their 65th birthdays, when Person A and Person B withdraw their funds and pay any taxes due, Person A is left with 39% more money ($70,080 vs. $50,311).

- Put the two effects together (i.e., the 22% effect and the 39% effect), and investments through a 401(k) improve the total amount of money Person A will have at retirement *by 78%!*

- But wait, there's more. Many employers have programs that match their employees' 401(k) contributions. That's right, if you put in $1,000, they will put in an additional $1,000, *for free* (to you)—i.e., it comes in addition to your salary. And, like your contribution, it is not taxed until it is withdrawn at retirement, so it also gets that 39% boost. Now, most employers have a maximum figure they will match, so you may not get matched for every dollar you save, if you save a lot. But free money is free money—and free turbocharged money is spectacular.

But what if your employer does not offer a 401(k) plan, or you are self-employed? That's where the second type of plan (or vehicle from your point of view) comes into play. Regardless of whether your employer has, and you participate in, a 401(k) program, you can individually create the same type of tax benefits through an *individual retirement account* (IRA). Just like with a 401(k), the amount you contribute is deducted from your current income for tax purposes, and the earnings are not taxed until you withdraw the money. The maximum amount you can contribute to such a plan each year is smaller ($6,000 for the IRA, vs. $19,000 for a 401(k), in 2019), and there are some differences in the details, but by and large, you can think of it as the same kind of program.

In summary, based on the importance of before-tax versus after-tax savings, your retirement savings strategy should have three components:

- First, find out if your employer matches contributions to a 401(k) plan and really push yourself to contribute at least as much to it, to maximize the free money you get

- Next, keep placing retirement savings into the 401(k) and/or IRA until you hit either your own 10% to 15% of income goal or the combined dollar limits set by the government

- Finally, if you reach the limits imposed by the government, save the remaining part of your 10% to 15% goal on an after-tax basis—but keep those savings in a separate pocket from all your other savings.

~

As noted at the outset of this chapter, no new graduate likes the idea of saving money—after all, you've been waiting for years to have an income so that you can afford to buy fun things, not put money away! However, I hope I've convinced you that savings are something that you cannot do without, and the sooner you get started, the better off you'll be in the long run.

ENDNOTES

1 "Ultimate guide to retirement," CNN Money, n.d., money.cnn.com/retirement/guide/basics_basics.moneymag/index7.htm. Accessed November 19, 2019.

2 Kathleen Elkins, "1 in 6 millennials have $100,000 saved—here's how much you should have at every age," CNBC, February 5, 2018, www.cnbc.com/2018/02/05/1-in-6-millennials-have-100000-heres-how-much-you-should-have-saved.html. Accessed November 19, 2019.

3 "What Are the Tax Brackets?" H&R Block, n.d., www.hrblock.com/tax-center/irs/tax-brackets-and-rates/what-are-the-tax-brackets/. Accessed November 19, 2019.

CHAPTER 7

Investing for Retirement

In the previous chapter, I introduced the idea that much, or even most, of the money you will have at retirement will actually not come from the money you saved directly, but from the earnings on that money, which come in the form of interest or stock market gains and will build up over time, especially if you began setting aside money in your early years. I also introduced you to the three types of accounts—401(k) accounts, individual retirement accounts (IRAs), and your after-tax savings—in which you will save money.

However, just putting money into those accounts does not automatically start that wealth-generation process. Rather, once money is put into an account, *you must direct how that money is to be invested*, because it is the specific investments you buy that actually perform the work of increasing your wealth.

You may feel uncomfortable with the subject of investments. Most adults are. The field appears to be particularly complicated and filled with jargon. The advice you get can be confusing and contradictory, and even self-serving on the part of the advice givers. There seem to be a million different terms that just confuse you.

In this chapter, I will cut through all the clutter and describe for you, in everyday language, what you need to understand to make your investment decisions. Frankly, in order to make wise decisions, you only need to understand three things:

- The basic idea of investments

- The types of investments available to you

- A few restrictions on which types of investments are allowed in each type of account (i.e., 401(k), versus IRA, versus after-tax savings).

Finally, in case you want to understand more about how investments get valued and why stock prices go up and down, an appendix to this chapter explains all of that, so you can have the confidence to push back if some alleged financial expert tries to confuse or intimidate you.

THE BASIC IDEA OF INVESTMENTS
· · ·

An investment is simply anything that you put money into with the hope of getting back more money later. So, if you were to buy items at a yard sale, hoping to sell them for more on eBay, you can be said to have made an investment in those items. If you were to buy raw materials and pay someone to mix those together into candy you hope to sell, you can be said to have invested in both the material and the labor. (Of note, if you do the mixing yourself, you are not considered to have invested your own labor, at least not in financial terms; only an exchange of money counts as investment.) Similarly, if you were to purchase a property and simply hold onto it in order to sell it later, you are said to have invested in that property. Or, if you were to purchase a share of stock, you are said to have invested in that stock.

The defining characteristic of an investment is that you intend only to make money on an item, not use the item for your personal consumption. (There are situations where your motivation is part consumption and part investment—such as when you buy a house to live in, but that you also hope will increase in value over time—but the IRS treats these items differently.)

So, what makes a good investment? Simply put, *people would like to earn a lot of profit for every dollar they invest, without incurring much risk that they will lose the money they invested.* The profit per dollar of investment for every year your money is tied up in the investment is referred to as the investment's *rate of return* (or simply return, for short). For example, if you invest $200 for a year, and you get your $200 back plus $10 in profit, your rate of return would be 5%, because $10 is 5% of $200.

What may surprise you is how just a few percentage points in your rate of return can make a huge difference in how much profit you end up with if the money is invested for a long time (such as in retirement savings). Rate of return matters a little even if the time is short, but it matters a lot if the time involved is long. To illustrate:

- Let's pretend you want to save $1,000 for a year. You are choosing between two investments, one of which will earn 7% and another that will earn 8%. That does not sound like a big difference, and it's not. At the end of the year, you will have either $1,070 or $1,080, based on your choice.

- But now, let's pretend you are investing for your retirement, which is 30 years away. Upon retirement, the 7% investment will be worth $7,612, whereas the 8% one will be worth $10,062. That's right, the 1% difference in return makes a difference of $2,450—i.e., a 32% difference in how much cash you will have at the end.

- Differences in rate of return matter more the longer the investment lasts—and the difference keeps getting bigger, in both dollar and proportion terms, very quickly. If the two investments described above lasted for 40 years instead of 30, those repayment figures would be $14,974 versus $21,724, a difference of $6,750, or a whopping 45%, in cash.

No one knows the future, so all investments are based on guesses about what will happen. In effect, investors trade off expected returns against perceived risk.

- An investment with low returns (i.e., relatively low profits compared to how much you invested) and low risk can be seen as good.

- An investment with high returns and high risk can also be seen as good.

- An investment with high returns but only low risk is great.

- An investment with low returns but high risk is obviously bad.

In the next section, we will discuss the specific numbers for various types of investments.

TYPES OF INVESTMENTS

· · ·

As you can see from the previous section, the subject of investments is very broad. However, for the purposes of this chapter, we are interested only in the major types of investments you can and should make with the funds you are saving specifically for retirement. So, while you could technically use your after-tax savings to invest in a personal business, artwork, or anything else you fancy, this chapter will stick with the more conventional types of investments that people typically choose when saving for retirement.

The six major categories of investments you should understand are:

- Bank accounts

- Bonds

- Stocks

- Mutual funds and ETFs

- Commodities

- Options, derivatives and other exotic investments.

BANK ACCOUNTS
You are undoubtedly familiar with bank accounts (or instruments, as investments are sometimes called)—namely, *savings accounts*, *money market deposit accounts* (MMDAs), and *certificates of deposit* (CDs). They are available from any bank, savings and loan, or credit union. While they might be a satisfactory place to park money while you save for a year or two for a particular purchase, they are poor choices for long term investment such as retirement savings.

On one hand, they involve almost no risk. Assuming your bank, savings and loan, or credit union is insured by the FDIC (and about 97% of such institutions are), your deposit is insured by the U.S. government up to a value of $250,000, so even if the institution where you have a deposit goes bankrupt, you will not lose any of the money you invested. (Theoretically, you can lose the interest it owes you, but even that has rarely happened.)

On the other hand, they provide terribly low rates of return, even when you take into account their low risk. How bad are they? Well, to illustrate, on December 2, 2019, J. P. Morgan Chase (the largest bank in the country) offered a rate of 1.01% per year if you opened a large CD for the next ten years. That same day, the interest rate on ten-year U.S. government bonds (i.e., if you bought a CD directly from the government) was 1.82%. That's right, almost double the bank's rate, with less risk.

BONDS

Bonds are essentially loans to large companies or to the government. The loan is broken into separate chunks (such as $1,000) and sold as individual bonds. The company or government (the *issuer*) pays the person owning the bond (the *bondholder*) interest along the way, and then repays the loan amount (the *principal*) at the end. A bond can be of any length of time the issuer chooses, but the most common time periods are one year, five years, 10 years, and 30 years.

How high the interest rate on the bond will be is based on how much the potential buyers demand at that particular moment in order to lend this particular issuer the money for the length of time the issuer needs it (more on this in the appendix at the end of this chapter). Sometimes, there is a lot of money in the economy, so interest rates in general are low. At other times, there is less money available, so interest rates are generally high. As to whether this particular bond needs a higher or a lower rate than other bonds being offered to investors at the same time, if the potential buyers perceive there to be more risk, they demand a higher interest rate. They also tend to demand a higher interest rate when the issuer wants to borrow the money for a longer period of time.

As we saw in the prior section, bonds tend to pay you more than bank deposits, even when they are no riskier than bank deposits. That is because it costs the issuer less to sell a bond than it costs a bank to attract bank deposits (which generally requires putting up bank branches etc.).

Another advantage of bonds is that you do not have to buy them from the issuer or hold onto them until they *mature* (i.e., until the date when the issuer is required to pay them off). Rather, bonds are bought and sold in a marketplace analogous to the stock market called, not surprisingly, the *bond market*. That means you can buy a bond that has, for example, exactly 7 years and 225 days left to maturity if you want to, and then sell it 421 days later if you like. This aspect of bonds is referred to as being *highly liquid*.

If you purchase a bond when it is issued and hold it until maturity, you will earn exactly the rate of return that is stated by the interest rate on the bond. However, if you buy it later or sell it earlier, you might achieve a higher or lower rate of return. That is because the current value of a bond at any point in time may be higher or lower than the amount of the principal that is owed at the end. This, too, is explained in the appendix, but to illustrate the point, imagine a company issues a $1,000 bond at a time when potential investors think the company is quite solid. They have no doubt the company will pay off when the bond matures. But something happens to the company along the way, and investors are now worried they won't get repaid. They might be willing to sell the bond for $750. Someone else has more faith in the company and buys this bond for $750, and then he/she collects the $1,000 when the bond matures. This is a great deal!

Or, imagine that a company issues a $1,000 bond when interest rates are high, so they agree to pay investors a 10% return. That means the company is committed to paying $100 of interest every year until the bond matures. Then, imagine that interest rates in the market drop, and someone is now willing to pay a purchase price to buy that bond from the original bond-holders wherein the new bondholder would earn a 5% return. That purchase price would be higher than $1,000.

So, changing interest rates and expectations about the issuing company's future performance can make the current price for which the bond can be sold go up or down. But if you purchase the bond when it is issued and hold it to maturity, you will indeed receive precisely the rate of return that the interest rate states—so long as the issuer is able to repay the bond on time.

Even though the prices of bonds go up and down, the prices tend to move only moderately, so bonds are considered a low-risk investment category.

What rate of return can you expect on a bond? The basic answer is that for a bond that is considered to be low-risk, the rate of return has averaged about 2% above the rate of inflation (e.g., 4% during a period of 2% inflation, or 5% during a period of 3% inflation).[1]

With respect to your retirement account, bonds are useful as a safety-net investment. But they won't help your account grow very fast, and therefore (for reasons I will discuss below) they should probably represent only a small portion (or none) of your retirement investments when you are still in your 20s.

STOCKS

Stocks (or more precisely, *shares of common stock*) are units of ownership in a company; investors who own those shares of stock are called *shareholders*. How much ownership each share represents depends on how many shares the company issues. Some companies issue only a few shares, while others issue hundreds of millions, or even billions, of shares.

Two companies of exactly the same size and market value might issue radically different numbers of shares. For example, imagine two companies that are each worth one billion dollars in total. One might have issued 100 million shares, so each of its shares are worth $10 each. The other might have issued only 20 million shares, so each of its shares are worth $50. A company with a higher share price is not necessarily worth more than one with a lower share price. What matters to you, the investor, is simply whether the share price of the company you invest in goes up or down from the price at which you bought it.

When a company makes a profit, it decides whether to immediately hand over some of that profit to shareholders, or to hold onto the money and invest it in more equipment, inventory, etc. in the hope of making even more profit in the future. If the company passes some or all of the profit during a given period to shareholders, that is called a *dividend*. So, there are two ways a company can make money for you as a shareholder. One is by paying out dividends. The other is by convincing the stock market (i.e., all of the current stockholders and all the other investors who are watching the company and considering buying shares) that it will pay out so much dividends in the future that the shares are actually worth more than their current price, so everyone should want to buy more shares—and therefore bid up the price of the shares in order to be the lucky buyer.

Stock prices go up and down as investors change their minds about how optimistic to be regarding the company's future. Just how much the prices go up and down is referred to as the stock's *volatility* (or the market's, if you are referring to all stocks combined).

Here's the key thing about stocks: Over the long term, prices for the stock market as a whole go up enough that on average, investors earn about a 7% annual rate of return above the rate of inflation,[2] which is much better than bonds' average return of 2% above inflation. However, there are two caveats:

- First, notice the words "*over the long term.*" Stocks achieve their growth via a path that goes up and down a lot during various shorter periods. There can be periods of two to five years when stock prices go down, not up. That can be very unnerving for investors.

- Second, not all *individual* stocks go up 7% when the *overall market* goes up 7%. An individual company's stock may shoot up like a rocket, or it may tank (i.e., decline significantly in price), depending on how investors are feeling about that particular company's stock.

There are thousands of people whose full-time job is predicting the fortunes of individual companies and, therefore, the future price of those companies' stocks.

What does all this mean for your retirement investments?

- First, stocks are a good investment for your retirement accounts when you are young, because you have a long time until retirement for those stocks to grow at an average rate of 7%, including plenty of time to more than make up for any short periods of low growth or decline.

- Second, if you choose to invest in any particular stock (rather than buy a cross-section of many stocks that will collectively reflect the stock market as a whole, as we will discuss below), remember that you are betting you know something about that particular company that all those full-time professionals I just mentioned don't already know. If they already know the same thing, they will have already bid the company's stock price up or down before you could get a bargain.

Stocks are easy to buy and sell. They are extremely liquid and can be bought and sold by any stockbroker you see in television advertisements, such as Schwab or TD Ameritrade.

MUTUAL FUNDS AND ETFS

Many years ago, someone recognized the inconvenience of having to buy many different individual companies' stocks to achieve his/her goal of having a collection of stocks, called a *portfolio*, that would mirror the performance of the stock market as a whole rather than the unique fortunes of a single company. In addition, someone recognized the same inconvenience of having to buy many different individual companies' bonds to even out the odds of any one particular company defaulting on its bonds.

From these insights, *mutual funds* were born. In a *stock mutual fund*, a *fund manager* gets a number of investors (sometimes millions of investors) to put money into a joint pool of funds. The manager then chooses several stocks to invest in, according to a set of rules that he/she has promised to follow. For example, the stocks could mirror the stock market as a whole— that is, the manager buys only those stocks that comprise the Dow Jones Industrial Average (also called the Dow Jones or the Dow, a widely followed indicator of stock market prices), or those that comprise the Standard and Poor's 500 (or S&P500 as it is often called), which is another indicator of stock prices for the market as a whole. As a second example, the manager might invest in stocks he/she personally believes will do well, but only from a particular economic sector, such as a certain industry. There are literally thousands of variants of rules that mutual fund managers have promised to follow.

In a mutual fund, the change in value of the fund as a whole is simply the sum of the changes in value of all the stocks in the fund. In a so-called *actively managed fund*, which is described here, the manager's job is to buy/sell stocks as if he/she personally owned the pool of money, using his/her knowledge and research to try to make as much money as possible for the members of the fund, consistent with the rules of that particular fund. All the investors share the gains and losses equally, based on how many shares of the fund each investor owns. The large majority of mutual funds allow investors to purchase and sell their shares of the fund (i.e., alter the amount of ownership they have in the fund) every day. So, as you can imagine, every day, the fund conducts a re-accounting of which shares it happens to hold on that particular day, and therefore which mutual fund shareholders are entitled to the gains and losses from that particular day.

Mutual funds for bonds (called a *bond mutual fund*) work exactly the same way, except that the fund manager is buying and selling bonds, not stocks.

As you might imagine, mutual fund managers expect compensation for their work. This comes in two forms: (1) a commission (called a *load*) for purchasing shares in the mutual fund, and (2) an *annual management fee*.

While not all mutual funds charge loads, and some even waive the load if you invest through your 401(k), front-end loads are typically 3.75% to 5.75% of the amount you invest.[3] As for annual fees, they typically average between 0.5% and 1.0% of your total portfolio value but can run as much as 2.5%.[4]

Loads and annual management fees are one of the disadvantages of a mutual fund. Remember the example from the beginning of this chapter in which I demonstrated how much of a difference in retirement savings resulted from just a 1% difference in rates of return? That phenomenon also takes place inside a mutual fund. Only if the manager, through his/her smarter-than-average choices of stocks, can outperform the market as a whole by more than the cost of his/her compensation (in the form of loads and annual management fees) does the mutual fund perform better than the market as a whole. Some do, but most don't—on average, mutual funds slightly underperform the market.

In light of this, someone decided it might be a waste of money to even *try* to outperform the market. Why not just purchase exactly those stocks that make up those well-known indices (such as the Dow or the S&P500) in exactly the right proportions to mirror the behavior of the index? The result was so-called *index funds*. Today, there are hundreds of such funds that mirror dozens of different indices, from broad market indices like the Dow and the S&P500 to much narrower ones that mirror only specific segments of the market, such as small companies only, large companies only, U.S. companies only, foreign companies only, certain industrial sectors, etc. Index funds are also available for bonds, with an equal ability to follow only segments of the bond market (such as government bonds, high-yield bonds, etc.).[5]

Index funds have very low commissions and management fees relative to other mutual funds. For example, a typical index fund has annual management fees of 0.2%.[6] For you, this means you should only invest in so-called actively managed mutual funds (i.e., funds other than index funds) if you believe the particular manager is among the minority of such managers who can outperform the market as a whole.

Ultimately, someone went the next step and created something called *exchange traded funds* (ETFs). These are like index funds, but they are managed primarily by computers and have even lower annual expenses. Some charge annual management fees as little as 0.03%. They also have somewhat better tax treatment if you are investing your after-tax savings rather than investing through a 401(k) or IRA.

COMMODITIES
Commodities are generally raw materials or agricultural products that are bought and sold in great quantities, such as gold, silver, wheat, corn, etc. For reasons explained in the appendix, investors get in between the original producers of the commodities and the ultimate users of them. They buy and sell the commodities along the way, hoping that supply and demand for the commodity will change so the price will go up during the period they own it or down during the period between the moment they sell it and the moment they actually have to deliver it.

Now, to be more specific, most investors do not actually buy the commodity itself. Instead, they buy and sell *contracts* for the commodity to be delivered at some specific location at a specified later date. That way, they can buy and sell the contracts back and forth, and only the one holding the contract on its expiration date (usually, the end user) actually has to worry about the physical commodity itself.

At the risk of offending advocates of commodities (who generally have something to gain if you choose to invest in commodities), I suggest you refrain from investing your retirement funds in these types of assets (either directly or through a commodities mutual fund) unless and until (1) you have learned about not only commodities trading in general but also about what drives supply and demand for the particular commodity you are interested in, and (2) you have the time and interest to actively manage your investment.

Why this caution? First, unlike both stocks and bonds, commodities contracts are not inherently productive. Stocks and bonds produce dividends or earn interest, which means the average investor wins over the long term. A commodity just sits there. Therefore, it has no underlying bias to make money—so for one person to win, another has to lose. Next, there are just as many studies refuting the advocates' arguments for adding commodities to your portfolio ("inflation hedge!," "great source of diversity because their returns are not correlated with the stock market!") as there are studies supporting those arguments.[7]

There is plenty of time later in your career to speculate in commodities if you want to. In your first years out of college, other asset classes provide plenty of equally attractive opportunities with less effort and risk.

OPTIONS, DERIVATIVES, AND OTHER EXOTIC INVESTMENTS

If you are interested, the appendix provides an explanation of these types of investments. I believe you should not consider them for your retirement investments at this point for the same reasons as my point of view on commodities—only more so.

RESTRICTIONS ON INVESTMENTS
IN 401(K) ACCOUNTS AND IRAS
• • •

While you are free to invest your after-tax savings in anything you want, the federal government places certain restrictions on the types of investments you can make through your 401(k) account and your IRA (in return for the tax advantages of allowing you to invest those vehicles).

Frankly, you don't need to worry about government restrictions on 401(k) investments, because there is actually an even tighter restriction you will be subject to. When an employer offers 401(k) accounts to its employees, that means the employer has set up a master plan with a financial institution that governs the administration of all the accounts within the plan. (That is good, because that enables the plan to negotiate huge discounts on front end loads, etc. from the various mutual funds where the money will actually be invested.) However, it means the only investments you will be able to make are the ones that appear in the menu of options provided by the 401(k) plan administrator (and every one of those investments will already have been vetted for compliance with any government regulations). This is not a very confining restriction. In order to be attractive to potential employer clients, most financial institutions offering 401(k) plans have gone to extremes to make it possible to choose from massive numbers of alternative mutual funds, etc. If the plan allows for a 401(k) self-directed brokerage account (which many do not), you can invest in the stock or bonds of specific individual companies.[8]

As to your IRA, you have much more—but not complete—personal discretion. But there are a few things that are prohibited. You cannot lend yourself money, and you cannot invest in life insurance, highly speculative options and derivatives, antiques or collectibles (such as art), real estate that you intend to personally use (like a vacation house you might rent out part of the time), and most coins.[9] Consider it a small price to pay for the great tax breaks associated with an IRA.

⁓

You now know the basics about investing for your retirement, including the basic idea of investments, the types of investments available to you, and a little bit about the few restrictions on which types of investments are allowed in each type of account. If you'd like to move on to the next chapter at this point, feel free to do so. Or, if you'd like to develop a more robust understanding, stick around a little longer and dive into the following appendix.

APPENDIX

UNDERSTANDING FINANCE IN 30 MINUTES

• • •

As you consider various types of investments, it is helpful to understand what lies behind them, what causes a particular class of asset to exist, what determines whether its price goes up or down, etc.

People who work in finance (or who are finance majors) like to promote the idea that finance is byzantine and that you wouldn't understand. In fact, the principles that underlie these investments are quite straightforward. It is only the embellishments that are complicated. Here is a primer to help you understand the basics.

THE MOST IMPORTANT CONCEPT IN FINANCE: COMPOUND INTEREST (AND THE RELATED CONCEPTS OF PRESENT VALUE AND FUTURE VALUE)

All of finance—stocks, bonds, or your own investments—is about how the value of things changes over time. Every financial instrument or product (e.g., making a loan, making a bank deposit, holding stocks or bonds, making investments in commodities, etc.) is based on the idea that someone puts cash in now hoping to get more cash back in the future. Finance addresses the question of the relationship between how much money someone has now and how much they will have in the future.

The core question is this: How much money should someone receive back at some specified point in the future (e.g., one year from now) in order to compensate him/her for giving up the ability to use that money in the meantime?

The answer is that the value of money today vs. later is connected by the *interest rate* that is required, given the level of *risk* that is involved in the investment (the risk is that something will go wrong, and the investor/lender will not get his/her money back at all).

Let's start with a simple example, and then we will make it more complicated:

- Krista is willing to lend Zoe $100 for a year, but she demands a 20% interest rate in return. Therefore, one year later, Zoe owes Krista $120—the original loan amount, called the *principal* of $100, and the *interest* of $20 (being $100 times 20%).

- Zoe says, "Can we make it two years instead?" Krista agrees. But at the end of two years, Zoe then owes Krista $144, not just $140 as you might have expected if you add together the principal of $100 and two years of interest of $20 each.

- The reason for the difference is called *compound interest.* You see, at the end of the first year, Zoe already owed Krista $120 (as we saw in the example above), even though their contract did not specify that Zoe had to pay it back at that time. Therefore, in the second year, the interest is calculated by multiplying the interest rate (20%) by the new amount Krista is owed at the end of the first year (i.e., $120).

- The result is that, due to compound interest, Zoe owes another $24 in interest (not just $20) in the second year. Add that to what she owed at the end of the first year (i.e., $120), and you get $144.

- The $100 is called the *present value* and the $144 is called the *future value.* They are considered to be equal in financial terms (just separated in time), because Krista is apparently equally happy to have $144 in her hand two years from now as to have $100 in her hand today.

The same compound interest formula can be run forward in time (equating a value today to a value in the future) as well as backward in time (equating a value in the future to a value today). For example:

- Krista's other friend, Hailey, asks to borrow as much money as Krista is willing to lend, and she promises to repay Krista exactly $10,000 in three years' time (when Hailey will inherit that much money).

- This time, Krista demands that she earn a 25% *rate of return* (rate of return being another name for interest rate) each year for those three years.

- Krista can calculate how much she would be willing to lend Hailey now in order to get back $10,000 three years from now having earned a 25% rate of return. Take the $10,000 and divide it by 1.25 (i.e., 1 plus the interest rate of 25%) to see the value two years from now, then divide the result by 1.25 again to see the value one year from now, and finally divide the result by 1.25 again to see the value today. The result is $5,120. So the $10,000 is the *future value* and the $5,120 is the *present value.*

- To check that this is right, assume Krista lends Hailey $5,120 today and calculate how much Hailey would owe Krista in three years. Multiply $5,120 x 1.25 x 1.25 x 1.25, and it equals exactly $10,000.

Using this same logic, we can relate any amount of money at any point in time to an amount of money at any different point in time by working the formula backward and forward.

There are lots of different (and complicated) ways the present value formula can be applied. For example, what if the loan pays the interest each year in cash but only pays the principal back at the end? If I wanted to borrow exactly $67,235 at an interest rate of 4.75% and pay the entire loan back—including interest—in five equal annual payments, how much would I have to pay each time? The underlying arithmetic is always the same. There are formulas that shortcut the calculations, but they are all mathematically equivalent to taking every payment and calculating the future value back to the present value or vice versa.

These concepts underlie everything in finance, from stocks and bonds to commodities and all the weird-sounding concepts you occasionally hear about: *puts, calls, derivatives, swaps, forward contracts, mortgage backed securities, synthetics,* etc.

Now, there's one final related concept you need to understand, called *net present value.* Let's return to Krista's loan to Hailey:

- Pretend Krista has several different places she could invest her money and earn a 25% return.

- In that case, has Krista really done *herself* a favor for having lent $5,120 to Hailey? Not really. She has maintained her wealth, but she has not actually made herself better off, because of that equivalence of present value and future value that we discussed earlier.

- Krista only does herself a favor and *creates wealth* for herself via the transaction with Hailey to the degree that she either (1) gets paid back *more* than $10,000 in return for her lending $5,120 or (2) she lends *less* than $5,120 but still gets $10,000 in repayment.

- For example, pretend Krista agrees to lend Hailey only $4,500, while getting a promise from Hailey to repay her $10,000 (which is worth $5,120 to Krista, according to the formula above). If she only lends $4,500, but the present value of the $10,000 she will get back is $5,120, then Krista has $620 in present value left over. In finance terms, that extra $620 is referred to as the *net present value* of the transaction to Krista. It is the size of the *profit* Krista gets for having engaged in the transaction. (But of course—and many finance people forget this—it is really only the *expected net present value* at the time Krista makes the loan. It doesn't become a real profit until Hailey actually repays the loan! If Hailey doesn't repay, Krista actually has a $4,500 loss.)

UNDERSTANDING BONDS

A bond is just a loan. A company wants to borrow a lot of money, but rather than borrow it from a single bank, the company creates loan contracts (called *bonds*, usually in the amount of $1,000 each) and sells them to a lot of different investors (called *bondholders*). The contracts specify when the company will pay back the $1,000 (the *principal*), and also any payments during the meantime, based on the *interest rate* it specifies in the contract. So, for example, a bond could last ten years, and the company could promise to make interest payments of $50 every year along the way. That bond would be said to carry an interest rate of 5% (because $50 is 5% of $1,000). Very importantly, note the contract technically specifies $50, not 5%. This matters, because even if someone else buys the bond from the original bondholder (e.g., if the bondholder gets desperate for cash and sells it at a bargain price to a friend), the $50 and the $1,000 are still owed to whoever holds the bond. Therefore, the rate of return for the new bondholder may turn out to be different from 5%.

How are interest rates determined? Theoretically, a borrower and lender could negotiate any rate they can mutually agree on, which may be ridiculously high or ridiculously low, but in the investment world, rates are usually determined by looking at three factors: (1) *base rate*, (2) *time*, and (3) *risk*.

- First, let's look at the base rate.

» For lending money for one year under conditions where there is no inflation and investors believe they face no risk that they won't get their money back, they typically like to earn about 1% to 2% per year.

» That is the rate paid on short-term U.S. Treasury bonds (which are essentially riskless) when there is an expectation of almost no inflation. The exact rate goes up and down a little as the economy changes.

• Next, there is time.

» Except in unusual circumstances, investors demand a higher interest rate (i.e., more money each year) if they have to tie up their money in an investment for a longer period than a short period. How much more is measured by the *yield curve,* which is simply a chart that shows how much interest is required for a loan of one year, two years, five years, etc.[10]

» Generally, the longer the time period, the higher the required interest rate. Depending on how worried investors are about the future, they will charge a higher interest rate for investing the money for a longer time.

» What makes investors worry? One of the most important factors is inflation. Investors need to earn back that 1% to 2% *above* the rate of inflation. This is logical, because if you had $100 to lend today, you would not want to lend it out for a year at a 2% interest rate if you thought prices were going to rise 10% during that same time period—the $102 you would get back at the end of one year would buy as much as $92.72 could buy today. You would be worse off for having given up your money for a year!

» So, the expected inflation rate gets added to the base rate. How much gets added is based on what investors think the inflation rate will be for each year in the future.

• The third factor is risk.

» Not surprisingly, investors or lenders demand a higher interest rate when they believe there is a higher chance they might not get their money back. In the case of Krista and Zoe, it is up to Krista to determine how concerned she is and, therefore, how much interest she demands. In the case of the investment world, the additional return is referred to as the *risk premium*.

» The risk premium is how much additional return (over the *risk-free rate*, which is the interest rate for U.S. government bonds for the same length of time) is expected from an investment that is considered to have a particular level of risk. Like the yield curve, the risk premium goes up and down as investors feel more or less confident about the future of the company that issued the bond.

> › The first factor in investors' confidence has to do with the economy as a whole. If times are good, strong companies (so-called *AAA credits*) can borrow money at a credit risk premium of about 1%. Companies that are good but not great (so-called *BAA credits*) must pay an extra 1% (so, 2% in total). But during recessions, investors are less confident, so these risk premiums can jump to as high as 2.5% for AAAs and 7% (in total) for BAAs.

> › The second factor in investors' confidence is based on how well the specific company itself fares versus other companies. If a mediocre company is performing very well, investors might upgrade it, meaning they assign it to a better risk category (e.g., from BAA all the way up to AAA, although that would be a big jump). That reduces the required risk premium, leading to a lower necessary interest rate (and as we saw earlier, a small difference in interest rates can make a big difference over time). Of course, the opposite can occur as well. If the company performs badly, investors lose confidence that the company will have the funds to meet its obligations, and the company is downgraded.

So, what does all this mean for you if you invest in bonds, or buy a mutual fund that invests in bonds?

Look back at the first paragraph in this section. Remember that the company issuing the bonds has to offer to pay the interest rate (set by all the factors I have just discussed) so that investors will buy the bonds. But, as I noted, the company locks in the payments it will make for all the time the bond is still outstanding at the moment it sells the bond. The $1,000 and the various $50 payments are locked in. And if you buy the bond from the issuer and keep it until maturity (i.e., when it pays back the principal—the $1,000), you will indeed make the 5% rate of return.

However, very few bondholders actually hold a bond until its maturity if the bond is a long one (e.g., longer than three years or so). Instead, the average bond gets bought and sold many times along the way. If you buy into a mutual fund of long maturity bonds, I guarantee the mutual fund will be buying and selling bonds all the time. Why? Because the bond itself becomes more and less valuable as interest rates in the economy change and as the perceptions of the credit risk of the company (i.e., the odds the company will be able to make the payments it has promised) improve or worsen.

Remember the figures from earlier about how much difference a 1% change in interest rates can make? That's why investors are always buying and selling bonds. They are trying to buy up bonds on which they estimate (i.e., guess) the interest rate is about to drop and sell the ones on which they estimate (i.e., guess) the interest rate is about to rise. They are each trying to out-guess everyone else as to the direction of movement. That's right, although they will boast about employing lots of analysis and statistics and mathematical models to make their estimates, it all comes down to a grand guessing game.

UNDERSTANDING STOCKS

Owning *stock* (which is measured in *number of shares*) refers to owning a part of a company.

The financial aspects of stocks work very much the same way as they do for bonds, but the guessing is more difficult, and the focus is on the potential to exceed the required rate of return (and so create wealth, as we discussed in the first section of this appendix).

Like bonds, stocks are valued based on the cash payments an investor hopes to get and the rate of return that the investor hopes to make. However, there is more uncertainty about whether the investor will indeed get those cash payments, so the investor uses a much higher interest rate (and still hopes to earn even more than that).

As you probably know, owners of a company get the money that is left over once everyone else (including bondholders) have been paid. The leftover amount can swing quite wildly with even small changes in the company's fortunes, because most of the people who get paid first receive a fixed amount of money, even if the revenues of the company move up and down.

To see this, imagine a company in the following situation:

- In a certain month, the company sells 500,000 items for $10 per item. Its revenues are $5 million.

- The raw materials cost $3 per item (a total of $1,500,000), and it pays its workers $2.5 million.

- Therefore, the company makes an operating profit that month of $1,000,000.

- However, the company has to make bond payments of $500,000 per month to pay back the bonds it sold in order to buy its factory.

- So, in that month, the company has $500,000 left to pay its shareholders (yay!).

- Alas, the next month, sales fall by 10% to 450,000 units.

- Raw material costs drop to $1,350,000, but the company is unable to reduce its labor costs of $2.5 million, because 10% is not much of a change in production, and if the company fires some of its workers, it won't have enough skilled and experienced workers available if the volume returns to normal next month.

- The company's operating profit falls to $650,000, but it still has to make the bond payment of $500,000, so the amount of money to distribute to its shareholders is only $150,000.

- That's right, a 10% drop in sales caused a 70% drop in payments to shareholders.

To a greater and lesser degree, this phenomenon holds for all companies. Because shareholders get only the leftover funds, the size of their return is much more volatile. That has two implications: (1) it is much harder to forecast the cash payments and (2) investors demand a much higher (forecasted) rate of return in order to be willing to invest.

How much higher? On average, over the long term, stocks have resulted in returns to investors of about 10% before inflation, or about 7% to 8% after inflation. So that is a starting point for investors' expectations for an average-risk company. They expect more if the prospects for the company are considered riskier. And remember, the returns I just quoted are *over the long run*. There are periods in which the returns are actually higher, and periods in which they are lower, or even negative.

Now, let's discuss what a stock is in a more literal sense. When a company is first started, the money to start it usually comes from one or a few people. Who owns what portion of the company is based on a negotiation among those who contribute the idea, those who will lead the company, and those who put up the money. No one talks about shares of stock at this stage; they simply speak in terms of what percentage of the company each person owns.

Later, when (and if) the company gets larger, it may need money to expand (e.g., to buy new stores, or to build a new plant). The amount may be more than the company can pay for out of its current profits, and more than the people who originally funded (and own the company) can afford to invest.

In those cases, the company can raise funds from the stock market. This is called *going public* through an *initial public offering* (or IPO). Here is how that works:

- The company first creates *shares* (where every share represents a proportion of the company that is the same as every other share). The number of shares can be basically any number the company wants. For example, the same company could choose to issue 100 shares, in which case each share represents 1% ownership, or it could create one million shares, in which case each share would represent 0.0001% ownership.

- The company distributes all of these shares among the current owners in proportion to the percentage of the company they each own.

- Let's pretend that a company called Bob's Business creates one million shares. The company then determines how much money it wants to raise. In the case of Bob's Business, it is $10 million.

- The executives and the board of Bob's Business create *projections* (also called *pro formas*) of how much cash the company will return to its owners each year for the next many years *if* it can sell enough new shares to raise the $10 million it needs. (Projections and pro formas are estimates, which in turn are euphemisms for guesses. You read that right—guesses. You will notice a lot of guessing in this section.)

- Next, they calculate the present value of all of those cashflows—just as you saw earlier—using the rate of return they guess investors would demand in order to be willing to buy the shares. (We will discuss below how they come up with this rate of return.) Let's pretend the present value answer is $50 million. That means (if you believe the guesses) the new investors would need to own 20% of the company for them to be willing to invest $10 million. Said another way, 20% of the present value of $50 million is $10 million, the same as the amount to be invested.

- Given the new investors must own 20% of the company, and there are 1 million shares already outstanding, the new investors must receive 250,000 shares in return for their investment. (The math here is that the number of new shares divided by the total shares must be 20%. The total number of shares equals the number of new shares plus the number of shares that were already outstanding. The number of shares that are already outstanding is one million. Thus, the number of new shares works out to be 250,000.)

- What's the price of the shares? The answer is $10 million divided by 250,000, or $40 per share. By the way, that means the already outstanding shares are worth $40 million in this calculation. Add that to the $10 million for the new shares, and you get the $50 million total valuation we started with above.

- The company's executives hire an *investment bank* to manage the process and to help the company find investors who will be willing to purchase the shares. The investment bank arranges for the company executives to conduct a *roadshow*, in which they travel around to various potential investors and *pitch* the investors on why this investment will be a good idea, because the company will generate even more cash than those previous guesses.

- The potential investors do not necessarily believe the company's projections. Instead, each potential investor goes away and develops its own guesses and calculates its own view of the value per share using the same methodology I described above (albeit with different assumptions and its own view about how much return it would require).

- Based on this process, each important investor decides how many shares he/she is willing to buy (if at all) and what the maximum price he/she is willing to pay per share. This type of bid is called a *limit order,* and these types of bids determine the actual price the shares are eventually sold for. Smaller potential investors may offer to buy certain amounts of shares at whatever price is eventually set (these are called *open bids*). Both kinds of bids are sent to the investment bank.

- The investment bank then builds what economists call a *demand curve* for the stock. Imagine you draw a bar where the price one investor would pay determines the height of the bar, and the number of shares he would buy determines the width. Now do the same for every potential investor the company met with. If you arrange the potential investors in order from the one who would offer the highest price to the one who would offer the lowest price, you get a downward sloping staircase that resembles a curve, which in this case is the demand curve.

- In the case of Bob's Business, the investment bank might report to the executives, "We have a potential investor who is willing to pay $50 per share, but he will only take 100,000 shares. That will only raise $5 million. We have a second bidder who will pay $45, but he, too, will only take 100,000 shares. Therefore, between them, that would be 200,000 shares at an average of $47.50, or $9.5 million. (The regulations for this process dictate that all shares in a single offering must be sold at the same price; so in this case, all of the shares would be sold at $47.50). To get to the full $10 million, we need a third bidder." The investment bank reports the third bidder will buy 50,000 shares but will pay, at most, $40 per share. That means 250,000 shares at $40 per share will raise the necessary $10 million.

- Which would you rather have? Ten million dollars in cash at a cost of 20% of your company or $9.5 million in cash at a cost of 16.7% of your company? (In the latter case, the new investors would hold 200,000 shares out of a total of 1,200,000 shares, or 16.7%.) The company decides on the former, and the shares are sold to the three investors. Bob's Business is now a *public company,* because it is simultaneously *listed* (i.e., registered for trade) with a stock exchange (e.g., the New York Stock Exchange, the London Stock Exchange, or NASDAQ).

In the real world, there are usually fifty to a hundred separate large investors who purchase shares in an IPO.

The new investors have no intention of holding onto the shares long enough to collect those projected cash payments. Rather, they hope other potential investors (such as you) will think the company is worth more than $10 per share, and offer to buy shares from them for a higher price than $10. In fact, many of them make their shares available on the stock market immediately. For example, they may offer shares to anyone on the exchange for $10.50.

Then and forever, the price of the stock becomes the result of hundreds or thousands of separate guesses about the future of the company and what the company (and its individual shares) are worth to them. Some investors (called *fundamentals traders*) build their own models of future cashflows and set their own demanded interest rate for the present value calculations. Others simply assume yesterday's price was somehow correct, and that if good news comes out this morning, then the stock is worth more than yesterday's price. Some don't have a view of the value but believe they can spot patterns in the stock's price movement that they can capitalize on. For example, one might notice that this stock's price goes down three consecutive days and then usually rises on the fourth day. So she waits for times when the stock has fallen three days in a row and then buys. There are hundreds of approaches.

There is also a constant stream of information coming out that might affect any investor's views of the company. Interest rates go up and down. Trade barriers get created or removed. Competitors come out with new products. The company cuts prices in the hope of getting more volume, but it does not know yet whether the gambit will work. Therefore, every investor who is paying close attention revises her view about the value fairly often.

All in all, you should understand there is nothing magical about a stock's price on any given day. It is simply the result of two staircases like the one I described in the IPO process. The first staircase (the *bid* staircase) is the result of potential investors who are willing to buy a certain number of shares at a certain price. It is the one we discussed above during the IPO. The second staircase (the *offer* staircase, which is upward sloping like a supply curve) is the result of investors who currently hold the stock but are willing to sell it today at a certain price. If the staircases cross (meaning the highest price that any potential investor is willing to pay exceeds the lowest price at which a current shareholder is willing to sell), then a sale is made, and the price is publicly reported. (Those are the prices you see in media channels that follow the stock market.) If the staircases do not cross, no trade takes place until someone on one side or the other gives in.

Note the oddity here. The price is set by the selling shareholder who *least* values the company. The 99% of shares that did not sell are in the hands of investors who are (for the moment) convinced the company is worth more than that. Their opinion counts for nothing in the report of the day's stock price.

Day after day, the stock trades back and forth among investors pretty much forever, unless the company goes bankrupt or is bought by another company. Sometimes, the company decides it needs to raise even more money. If so, the board of directors authorizes it to create more shares and to sell these additional shares in pretty much the same way as was done in the IPO. This process is, not surprisingly, called a *secondary offering*. There are no limits as to the number of times or amounts for which the company can raise funds in this way, as long as they can find additional investors who want the shares enough to pay a good price for them.

So, stock prices are the result of hundreds or thousands of people guessing and changing their minds each time they learn new information. But don't make the mistake of thinking these are dumb guesses. Many academic studies have shown it is very difficult to consistently make better guesses than the stock market does (as whole). And big investors spend millions of dollars every year trying to improve their particular approaches.

But all of them rely on one thing: information. To beat the stock market, you need to look for information about a company's performance and its competitive advantages over rivals that other potential investors have not yet noticed, and then you must act before everyone else finds out the same thing.

UNDERSTANDING COMMODITIES

In the investment world, commodities are simple physical things that (1) are produced and used (in vast quantities) by many independent parties and (2) can be graded so they can be considered reasonably uniform in quality no matter where they are or who produced them. If those conditions hold, there will be opportunities to potentially make money buying, holding, and selling them, as supplies and demand fluctuate up and down.

For example, gold is produced by many mines around the world and used by thousands of jewelers (75% of newly-mined gold usage) and industrial companies (who use it in certain electronics, etc.). While gold can be diluted (e.g., 14 karat, 18 karat), pure gold (i.e., 24 karat) is the same regardless of where it was mined. So long as there is a reliable process for determining a particular bar of gold is pure, you do not particularly care which bar you own. The price of gold can go up and down depending on whether the collective output of gold mines around the world is high or low this month and whether the fashion world is in a mood for lots of jewelry this year. So, an investor can make (or lose) money buying and selling gold in different places.

There are now exchanges that facilitate the buying and selling of dozens of different commodities, from metals to oil to farm products such as wheat or corn. Even currencies (such as the U.S. dollar and the British pound) can be traded against each other. The only two rules that determine whether something is a tradable commodity are the two listed above.

Commodities become a financial instrument when someone writes a contract that entitles the holder of the contract to a certain quantity of the commodity without having to actually take physical possession of the commodity itself. The contract can then—before it expires—be bought and sold without the item actually moving around. In fact, for many commodities (particularly food products, which can spoil), the contract does not specify that you own the commodity today; instead, it is a promise to deliver a specified amount of the commodity at a specific place at a specific time in the future.

How is that helpful? Let's take a look:

- Imagine you are a farmer who is planting a field of corn today. You can sell a contract today to deliver the majority of what you believe the field can produce at the time in the future when you expect the corn to be ready for harvesting.

- That does two things for you: (1) it gives you cash now, and (2) it locks in the price you will receive such that you do not have to worry you will do all the work only to discover there is an oversupply of corn at harvest time, making prices are so low you wished you had not planted corn at all.

- The buyer of the contract may not be a company who will actually use the corn, but an investor. The investor is betting that, as the time to take delivery of the corn gets closer, the price of corn (to be delivered at the time and place specified by the contract) will rise. The investor will then sell (hopefully at a profit) the contract to a company that actually needs the corn.

- Alternately, the investor may decide to sell the contract to a second investor sooner than that, leaving it to the new investor to sell it to the ultimate purchaser of the physical corn itself. Only the investor or company holding the contract on its expiration date actually has to worry about the physical corn itself.

Investing in commodities involves the same concepts as investing in stocks and bonds: putting cash in now, guessing how much cash you will get back when it comes time to sell, and calculating the value by comparing the future cash you will get with the cash you have to pay out by using the present value formula we learned earlier. Remember, you are guessing at what the future payment will be. Like stocks, there are many large investors who are trying to make better guesses than everyone else. So, to win in a commodity investment, you must ask yourself what information you have that they do not have, or what better conclusion about future prices can you reach by using the same information everyone has available. If your answer is nothing, then you are not really investing, you are gambling, because you are simply hoping that your guess about the direction of future price changes will randomly be correct, just as someone does at the roulette wheel.

UNDERSTANDING OPTIONS, HEDGES, SHORTS, SWAPS, DERIVATIVES, ETC.

A deep dive into all the types of instruments in the financial world lays beyond the scope of this book, but I can give you an idea of what they are all about. The vast majority of these instruments derive from stocks, bonds, and commodities. Think of them as consisting of either: (1) little insurance contracts that can insure the policyholder for a specified period of time against the price of the stock, bond, or commodity changing in a way that would hurt them financially; or (2) the exact opposite, a way to make a lot more money if you guess right about certain events than you would if you bought the underlying stock, bond, or commodity—but to lose a lot more money if you guess wrong.

To get an inkling of how this can work, let's look at an example of the first of these two categories, the insurance contract type:

- Imagine you bought a share of stock for $50, and now it is worth $100. You can sell it and get $100. (Yay!)

- What if you think the price is going to go higher? Then you need to hold onto the share. But the price might go down instead. (Yuck.) What to do?

- Another investor offers you a deal—called a *put option*—in which you will be the *purchaser* of the option and he will be the *writer.* He says, "You pay me $3, and I guarantee that regardless of what happens to the price of the stock, you can sell it to me for $90 at any time within the next 90 days. That way, if the stock goes up, you just sell the stock to someone else for whatever the market price is. If it goes below $90, you sell it to me for $90 [or "put it to me," in the lingo of finance]. You might lose a little money versus selling it today for $100, but at least you get to keep $90 (minus the $3 I'm charging you to write the put option), no matter how low the price goes. I'm stuck with having to buy your share for a higher price than I can sell it for on the market."

- Behind the scenes, the put writer has done a lot of mathematical calculations (guessing based on recent price behavior of the stock) that the odds the price will go to less than $90 are small—small enough that if he writes many similar contracts (i.e., on various stocks at various prices), on average his fees will exceed the losses he will incur when some of his contracts result in his losing money.

Stepping back from the specifics of any one transaction, what is taking place here? Someone (the *option writer*) has created a financial instrument (the *option*) that breaks apart some of the financial features of the underlying share of stock (i.e., the adverse impact of a price fall, which the purchaser of the contract no longer bears) from other features (in this case, a price rise, wherein the purchaser of the contract gets to keep the benefits). And to make that disaggregation work, he charges a fixed fee. Unlike the purchaser, the writer is not protected. He is deliberately absorbing risk of a large but unlikely loss in return for a guaranteed up-front fee, just as an insurance company does when selling you a life insurance policy.

The exact opposite of a *put* option is a *call* option. It is purchased by people who fear the effect of price rises. Who might want a call contract? Think about the commodity market. There are many people, such as the makers of breakfast cereals who might want to be protected against the price of corn or wheat rising.

Imagine all the ways someone could break apart all the features of the underlying bonds, stocks, and commodities. You can break price changes into falls versus rises (as we did above). You can break big changes in prices from small ones. You can break short time periods from long ones. You can swap your risk for my risk. Etc., etc., etc. There are hundreds of varieties of such instruments out there. That is what options, hedges, shorts, and derivatives are all about.

Finally, though, you should be aware that the prices and returns associated with these types of instruments can behave in very odd and extreme ways that are not predictable to someone not schooled in them. Therefore, my advice is to avoid them unless and until you invest the time to understand them in detail.

～

The investment world is full of jargon and complexities. But almost all of these are relatively small wrinkles on a few fundamental concepts. If you understand the concepts in this chapter, you will know enough to understand the explanations of all the wrinkles—at least the all of the ones relevant to you. If you cannot understand a wrinkle, then that may be a sign that the investment is not right for you.

ENDNOTES

[1] Joshua Kennon, "What Is a Good Return on Your Investments?" The Balance, June 25, 2019, https://www.thebalance.com/good-rate-roi-357326. Accessed December 14, 2019.

[2] Trent Hamm, "Average Stock Market Return: Where Does 7% Come From?" The Simple Dollar, October 29, 2019, www.thesimpledollar.com/investing/stocks/where-does-7-come-from-when-it-comes-to-long-term-stock-returns/. Accessed December 14, 2019.

[3] Troy Segal, "Front-End Load," Investopedia, April 10, 2019, www.investopedia.com/terms/f/front-endload.asp. Accessed December 14, 2019.

[4] J. B. Maverick, "What Is Considered a Good Expense Ratio?" Investopedia, September 9, 2019, www.investopedia.com/ask/answers/032715/when-expense-ratio-considered-high-and-when-it-considered-low.asp. Accessed December 14, 2019.

[5] Adam Levy, "10 Types of Index Funds Every Investor Should Know About," The Motley Fool, March 19, 2019, www.fool.com/slideshow/10-types-index-funds-every-investor-should-know-about. Accessed December 14, 2019.

[6] J. B. Maverick, "What Is Considered a Good Expense Ratio?" Investopedia, September 9, 2019, www.investopedia.com/ask/answers/032715/when-expense-ratio-considered-high-and-when-it-considered-low.asp. Accessed December 14, 2019.

[7] Suzanne McGee, "Five Myths About Commodities Investing," Wall Street Journal, June 11, 2019, https://www.wsj.com/articles/five-myths-about-commodities-investing-11560132781. Accessed December 14, 2019.

[8] Kailey Hagen, "Can You Invest Your 401(k) in Individual Stocks?" The Motley Fool, May 17, 2019, https://www.fool.com/retirement/2019/05/17/can-you-invest-your-401k-in-individual-stocks.aspx. Accessed December 14, 2019.

[9] Mark P. Cussen, "5 Investments You Can't Hold in an IRA/Qualified Plan," Investopedia, November 23, 2019, www.investopedia.com/articles/retirement/11/impermissable-retirement-investments.asp. Accessed December 14, 2019.

[10] Today's yield curve can be found at www.treasury.gov/resource-center/data-chart-center/interest-rates/Pages/TextView.aspx?data=yield. As of this time—late August 2019—the yield curve is shaped in an unusual way that happens only occasionally. It is inverted, meaning the interest rate for longer-term bonds is higher than the interest rate for short-term bonds. This happens when investors think there is a danger of higher inflation in the short run but less danger of inflation in the long run.

CHAPTER 8

The Legal and Health
Aspects of Sex

A 2017 survey by DrEd.com found that 66% of participants had had a one-night stand at least once in their lives.[1] The average American male reported seven such encounters, and the average American female reported six. A majority found their partners in a bar, while clubs and on-line dating apps were also common sources. Of course, these statistics do not include sex between couples who dated only briefly.

So, it is highly likely you participate in casual or near-casual sex. That's fine, but what should you know before you act?

In sex education, or in your everyday life, you learned a lot about the physical and romantic aspects of sex—but odds are, your knowledge of three critical aspects of sex is incomplete at best and completely unfounded at worst. Ask yourself: What do you know, with confidence, about the following three questions?

- What does and does not constitute *informed consent*?
- If the sex is unprotected, what are your odds of contracting a sexually transmitted disease?

- If a woman gets pregnant, what are the two sex partners' rights, roles, and financial responsibilities for what happens as a result, both before and after the baby is born?

FOR THE LGBTQ COMMUNITY
Homosexuality Between Consenting Adults

To address a fourth question, homosexuality between consenting adults has been legal in every state of the United States since at least 2003, when the Supreme Court invalidated sodomy laws in the 14 states that still had such laws. However, a number of states still retain various such statutes on the books.

INFORMED CONSENT
· · ·

Presumably everyone is familiar with the general principle that sex between two people is legal only when both parties consent to the acts taking place. However, how is that general principle translated into practice? There are four elements you need to know.

- Which acts constitute sex for the purpose of requiring informed consent?

- What is the law concerning the age of consent?

- Who is judged incapable of providing consent, such that if you have sex with this person, you are criminally liable, regardless of what he/she permitted at the time?

- How must consent be communicated to meet the required legal standard?

This section will provide you with a general framework that should serve you under most circumstances. However, be aware that if you push the edges in any of the four areas, the specifics of the laws (and the penalties associated with them) vary from state to state.

WHAT ACTS ARE COVERED

Sex can be a broad term, particularly when it comes to defining which acts are prohibited without a person's consent.

While some state definitions vary, in general, sexual acts occurring without consent that do not involve penetration come under the heading of sexual assault. These include unwanted touching of sex organs (directly or indirectly through clothing), forced physical contact with secretions and excretions, or the forced witnessing of sexual acts by others.

Any unwanted oral, anal, or vaginal penetration is classified as rape. In most states, any degree of penetration with any object (any body part or otherwise) can qualify as rape.

THE AGE OF CONSENT

Under the law, children are not able to legally consent to sex, no matter what they say or how they act.

Having sex with a person who is underage is considered statutory rape, which is a felony. The legal theory is the same as the one that says children cannot legally bind themselves to a contract. They have not reached an age of mental capacity to fully understand the potential consequences of their decision.

Having said that, most states establish the age at which a person can legally provide consent to sex at an age that is lower than the so-called *age of majority*, which is the age at which they can bind themselves legally in contracts, etc., typically 18. More specifically, although the age of majority is typically 18, as of 2019, 30 states set the age of consent at 16, and 7 states set the age of consent at 17. The remaining 13 states (including California, Florida, and New York) set the age of consent at 18.

Having sex with someone who is under the age of consent is considered *statutory rape* and is a felony. Conviction under such laws can result in imprisonment, and usually results in the offender being labeled as a sex offender, which carries with it another set of enduring legal burdens.

Of note, the full legal situation regarding age of consent is a little more complicated. Just over half of the states have some version of a close-in-age exemptions from the basic age of consent laws. These laws, often referred to as

Romeo & Juliet laws, partially or fully exempt the couple from age of consent laws if one or both is underage but the two are close to each other in age (such as a 19-year-old having sex with a 17-year-old in the state of Delaware, where the age of consent is otherwise 18). Romeo & Juliet laws come in a variety of forms (e.g., marriage exemptions, different age restrictions, and whether these laws fully offset the age of consent law or simply reduce the penalties involved). Therefore, given that you, as a new college graduate, are most likely over the age of 21, if your potential partner is under the age of 18, you need to understand the law in your particular state.

FOR THE LGBTQ COMMUNITY
Potential Exclusion from Romeo & Juliet Laws

Gays need to be aware that if you are over the age of majority and your same-sex partner is under the age of consent, in some states you will *not* be protected by their Romeo & Juliet laws that provide for reduced charges and penalties if the members of the couple are close in age.

JUST SO YOU KNOW
Is Statutory Rape Actually Prosecuted?

An analysis of the National Incident-Based Reporting System (NIBRS), using data from 21 states, indicated that 7,557 statutory rape incidents were reported to law enforcement from 1996 through 2000.[2] That is approximately 72 incidents per state per year.

Given that a separate source estimated that 7 million incidents of underage sex take place each year (an average of 140,000 per state), the rate of reporting appears to be exceptionally low.

That said, scattered data from a small number of states shows the number of prosecutions to be in the same ballpark as the above average number of reports. Thus, I would suggest that while the probability of an incident getting reported is low, if the incident is reported, the police and prosecutors will likely take the report very seriously.

Studies by Brittany Logino Smith and Glen A. Kercher of the Criminal Justice Center of Sam Houston State University have shown that many jurisdictions will pick and choose which cases they want to investigate and prosecute. For example, they wrote that "In some states it is common to only prosecute the male in events where both parties in a heterosexual relationship are below the age of consent." They also wrote there had been large inconsistencies among the decisions of prosecution and sentencing of these cases, and there had been accusations that minority males who have sex with minority women resulting in pregnancy, or who have sex with white women, have faced the brunt of enforcement.[3]

BEING CAPABLE OF GRANTING CONSENT

There are reasons other than age why someone may not be legally able to consent to sex. If you have sex with a person under any of these conditions, you are guilty of sexual assault or rape under the law.

Some people are semi-permanently or permanently considered to be unable to provide legal consent. While states vary as to which conditions permanently prevent an individual from being able to give legal consent, the categories commonly include mental disability, agedness, and certain physical disabilities.

Other persons are legally considered to be temporarily unable to give consent. Agreement to have sex is not always considered to be legal consent. In general, you should consider that consent was *not* given if:

- Agreement was given due to force or threats.

- Agreement was given out of fear. The definition of fear extends beyond just fear of physical harm. Fear of retribution, termination of employment, financial fear, and other kinds of fear also legally negate consent.

- Agreement was given due to one person being in a position of authority over the other.

- Agreement was given based on fraud. This provision is why consent is often referred to as *informed* consent. While there is some ambiguity as to where exaggerating ends and fraud begins, clear deception about an important factor in the person's decision to consent constitutes fraud. For example, if you do not inform your partner that you have an STD, this is fraud. If you deliberately damage a condom, this is fraud. If it is clear the person agreed to have sex because he/she believes you are someone you are not (e.g., a close friend of a rock star), this is fraud. Fraud legally negates consent. Therefore, while you might believe you have the other person's consent, that consent can be *retroactively* removed if you have engaged in fraud.

- The person agreeing to sex was unable to understand the decision he/she was making because he/she was too drunk or too strongly under the influence of drugs.

- The person changes his/her mind part way through the sexual activity. The law holds that consent must be continuous throughout the sexual activity. A person is legally permitted to change his/her mind at any time, and if so, the sex must stop.

- Any of the sex acts took place after the person lost consciousness. Importantly, this holds true even if the person had previously given consent while being conscious. As mentioned above, consent must be continuous throughout sex. Unconsciousness means the consent does not continue.

WHAT CONSTITUTES GIVING CONSENT

Assuming both partners are of legal age and able to give consent, the most pressing question is, "How do I know the other person has given his/her consent to proceed to the next level?"

On a human level, the obvious answer is not to presume. Wait until your partner makes it clear. For example, one university defines consent as "a *clear and unambiguous* agreement, expressed outwardly through mutually understandable words or actions, to engage in a particular activity." And it goes out of its way to state that consent can be withdrawn by either party at any point.[4]

But from a legal standpoint, the answer is quite murky. From jurisdiction to jurisdiction, there is little consensus on what counts as having provided consent. In fact, a June 2018 article found that half of the states do not even have a legal definition of consent.[5] Rather, these states rely on standards implicitly derived from other terms, such as *permission*. That means the standard that will be applied in individual cases is whatever the prosecutor thinks of your behavior and what the prosecutor can convince the jury to think of your behavior.

Even when states have a formal definition, it is open to interpretation. For example, California's definition is "Consent is defined to mean positive co-operation in act or attitude pursuant to the exercise of free will. The person must act freely and voluntarily and have knowledge of the nature of the act or transaction involved." It further specifies that the definition requires freely given consent or affirmative consent. Colorado's definition is "Consent means cooperation in act or attitude pursuant to an exercise of free will and with knowledge of the nature of the act." However, it does *not* require freely given consent or affirmative consent. Why does one require freely given consent or affirmative consent when the other does not, given the similarities in their basic definitions? And what is the meaning of the connective between the two uses of *or* rather than *and*? Surely you would want both, wouldn't you? In the case of Colorado, how is its definition consistent with not having a requirement for *either* freely given consent or affirmative consent?

Bottom line, the only safe strategy is one of proceeding only when you are highly confident that your partner wants you to.

JUST SO YOU KNOW
What Are the Statistical Outcomes When Sex Has Occurred Without Consent?

I certainly wish it were otherwise, the statistics for obtaining justice when there has been sex without consent are disheartening.

According to the Rape, Abuse and Incest National Network, only about five out of one 1,000 incidents of sexual violence (i.e., 0.5%)

results in the perpetrator being convicted of a felony (which, 90% of the time, also results in jail time). The largest problem is that 77% of incidents of sexual violence go unreported. Even if the incident is reported, the resulting conviction rate is only 2%, barely more than half the rate for assault and battery cases and only one-third of the rate for robberies.

Therefore, unfortunately, if you are sexually assaulted, your hopes of seeing justice are small. By far, your best strategy is to protect yourself by avoiding situations with partners you don't fully trust or where there can be any ambiguity about whether you give consent.

UNPROTECTED SEX: WHAT IS THE REAL RISK OF CONTRACTING A SEXUALLY TRANSMITTED DISEASE?

• • •

Most sex education classes and most government literature cover the symptoms of and remedies for sexually transmitted diseases. I therefore assume you already know about these.

However, those same classes and pamphlets deliberately create the impression that sexually transmitted diseases are rampant. One can easily understand their motivation for doing so—if it were your job to teach sexual health, or if your career were devoted to the prevention and/or treatment of STDs, you also would want to encourage the public to take extra precautions to protect itself.

However, in writing this book, I am dedicated to simply providing you with the facts, which should enable you to make informed decisions for yourself. Statistically, rates of sexually transmitted diseases in the United States— other than genital herpes—are surprisingly low. In this section, I will provide an overview of the statistical odds of a potential sex partner carrying an STD, and if your partner has an STD and you do not use protection (such as a condom), what are the odds that you will become infected.

How likely is it that the person you are about to have sex with has an STD? Unfortunately, the U.S. Centers for Disease Control and Prevention (more commonly called simply "the CDC") does not publish a unified analysis of all STDs. Therefore, I have compiled statistics from across their reports to provide a comprehensive picture. The specific statistics differ between two groups.

- Group 1 includes chlamydia, gonorrhea, and syphilis. These STDs occur episodically; that is, a person can be infected and then cured. The relevant measure is *incidence* or, roughly translated, 'What is the likelihood this person contracted the disease in the past year?"

- Group 2 includes HIV/AIDS, HPV, and genital herpes: These diseases generally affect a person for life, and that person can infect you throughout his/her life (unless, in the case of HIV/AIDS, he/she regularly takes certain recently-introduced prescription medicines). The relevant measure is therefore *prevalence,* or, roughly translated, "What is the likelihood this person has been infected in his/her lifetime?"

As to the Group 1 STDs, the CDC reported:[6]

- Among 20- to 24-year-olds, 4.1% of women were infected by chlamydia during the year, or one in every 25 women. The rate for men was 1.8%, or one in every 50 men. For gonorrhea, the rate was 0.7% for both genders (i.e., less than one in every 100). And for syphilis, the incidence rate was a very low 0.05% for men and 0.01% for women.

- For the next age bracket (25 to 29 years old), the rates were about half of those for 20- to 24-year-olds.

As to the HIV/AIDS, the CDC reported:[7]

- Among 13- to 24-year-olds, the prevalence is 0.1% (i.e., one-tenth of 1%). Among 25- to 34-year-olds, the prevalence is 0.5%.

- Across the population, the prevalence is approximately three-and-a-half times higher for males than females.

As to HPV, prevalence is not measured as comprehensively or as often as it is for the other STDs mentioned above. The best data available shows that during the 2011–2014 period, prevalence among females 14- to 19-years-old (who would be women between 20- and 28-years-old today) was 3.3%,[8] which is down significantly from earlier periods, due in part to the availability of vaccines against the worst forms of HPV. Further, as of 2018, the majority of younger females and males were being vaccinated, so the rates have probably declined even further.

As to genital herpes, prevalence is much higher. The data is more complex, because although most genital herpes is caused by the HSV-2 virus (which is directly associated with genital herpes outbreaks), it can be caused by the HSV-1 virus (which is normally associated with oral herpes but can cause genital herpes outbreaks).

Prevalence of the HSV-2 virus in the 14-to-49 age bracket was most recently estimated to be 15.9% for women and 8.2% for men.[9] Most are unaware they are infected. In fact, 87% of those infected have never received a clinical diagnosis. While HSV-1 may not result in genital herpes, its prevalence is higher. From 2015 to 2016, its prevalence in the 14-to-49 age bracket was estimated to be 50.9% for women and 45.2% for men.[10]

It is important to understand that rates of infection for the STDs described above vary significantly by race, socioeconomic status, and sexual preference. In general, rates are significantly higher in blacks and Hispanics than whites, significantly higher in less-educated segments of the population, and significantly higher in men who have sex with men than in either women or men who have sex only with women.

Keep in mind that although the statistics provided herein show averages, your particular circumstances may be quite different than the average, even for your location and demographic profile. STDs tend to run in pockets of society. That is, collectively, the people in a common geographic and social network tend to primarily sleep around within their pocket and sometimes—but less often—outside of that pocket. When a member of a network contracts an STD from outside the pocket, it then tends to spread within the pocket. Therefore, that pocket will have a much higher rate of infection, while other pockets with similar locations and demographics remain relatively disease-free. Thus, I advise you to pay close attention to any reports of STDs in your network and behave accordingly.

Equally important as the odds that your sex partner has an STD are the chances that he/she will transmit the disease to you if the two of you have unprotected sex. While the actual odds vary with the type of sex (e.g., oral, vaginal, anal) and the choice of sex partner (i.e., male-female, male-male, female-female) the following table[11], based on male-female vaginal intercourse, is indicative.

STD	MEN	WOMEN
Chlamydia	20%	40%
Gonorrhea	25%	50%
Syphilis	20%	30%
HIV	1%	1%
Genital Herpes	30%	50%

Thus, while the chances of becoming infected are usually less than 50%, they are not trivial.

Said in reverse, if you know or even suspect you carry an STD, engaging in unprotected sex places your partner at high risk of infection. That places you at high risk of legal liability should you fail to disclose that fact prior to sex taking place, as discussed above.

PREGNANCY: RIGHTS, ROLES, AND FINANCIAL RESPONSIBILITIES
• • •

Obviously, an additional potential consequence of unprotected sex between a man and a woman is pregnancy. In this chapter, I assume any pregnancy would be unwelcome (for a discussion of the opposite circumstance, in which a pregnancy would be welcome, see Chapter 13).

In the following pages, we will address two key questions and several related sub-questions: (1) "What are the odds of a woman getting pregnant?," and (2) "What are the legal rights and responsibilities of both the woman and the man should that happen?

WHAT ARE THE ODDS OF PREGNANCY?

You may have heard the statistic that a heterosexual couple trying to get pregnant has a 15% to 25% chance of succeeding in any particular month (with the variation based on the individual couple's circumstances). That statistic is not relevant to your situation.

Here is what is relevant: the chances of pregnancy from a single act of intercourse are a function of when that act occurs relative to the woman's ovulation cycle. If the act occurs more than a week before ovulation, there is virtually no chance of pregnancy occurring. However, the probability rises quickly thereafter. Five days before ovulation, the probability is 10%. Two or fewer days before ovulation through the day itself, the probability is 30%. After ovulation, the chances quickly fall back to zero.[12]

That said, you need to understand that women often do not know when they are ovulating. Some women predictably ovulate halfway through their menstrual cycle (i.e., 14 days before their period starts), but others do not. Ovulation can occur as early as the day after a woman's period if she has a short menstruation cycle. And for some women, it does not always happen on the same day of her cycle.

Also, be careful treating those probabilities too literally. They were developed through the analysis of steady couples. In contrast, there is a substantial body of research that indicates that one-night stands are particularly efficient at generating pregnancies—much more so than sex with a regular partner.[13] The cause lies within the biology of both women and men.

On the female side, women's estrogen levels decline sharply during ovulation, therefore leaving them more exposed to their internal testosterone, which makes them hornier—and a variety of studies have suggested that higher degrees of female lust and sexual satisfaction contribute to the likelihood of pregnancy.[14]

On the male side, a 2015 study published in the journal *Evolutionary Psychological Science* reported that men are aroused by a new sexual partner, and as a result produce more and healthier sperm than when they have gotten used to sleeping with that partner.[15]

So, if you are trying to avoid pregnancy, both of your bodies are conspiring against you.

If you have had unprotected sex and are not confident about being safe from pregnancy, you can consider an emergency contraceptive pill (ECP), the so-called morning after pill, which is a post-intercourse contraceptive available over-the-counter for as little as $10, or a copper intrauterine device (IUD). But do not wait. The effectiveness of ECPs and IUDs depends on how quickly they are used after intercourse. Also of note, I say "consider" ECPs or IUDs because their effectiveness depends on when they are taken relative to ovulation (e.g., recent studies have suggested that ECPs work only if taken before ovulation occurs, not if it has already occurred), and both methods can have side effects. That said, their labels often claim that they are 88% effective, so the benefits are potentially significant.

IF A WOMAN BECOMES PREGNANT, WHAT ARE BOTH PARENTS' LEGAL RIGHTS AND RESPONSIBILITIES BEFORE THE BABY IS BORN?

For better *and* worse, in cases where the couple is not married, the pregnant woman bears the full financial responsibility of the pregnancy, but she also has the exclusive right to make all decisions. Fathers are not obligated to pay for abortions or for prenatal care of the mother. However, fathers are also not granted any direct rights in the mother's choices that might affect her or the baby's health or the mother's decision whether to take the baby to term or abort the fetus. (If the father believes the mother is behaving in ways that harms the child, he can alert the authorities, such as a child welfare agency. However, any actions that are taken as a result are based on the agency's authority, not any paternal rights.) The father does not even have the legal right to see the results of medical tests, sonograms, etc., without the mother's permission.

The father is permitted to influence the mother's choices through informal means (such as expressing his desires) or through formal means (such as entering a contract to provide financial assistance in return for the mother making certain choices). However, the father is not permitted to use any form of coercion to influence the mother's choices.

With respect to the above decisions, it does not matter whether the father's paternity has been scientifically verified or not. However, establishing paternity does alter the rights and obligations of the father immediately upon birth (see the next section, below). Therefore, the question of establishing paternity— which is normally done at birth simply by filling in the father's name on the birth certificate—can arise during the pre-birth period.

Legally, the mother and the father each independently have the right to de- mand the assumed father's actual paternity be established or refuted. That is, a court, petitioned by either side, can compel the assumed father (and the baby, through the mother's blood) to take a paternity test. Therefore, an expectant mother can (through the courts) force a reluctant father to be tested. She can presumably also force a man who claims to be the baby's father, but whom she does not want to be so recognized, to be tested in the hopes of proving he is not the actual father. A potential father who believes he is not the actual father can force a test to clear his liability. And a father who wants a connection to the child can force a test to establish that he is, in fact, the father.

The testing itself requires DNA from both the father and the child. After birth, this is usually accomplished through swabs of the inside cheek of both the father and the baby. When the test is performed before birth, the mother provides a blood sample (and doctors are able to sort the baby's DNA from the mother's in the mother's blood).

The cost of a paternity test ranges from under $20 to over $2,000, depend- ing on whether the test is conducted before or after the birth of the baby (a blood-based test is more expensive than a cheek swab test) and whether the results will be legally binding (to be legally binding, all samples must be taken by a trained third-party collector).

If a woman becomes pregnant and does not want to have or raise a child, she may consider having an abortion. If so, here are several basic facts to know:

According to a 2017 study published in the American Journal of Public Health, 19% of women will have had an abortion by age 30.[16]

There are two basic technologies for an abortion:

- An in-clinic abortion, which involves a medical instrument placed in the vagina to gently suck the fetus from the uterus. The procedure itself takes about ten minutes, although the complete visit will take several hours.

- A medication abortion, which involves two pills. Again, the complete visit to the provider will take several hours.

Both abortion technologies have high success rates—over 95%—and neither requires a lengthy recovery time. A provider can discuss the pros and cons of each technology with you.

As to cost, Planned Parenthood estimates that the cost of an abortion during the first trimester is between $350 and $950, depending on where you live and where you have the procedure performed (e.g., in a clinic versus a hospital). Your health insurance may cover some or all of the cost.

You should assume the time window in your pregnancy during which you can obtain an abortion may be shorter than you hoped for (depending on what state you live in), and finding a provider and arranging for the procedure will take more time and hassle than you expect. As of mid-2019, seven states had only one clinic (Kentucky, Mississippi, Missouri, North Dakota, South Dakota, West Virginia, and Wyoming), and Missouri was actively attempting to close its clinic. Utah has two clinics; 15 states have three or four clinics; 9 states and the District of Columbia have five to 10 clinics; and the rest of the states have more than 10 clinics.[17] Furthermore, many states placed restrictions and/or administrative burdens on both the patient and the clinic administrators to prevent free and easy access to these clinics.

Therefore, it is best to begin thinking about what you want to do as early as possible.

JUST SO YOU KNOW
Does a Woman Have a Legal Right to an Abortion?

A woman's legal right to an abortion throughout the United States was established by the 1973 Supreme Court Case *Roe vs. Wade.* However, if you are pregnant and considering an abortion, you need to do some research and make your decision quickly, because (1) that decision and subsequent ones allow individual states to impose restrictions, many of which make it much more difficult than you would hope to qualify for an abortion and to find a provider, and (2) as of the writing of this book, a number of states have deliberately passed severe restrictions on abortions and abortion providers in an attempt to cause a legal crisis and force the current Supreme Court to revisit the *Roe vs. Wade* decision. Their hope is that the current conservative majority in the Supreme Court will modify or reverse the 1973 decision, which would change the law throughout the country.

Therefore, no matter where you live, you should know there is a possibility the legality of abortion could be eliminated.

IF A WOMAN BECOMES PREGNANT, WHAT ARE BOTH PARENTS' LEGAL RIGHTS AND RESPONSIBILITIES AFTER THE BABY IS BORN?

Once the birth occurs, roles and responsibilities become more complex for both the father and the mother of the baby.

That said, it is important to note that *any* roles and responsibilities on the part of the father depend on his established paternity, either through his name appearing on the birth certificate (which usually happens in cooperative situations) or via DNA testing (which usually happens in uncooperative situations). Both methods have permanent legal standing. That is, once a man agrees to be identified as the father on the child's birth certificate, he cannot later evade his legal responsibilities as the father, even if a later DNA test shows he is not the biological father. While this might seem unfair to the father, the courts look to protect the most vulnerable party (i.e., the baby) in preference to overprotecting the rights or preferences of parents. Therefore, if a man has accepted the responsibility associated with being the father, he is seen as owing it to the child to continue. Every once in a while, the media will report that a man is attempting to challenge this in court, but the story almost always focuses on his losing the case.

As to roles and responsibilities, the combinations of potential circumstances are many, based on which parent wants or doesn't want various roles, rights, and responsibilities, and/or which parent wants or doesn't want the other parent to have various roles, rights, and responsibilities. I cannot hope to cover all of the possibilities here, so this section must necessarily be limited to broad principles, as follows:

- Assuming there is no involvement by a child welfare agency (i.e., the mother being considered unfit), if the mother wants to raise the child, she will be allowed to do so. She will also bear financial responsibility for the child (although not necessarily sole responsibility, as we will discuss below).

- If the father wants partial custody, the courts will probably allow it. It will certainly come with financial responsibilities. (The court will decide how much, if the parents cannot agree.)

- If the mother wants to raise the child and the father wants no role, the father still bears financial responsibility for child support.

- If the mother wants to put the child up for adoption (which can be an involved process and is therefore best started during pregnancy), she can usually do so. However, the father has the same legal rights to a child as the mother, so he can sometimes prevail in stopping an adoption (e.g., if he wants to raise the child).

- The biological mother typically works with an adoption agency to choose the couple who will become the adoptive parents. Therefore, if the mother's relatives (e.g., the baby's grandparents, or an aunt and uncle) want to adopt the baby, that can usually happen. However, because the father has rights too, it is possible he could object to the mother's choice of adoptive parents (e.g., if the preferred couple will not permit him to visit the child). In this case, the court will decide the outcome.

~

In summary, if there are substantial disagreements between the mother and the father, you will definitely need an attorney, because a court may well be your only option for resolution. The laws vary by state, and the outcome is heavily dependent on the particular circumstances of the case, as the court's focus will be on what is in the best interests of the child, not what either parent happens to prefer.

ENDNOTES

[1] Kasandra Brabaw, "This Is How Often People Actually Have One-Night Stands," Refinery29, June 6, 2017, www.refinery29.com/en-us/2017/06/157756/one-night-stand-casual-sex-facts. Accessed October 22, 2019.

[2] "Statutory Rape Crime Relationships between Juveniles and Adults: A Review of Social Scientific Research," *Aggression and Violent Behavior*, 2007.

[3] "Adolescent Sexual Behavior and the Law", Crime Victims Institute, Criminal Justice Center, Sam Houston State University, 2011. www.crimevictimsinstitute.org/documents/Adolescent_Behavior_3.1.11.pdf

[4] University of Michigan Policy & Procedures on Student Sexual & Gender-Based Misconduct & Other Forms of Interpersonal Violence. studentsexualmiscon-ductpolicy.umich.edu/content/1-consent

[5] Kimberly Lawson: "Half of the Country Doesn't Have a Legal Definition of Consent." www.vice.com/en_us/article/bj3p35/state-definition-of-consent-legislation

[6] Table 1, "Sexually Transmitted Diseases—Reported Cases and Rates of Reported Cases, United States, 1941–2018," in Centers for Disease Control and Prevention, *Sexually Transmitted Disease Surveillance 2018* (Atlanta: U.S. Department of Health and Human Services, 2019), 72–73.

[7] See Table 7 in Centers for Disease Control and Prevention, *Estimated HIV Incidence and Prevalence in the United States, 2010–2016*, HIV Surveillance Supplemental Report 2019, 24, no. 1, www.cdc.gov/hiv/library/reports/hiv-surveillance.html.

[8] See National Profile-Overview in Centers for Disease Control and Prevention, *Sexually Transmitted Disease Surveillance 2018* (Atlanta: U.S. Department of Health and Human Services, 2019), 1–38.

[9] "Genital Herpes: Detailed Fact Sheet," Centers for Disease Control and Prevention, https://www.cdc.gov/std/herpes/stdfact-herpes-detailed.htm.

[10] "QuickStats: Age-Adjusted* Trends in the Prevalence of Herpes Simplex Virus Type 1 (HSV-1) and Herpes Simplex Virus Type 2 (HSV-2) Among Adolescents and Adults Aged 14–49 Years—United States, 1999–2000 Through 2015–2016," Centers for Disease Control and Prevention, February 16, 2018, Weekly, 67, no. 6: 203, https://www.cdc.gov/mmwr/volumes/67/wr/mm6706a7.htm.

[11] "Not for Men Only: Sexually Transmitted Diseases," Male Health Center, n.d., http://www.malehealthcenter.com/c_std.html#overview. Accessed October 21, 2019.

[12] "Your Fertility right time for sex," Your Fertility, July 29, 2019, https://www.yourfertility.org.au/everyone/timing. Accessed October 22, 2019.

[13] Clare Goldwin, "Why you're far more likely to get pregnant from a one-night stand . . . as the Archbishop of Canterbury's mother proves," Daily Mail, April 13, 2016, https://www.dailymail.co.uk/femail/article-3538519/Why-far-likely-pregnant-one-night-stand-Archbishop-Canterbury-s-mother-proves.html. Accessed October 22, 2019.

[14] Ibid

[15] Ibid

[16] "Abortion Is a Common Experience for U.S. Women, Despite Dramatic Declines in Rates".. Press Release by Guttmacher Institute: https://www.guttmacher.org/news-release/2017/abortion-common-experience-us-women-despite-dramatic-declines-rates

[17] Mehreen Kasana, "How Many Abortion Clinics Are in My State? It Varies Widely," Bustle, May 30, 2019, https://www.bustle.com/p/how-many-abortion-clinics-are-in-my-state-it-varies-widely-17928303. Accessed October 28, 2019.

PART III

Potential Early Setbacks That Are More Likely Than You Think

CHAPTER 9

You Quit or Get Fired

According to the Bureau of Labor Statistics, the average person changes employers 4.2 times between age 23 and age 32.[1]—so it is clearly in your best interest to become knowledgeable about the process of changing jobs. In some respects, being good at changing jobs is the same regardless of whether you quit, are laid off, or get fired. In other ways, what it takes to be good is different depending of which of those events occurred. Here's what you need to know, and how to form a game plan, when it happens to you.

LONG BEFORE IT HAPPENS...

One of the biggest mistakes many first-time (or second- or third-time) job changers make is that they are not prepared for the event. By this, I do not mean they were caught off guard at the moment it happens. Rather, they failed to recognize that successfully changing jobs relies on three types of resources that cannot be put in place quickly—they must be built up over months, or even years—each of which we will explore in turn below.

FINANCIAL RESOURCES

In Chapter 6 I showed you how to calculate an average time that you might be between jobs if you were to lose your job today or quit before you have another job lined up. I showed you that the average person needs about four to six months to find a new job, and the range of times varies quite a bit around that average. If the average person changes employers over four times between ages 24 and 32, that means they change jobs an average of every 26 months during that period—and if they are unemployed for even four months each time, that means they have an average of only 22 months to save up enough to carry them through four months of unemployment.

While you can reduce your spending while unemployed, and perhaps rely on your parents for some assistance, it is clear you need to have a serious savings plan in place from the beginning of your career (or a reason to be highly confident that you will be the exceptional graduate who stays in his/her early jobs for an unusually long time). So, don't ignore the lessons of Chapter 6.

A PERSONAL NETWORK

Both to accelerate your career progress and to protect yourself in the event of a career setback, you need a network of colleagues in your industry that extends beyond your current employer.

Various outplacement and alumni career services surveys report that 65% to 85% of job seekers find their positions through networking.[2] While that sounds high, there is no denying that personal networks are hugely valuable in such searches.

However, the best networks are not those that are built once you start looking for a job. Those are useful for contacts, but not credibility. In those networks, everyone knows you are selling yourself, looking for your next opportunity. The best networks are ones where you have demonstrated competence and knowledge when you were not seeking any favors.

Building personal networks take time, and you need to build two of them: (1) one inside your company, to open up new opportunities that lie beyond the purview of your current boss and your boss's boss, and (2) a second one outside your current company to open up other possibilities on the outside. The first network helps you for as long as you remain at a company, but it is rarely valuable once you leave—that's when you need the second one.

How do you build an outside network? Exposure, particularly to people whose job it is to know others in the industry. For example:

- If there is an industry convention, attend it. Go to the vendor exhibition hall and meet a lot of vendors. Show curiosity, intelligence, and knowledge of the industry. The vendors will be happy to talk to you even if you are not in a position to purchase anything, because most of the time, vendors at such conventions have a lot of time to kill while they're waiting for someone relevant to talk to. Later, these vendors can be particularly helpful to you. For example, you may hear of a company you could be helpful to, but you don't know anyone at that company. In contrast, your friend the vendor probably does—because part of every vendor's job is to know people at every company in the industry.

- If there is a local association for your profession that cuts across industries (such as forums for electrical engineers), attend the meetings and become active in the group.

- If your college has an alumni association in town, and there are a large number of graduates who have your same major, become active in that group, too.

In all of these cases, the key is to get exposure to people who move in circles that are related to what you do, but whose circles are outside of your company. Use the period when you are happily employed, and therefore need nothing anyone, to form some bonds and make some favorable impressions. That way, you won't be a stranger when it comes time to network and find interesting new opportunities.

AN IMPRESSIVE RÉSUMÉ

Everyone thinks the key to a great résumé lies in the writing. While good writing helps (as I discuss in more detail later in this chapter), the real power lies in the *achievements* the résumé reports. The best résumés speak of accomplishments, not just of the position you held. So when you're considering an assignment at work, think about whether the role can result in a significant accomplishment that is describable in a résumé. When conducting your work, think about how—if you do the work just a little differently—that work can be captured in a phrase that speaks to a tangible impact you've had, not just a bland description of your job duties.

IF YOU GET FIRED (OR LAID OFF)

. . .

No one likes to be fired. In addition to the loss of income, it can be a real blow to your self-confidence, particularly early in your career. That said, there are better and worse ways for it to happen.

First, it is important to distinguish between being fired for cause and being fired for anything else (such as job performance, absenteeism, etc.).

BEING FIRED FOR CAUSE

The definition of *for cause* is that the action was based on a "breach, misfeasance, or other inappropriate action of the other party."[3] In the employment world, it is usually considered to be a shorthand way to connote that someone has broken a fundamental principle of decency, such as fraud, stealing from the company, or being guilty of sexual harassment. It can even be considered vaguely suggestive of someone having committed a crime (or close to it), but the company might have chosen to forego the complications of actually involving the police. Therefore, it is a huge black mark, and if a reference call ever comes into the company, and the company says a person was fired for cause, it is very likely to prevent the caller from hiring that person.

Therefore, if a company ever says it is firing you for cause, and you believe this is unjustified, protest immediately. If the firing is, in fact, the cover-up of malfeasance by a manager toward you, you may choose to fight back quite strongly and involve an attorney.

On the other hand, even if you do not want a major fight, you may want to protest anyway. You might tell the company you accept being fired, but you want the record expunged of any mention of "for cause" or you (and your attorney) will insist on a hearing to clear your name. You are giving away nothing, because you are better off leaving the company anyway—i.e., even

160

if the firing was unfair, if the company were to overturn the firing, you would likely be stuck in a company in which the story has gotten around, and that would make your job difficult for you in many ways.

The company may accept the compromise, which is potentially better for both sides. For you, it is better to have the record in the HR office (who will receive those reference calls) to be clean. Further, in some states, you are not eligible for unemployment benefits if you are fired for cause.[4] For the company, it may be better to simply have the situation resolved. The managers get what they really want—you gone—without the possibility of a hearing that would expose their own failings.

BEING FIRED, BUT NOT FOR CAUSE
Being fired for anything other than cause also hurts your feelings, but your course of action should be different.

Understand that most often, it is not possible to get the company to change its mind. Exceptions can occur when the firing was simply an emotional outburst by a volatile manager in response to a momentary event. In this case, back away, give the manager time to calm down, and then approach him/her (if you still want to). Another exception can be when the manager who is firing you has sole discretion over the decision, and it is obvious he/she is torn over the choice he/she is making.

But if your company is one in which several people must be involved in the decision, it is rare that anything you say will change the decision. Firings are so unpleasant that companies avoid them as long as possible, and then they steel their resolve and purge themselves by taking the ultimate action. The person who actually delivers the news represents the collective will of a group and does not have the power to reverse the group's decision.

So, it is normally best to accept your fate but act in your own best interest, given the situation. To accomplish this, avoid being rushed into either of two severance pay traps.

The first trap comes in the form of, "We will allow you to quit, rather than be fired" or to comply when you are asked to resign. The enticement to accept this offer is that you can avoid the embarrassment of being fired—but the price for you (and the savings for the company) are high:

- First, if you quit, you will not be offered severance pay. Given that you may be unemployed for some time, you might need that money.

- Second, if you quit, you are generally not eligible for unemployment benefits. There are exceptions if you quit because the job was unsafe, the employer had not paid wages recently, etc.[5]

You must weigh the tradeoff, but you should not overreact to the "lack of embarrassment gambit." Here's why:

- It is not at all unusual to be fired (or laid off). In 2018, in the middle of a very strong economy, 21.9 million U.S. workers were fired or laid off.[6] Many years, the figure is far higher. One survey indicated that 37% of all workers had been laid off or fired at one point in their careers,[7] and almost half of those people reported that it had happened more than once. Therefore, job interviewers are unlikely to be frightened off by the fact that you are one of that 37%.

- Further, there are many reasons why people get fired, such as personality conflicts and legitimate disagreements about how a job should be done. Simply have a brief explanation of why you were fired that helps the interviewer understand your side of the story and perceive you were not acting unreasonably (if these are true, of course).

- Frankly, you don't have to worry very much about the company you are leaving bad-mouthing you to a prospective employer.

  » First, most companies these days have their HR department handle all official reference calls, not the specific managers you worked with—and the HR department almost always only has records, not war stories, to work with when describing the circumstances of your leaving.

  » Second, in order to avoid the risk of lawsuits from former employees alleging that the company made statements that hindered an employee's future career or earnings potential, many companies also have policies that prevent both the HR department and/or your former manager from saying anything about past employees beyond confirming the dates the employee worked there and what their job title was.

The second severance pay trap you need to avoid occurs frequently when companies are going through layoffs (but can occur in a simple firing situation as well). That trap is agreeing to a severance package that does not pay you what you are truly owed.

- If a company owes you back wages or unpaid bonuses, or has made previous representations that you have qualified for a future payment of any kind, then you must be very careful before agreeing to any severance package. Many (perhaps most) such packages contain a clause saying that, by accepting this payment, you are releasing the company from all future financial obligations to you. Some go so far as stating you will not sue the company for any reason.

- Again, every situation is different, and you may desperately need the short-term cash. But recognize the company is offering the current payment as a money-saving strategy on its part. If there is a substantial difference between the severance package and what you are truly owed, you may very well want to consult an employment attorney.

Not all firings are acrimonious, and not all of them involve either of the severance pay traps just mentioned. But even if your firing is simply a mutual parting of the ways, there are still other actions you can take in your own self-interest.

- First, see whether you and the specific manager you worked with can agree on a mutually consistent (and honest) description of why the split occurred, one that is supportive of both you and the company. If you can, then it becomes possible for you to have any future interviewer call the manager directly instead of making an official reference call.

- Second, see whether the company typically provides any outplacement assistance, such as coaching on résumé writing, introductions to executive search firms, etc. It may not, and it may not be willing to do so in your case, but it doesn't hurt to ask.

Finally, if you get fired, don't let it harm your sense of personal value to potential employers. As I said before, people get fired for all kinds of reasons.

- Being fired is rarely a function of your fundamental competence.

- Maybe you did not fail; it was just a matter of circumstances.

- Maybe you failed at a particular task, but that does not mean you will fail at other tasks, even related ones.

- Maybe you weren't trained or guided appropriately.

- Maybe you were part of an organization that you did not really care about, so it was impossible for you to care enough to perform at your best.

- And, keep in mind that people get fired at a particular point in time. You may have succeeded brilliantly for most of your time at that company, but there was simply one event that didn't go right. Try to have the emotional distance to understand that how the job ended is not the right measure of whether the job was a good experience or whether (on balance) you were a success there. It was just a point in time.

IF YOU (PLAN TO) QUIT
· · ·

When people want to quit their jobs, they are usually in one of two emotional states. With rare exceptions, the best course of action is the same for both states—namely, you should only quit your job *after* you have found a new one.

- In State 1, which applies to most people and most situations, job dissatisfaction is a creeping feeling. Day after day, you find the tasks less satisfying or you come to realize the opportunities are simply not what you had hoped for. Under these circumstances, this recommended course of action makes sense and is easy to commit to.

- In State 2, you suddenly hate being there. The urge to run screaming for freedom feels overwhelming—we have all experienced the emotion at some point of, "I'm done!" However, unless the situation is truly unbearable, it is rarely the best strategy to act instantly. Don't act on impulse until you have thought through what comes next. Remember the average time between jobs that were described earlier in this chapter? Ask yourself whether you would rather be unemployed for that length of time *right now* or still have your current job (without the mental stress of caring very much about succeeding in it) while you find a better one. Making up your mind to leave, but holding your tongue, helps you in two ways: (1) if you change your mind tomorrow, you still have the option of staying where you are, and (2) if you don't change your mind, your current job can pay you while you conduct your job search.

MOVING ON WITH YOUR LIFE
· · ·

Regardless of whether you quit, are fired, or get laid off, you need to move on with your life quickly. Here are four keys:

- First, adjust your budget, *immediately*.

  » Many people, when they are first unemployed, take a couple of weeks (or longer) before explicitly addressing their new financial situation and, during the interim, keep spending as if their situation has not changed.

  » The situation has changed, and there is no way to tell how long your new situation will last. It is time to immediately assess your resources (i.e., savings, family support, credit card limits, etc.) and adjust your spending accordingly.

- Second, check into unemployment benefits, *immediately*.

  » You are unlikely to qualify for unemployment benefits if you quit your job or were fired for cause. But if you were fired for other reasons or were simply laid off, you will likely qualify for unemployment benefits. These are effective immediately in some states and after a week in others. However, "effective immediately" does not mean "cash immediately." It might take two or three weeks to collect a check, so the faster you file, the faster you get paid.

  » Be aware that actively seeking work is a requirement for unemployment benefits. So be prepared to demonstrate that you have a résumé and are submitting applications for positions.

  » How much money you can collect varies by state. In some states, it is half of your previous income (subject to a maximum). The maximum duration for unemployment benefits across the country is 26 weeks, and it is shorter in some places.

» And, yes, unemployment benefits are subject to income taxes.[8]

- Third, think about your health insurance, *immediately*.

  » One of the frightening aspects of losing your job is the prospect of losing your health insurance coverage.

  » If you have health insurance through your work, it has probably already been paid through the end of your current pay period, as healthcare premiums are usually paid in advance. If you or your family have any pending healthcare needs, try to get them taken care of during that time.

  » After that time, healthcare coverage through your former employer is still (indirectly) available to you, but it comes at a cost. A federal law called COBRA (what it stands for in this case is irrelevant) requires the company that provided you with healthcare coverage at your former employer continue to be willing to provide you with the same coverage for up to eighteen months, so long as your former employer still has 20 or more people working there. You can cancel it at any time. However, there is a catch: You have to pick up the entire monthly cost of the coverage, plus a 2% administrative fee. That includes the portion that was previously being paid by your employer, which could have been as high as 80% or 100% of the monthly premium. So if you elect this option (you have about 60 days to decide whether to do so), that is one expense that will be going up dramatically at the same time your income is going down.[9]

  » Many people find it better to obtain coverage elsewhere, such as in a health insurance marketplace—the ones created under the Affordable Care Act (a/k/a Obamacare).

- Fourth, look for temporary jobs at the same time you are looking for a permanent job.

  » Once you complete the first flurry of activity associated with a job hunt (discussed below), there are often significant time gaps when you are waiting to hear back from potential employers.

» Many unemployed people make the mistake of assuming that these will be short and that it will be more useful to keep themselves available for interviews etc. Instead, look for small, flexible, temporary positions, perhaps even if they are below your capabilities.

» In some states, this can reduce (or even eliminate) your unemployment benefits if you get paid too much. In others, the earnings are a partial offset.

» However, even if a temporary job does lead to a loss or reduction of unemployment benefits, it may stop the clock running against the maximum duration or maximum amount of your benefits. And you never know whether you might need extra time to find your next position.[10]

BETTER RÉSUMÉ, BETTER JOB SEARCH

• • •

There are dozens if not hundreds of books that provide advice on conducting a job search. I will not try, in one part of one chapter, to replace them. That said, I have found that very few people, and apparently even few authors of existing books, know how to write a résumé that truly raises the likelihood you will secure a job interview—which, after all, is the primary purpose of a résumé.

A résumé is not a chronology of your life; it is an explanation of what is important for the reader to understand about you, *given the hiring criteria.* Think of it as a sales document that should present only those attributes of the product (i.e., you) that matter to the buyer (i.e., the résumé reader within your potential employer).

Let's take this philosophy and apply it to your résumé. Then, as a bonus, we'll apply it to your cover letter, and even to the interview itself.

WRITING YOUR RÉSUMÉ

When assembling your résumé, the first question you need to ask yourself is, "What job am I looking for, and how does that translate into how I should describe myself?"

- If you simply want the next job up the ladder from the one you just had, your focus should be on demonstrating coverage, namely, that you possess the full range of *experiences* necessary to succeed in this next position.

  » You should likely devote more of the available space on your most recent experience (which is presumably your most senior experience). You will want to include any designations and official qualifications you have. The accomplishments you want to highlight are the ones that most observers say address the most common challenges of your most recent job.

- However, if you are looking to change careers or industries, you will want a very different résumé. Here your focus should be on demonstrating you have the *skills* that are needed in the new career.

  » To be clear, that is not the same as demonstrating experience. In fact, if you try to write a résumé that focuses heavily on describing specific experiences, you will likely lose to other job seekers from the industry you are trying to enter, because they can point to more directly relevant experiences.

  » Instead, you should think about the skills the recruiter is looking for (e.g., intelligence, resourcefulness), and write your résumé to emphasize the display of these skills to a higher degree than other candidates might have (e.g., if you need to demonstrate raw intelligence, your high test scores or your most noteworthy academic achievements might figure highly).

  » You will probably devote less space to your most recent job and more space to various jobs you have held that relied more heavily on the specific skills you are trying to demonstrate. (To characterize your thinking: "In this job, I had to be resilient, and this shows I was. In this other job, I needed to be very caring about people, and here is the evidence that people loved me. Oh, and look at that academic record—that shows I must also be brilliant.")

Next, you need for your résumé to be convincing to the reader—but you need to think about who, or *what*, the reader of your résumé will be.

- In recent years, many jobs have been sourced through online job sites, such as LinkedIn.com, Indeed.com, CareerBuilder.com, etc. The recruiter uses these sites to source a few dozen of the most relevant résumés, and then he/she sorts through them by hand and interviews a handful of candidates.

- This process has turned some prior advice on its head.

  » Previously, I would have advised you to avoid self-complementary descriptors, such as "self-starter," "creative," and "results oriented," because declaring yourself to be proficient at something does nothing to convince the reader that you actually are. (In fact, at one firm I used to work for, there used to be a game of finding the résumé whose contents most belied its author's self-proclamation, such as someone who claimed to be a great communicator but sent a résumé was full of grammatical errors, or someone who claimed to be highly intelligent but listed a very poor grade point average).

  » Now, however, because computers are naively searching thousands of résumés for key words selected by the recruiter, you must include such descriptors, just to be among the ones selected for human review. So think: What are the key words the recruiters will most likely enter, and how can you unobtrusively plant them in your résumé?

- Once you are selected by the computer, you must then survive the human screening process, so your résumé must provide externally-observable, objective proof that your assertions are legitimate.

  » To refer back to the previous example, if you claim brilliance, then you should show high standardized test scores or academic awards, or refer to a situation where you solved a problem that many others could not figure out.

  » Or, if you claim to be a leader, you must demonstrate where others voluntarily followed you, or when you were selected to lead from a broad field of candidates, etc.

- In addition, your résumé needs to avoid any phrases that someone much less accomplished than you could legitimately use to describe themselves. For example:

» When a résumé reviewer reads "analyzed," "managed a database," "coordinated," "provided support," or "built a model," he/she has no idea whether you did so in a highly sophisticated way or just a pedestrian way—some high school interns could legitimately use these phrases when describing their summer jobs.

» However, they usually cannot use phrases such as, "discovered a new way to analyze sales data that improved sales of the office by 15%" or "coordinated two previously-antagonistic departments in ways that led to five new product breakthroughs."

» You must find a way to demonstrate, not just the dry list of duties you performed, but the sophistication you brought to that task and the success you achieved in it.

• Along the same line, do not clutter your résumé with unimpressive accomplishments. Everything you say that does not impress the recruiter counts against you. It's as if he/she silently says, "If that's the most impressive thing this person has to point out about himself/herself, he/she must not be very impressive."

• The final tip I can offer about impressing the human résumé screener is the 30-second test.

» Many résumé screeners will spend no more than one minute per résumé.

» Tougher still, if your résumé is not intriguing within the first 30 seconds, he/she usually will not grant you the second 30 seconds to search for whether you meet the rest of the job's requirements.

» So, look at both the content and the format of your résumé. Does it highlight the most interesting facets of your skills or experience, or are they buried in the details? Is it cluttered with nice-to-have information (such as personal interests) that might distract the reader for a few seconds? Even if the content is perfect, is it formatted in a way that is pleasing to the eye and makes it easy to find the critical information quickly?

» I suggest you have a friend or two look over your résumé for thirty seconds and circle the items that catch their eyes. Are those the items you want the recruiter to see first? If not, you need to redesign your résumé.

WRITING YOUR COVER LETTER

Now, what about your cover letter? It's easy to think cover letters don't matter anymore, because it seems like no one actually sends letters of *any* kind anymore, and many online jobsites don't require or, in some cases, even provide space for, cover letters.

But don't be naïve—whether your "cover letter" takes the form of an old school physical letter, or an email, or simply a quick note on LinkedIn, the right cover letter can make or break you, because it can be a key determinant of whether a recruiter or hiring manager ever actually reads that outstanding résumé you worked so hard to create.

- Most people put too much information, and the wrong information, in their cover letter.

- Do *not* take up any space to tell the recruiter how great his/her company is and how it would be good for your career to work there. While a brief compliment might be fine, the recruiter does not care how the company would be good for you (at least not yet anyway). He/she cares that you are good for the company.

- Your cover letter should be an enticement to look at the best parts (i.e., the most relevant parts) of your résumé, and nothing more.

USING YOUR RÉSUMÉ DURING THE INTERVIEW

Let's assume you have been selected for a job interview. Is your résumé's job done? No. Although you *write* the résumé strictly with a focus on *getting* the interview, you must now be proficient at *using* the résumé as a jumping-off point for an intriguing conversation during the interview itself. What conversation do you want to have?

- Interviewers often have a specific list of criteria they are searching for in a job candidate. You need to accurately guess what that list is, and then think through how you are going to make *all* of those points during the interview.

- Then, look at your résumé and think through how you can use its content to introduce those points.

» If the interviewer asks directly about the experiences or skills he/she is looking for, you can bridge to the résumé to demonstrate when and where you showed that skill or had that experience.

» If the interviewer asks you about one of the jobs you had, you can describe that job in terms of the skills or types of experience you believe he/she is looking for evidence of.

• Do not waste time describing anything more about the job than is necessary to set up the point about the skill or experience.

» The recruiter does not really care about those details, and you are wasting the time you need to make the rest of the points you need to cover.

» Literally millions of job seekers have had fun and fascinating conversations with recruiters, and then they have not received an offer because, at the end of the interview, the recruiter knew nothing about the candidate's qualifications with respect to some other key criterion.

~

Changing jobs, under any scenario, can be highly stressful. But if you get fired, or have a hard time finding a new job after you quit a previous one, remember that the world is large. No matter what happened before or is happening now, there are still plenty of employers who do not yet know anything about you. There are always more opportunities to be found!

ENDNOTES

1 Bureau of Labor Statistics, "Number of Jobs Held, Labor Market Activity, and Earnings Growth Among the Youngest Baby Boomers: Results from a Longitudinal Survey," U.S. Department of Labor, June 27, 2008, www.bls.gov/news.release/archives/nlsoy_06272008.pdf. Accessed December 26, 2019.

2 Bob McIntosh, "80% of Today's Jobs Are Landed Through Networking," Recruiting Blogs, March 26, 2012, recruitingblogs.com/profiles/blogs/80-of-today-s-jobs-are-landed-through-networking. Accessed December 26, 2019.

3 Your Dictionary, s.v. "for-cause," www.yourdictionary.com/for-cause. Accessed December 27, 2019.

4 "Guide to Claiming Unemployment Benefits," The Balance Careers, n.d., www.thebalancecareers.com/how-to-claim-unemployment-benefits-2058799. Accessed December 27, 2019.

5 "Collecting Unemployment When You Quit Your Job," The Balance Careers, n.d., www.thebalancecareers.com/collecting-unemployment-when-you-quit-your-job-2061011. Accessed December 27, 2019.

6 Alexia Fernández Campbell, "American layoff and firings are at a 20-year low," Vox, April 9, 2019, www.vox.com/2019/4/9/18300355/workers-layoffs-firings-rate. Accessed December 27, 2019.

7 Andrew Martins, "New Report Suggests Americans Familiar with Unemployment," Business News Daily, March 12, 2019, www.businessnewsdaily.com/11329-americans-familiar-with-unemployment.html. Accessed December 27, 2019.

8 "Guide to Claiming Unemployment Benefits," The Balance Careers, n.d., www.thebalancecareers.com/how-to-claim-unemployment-benefits-2058799. Accessed December 27, 2019.

9 Barbara Marquand, "What you need to know about COBRA Insurance," Insurance.com, October 25, 2019, www.insurance.com/health-insurance/health-insurance-basics/what-you-need-to-know-about-cobra.html. Accessed December 27, 2019.

10 Cynthia Myers, "Do Part-Time Workers Get Unemployment Benefits?" Chron, June 29, 2018, work.chron.com/parttime-workers-unemployment-benefits-10334.html. Accessed December 27, 2019.

CHAPTER 10

You Have a Serious Car Accident

By the time you turned 21, you had about 22% odds of having been in a meaningful car crash. The good news is that your odds over the next ten years are, in total, only about two-thirds as high. The bad news is that a car accident is different when you're an adult, it's your car, and it's your insurance policy. How you act after the accident, and how you and the other driver handle some of the legal issues, can have dramatic financial consequences—good or bad.

When you were a teenager, if you wrecked your car it was clear what you should do next: call your parents and do what they tell you—but now, everything is up to you. There are a number of actions that must be taken, a number that should be taken, and a number that can be taken. It is up to you to decide.

BEFORE THERE IS AN ACCIDENT
• • •

It is best that you take a few simple steps now to improve the outcomes when an accident occurs, because you will not be able to accomplish them after one occurs.

STEP 1: This is obvious but often overlooked: Ensure that you keep with you the three legal documents that are required in the case of an accident: (1) your driver's license, (2) your car's current registration, and (3) current proof of insurance.

» You already carry your driver's license with you every time you drive any car.

» But are you as diligent about the two other documents? The police usually demand to see them if they stop you for any purpose, and they will certainly demand to see them if you have an accident.

» And did you notice I said your car's *current* registration and your *current* proof of insurance? These documents are not permanent.

› The car registration is updated annually when you pay your car taxes or tag fees.

› The proof of insurance is the card or slip of paper your insurance company sends or emails you when you pay your policy premiums. It may cover as little as three months' time.

» In both cases, the *current* documents must be in the car. The police will not accept outdated documents as evidence you have the current ones buried in a stack of papers at home. Therefore, make sure you get the new ones into the car every time one arrives.

» By the way, you do *not* have to carry the title to your car in the car itself—in fact, it is a bad idea to do so, as it facilitates a thief's efforts to sell your car after they steal it.

STEP 2: Place a copy of the checklist of the steps that you should go through in the case of an accident (listed below) in your car, *now*.

» At this moment, the items may seem obvious, and you will think placing a list in the glove box is unnecessary. However, at the time of an accident, your mind will be flooded with thoughts and emotions, making it difficult to think clearly. I have been in several accidents in my life—and more often than not, I have later realized that I forgot one or more of the important steps.

STEP 3: Think, *now*, about hospitals and your car.

» Decide whether you have a preference for which hospital you do, or do not, want to be taken to if you are injured (as discussed in more detail below)

» Decide where you want your car to be towed if it is not drivable (probably a body shop that is on your insurance company's preferred list).

According to the National Highway Traffic Safety Administration, of the 6.5 million vehicle accidents in the United States in 2017, 4.6 million (or 71%) of those involved property damage only—that is, they did not involve injuries or fatalities.[1] Because injuries or fatalities change what you should do at the scene of the accident and afterward, I will first discuss property-damage-only accidents, and then cover what you should do differently when there are injuries involved.

ACTIONS AT THE SCENE
OF AN ACCIDENT AND AFTERWARD
· · ·

While you need to use your judgment about which actions to take and in what order, here are the major actions you generally will want to take at the scene of an accident:

• Stop—do *not* leave the scene of the accident.

» Every state has laws (referred to as hit-and-run laws) against improperly leaving the scene of an accident. For example, in Georgia, the law specifically requires all drivers to fulfill several obligations (listed below) before they are permitted to leave the scene.

» The crime of hit-and-run constitutes a misdemeanor if the property damage was light, or a felony if the damage was major or if someone was injured. Again using Georgia as an example, the fine for a misdemeanor hit-and-run ranges from $300 to $1,000 for a first offense. For a felony hit-and-run, the penalty includes one to five years in prison.

- Check for injuries—first, your own; then, your passengers; then, others involved in the accident.

  » If anyone is injured, you are required to render reasonable assistance (such as calling an ambulance—discussed below).

- Call 911 for an ambulance if there is any reason to believe one is needed.

  » This will be discussed in more detail below—but put it on your list.

- Do not move the vehicles (in most cases), but do secure the scene against the potential for additional wrecks.

  » You should not move a severely injured person (because it might cause more harm).

  » Further, you are not supposed to move the vehicles until the police arrive, unless the vehicles are causing a major traffic obstruction.

  » However, this means the vehicles may well be positioned in ways that render them vulnerable to additional collisions. Therefore, engage any emergency blinkers and take additional steps as appropriate (such as flares, waving a makeshift flag, etc.) to warn off approaching vehicles, provided those steps do not put yourself or others at additional risk.

- Obtain the names and telephone numbers of any witnesses.

  » Although the drivers are required to remain at the scene of an accident, witnesses generally are not. They could well decide to leave before the police arrive, particularly if there is a delay. Therefore, you want to get their contact information right away.

- Exchange information with the other driver(s).

  » This includes driver's license information (including the person's full name, address, and license number), and also their insurance information.

- Insist on an investigation by the police.

  » The more damage there is and/or the more injuries there are, the more important it is for the police to objectively establish what happened and who is at fault. This will matter greatly when you deal with your or the other driver's insurance company.

- Document the accident by taking your own photographs.
  - » This should include damage to both cars, as well as the scene of the accident and the location of the cars relative to each other so that it is clear who hit who, etc.
  - » You should also photograph the other driver, just in case he/she decides to suddenly leave the scene.
- Check the police officer's notes of his/her interview with you.
  - » If there is a significant error, it is much better to correct it then and there. Any attempt to correct it later will have much less credibility, as there would be a suspicion that you have been coached by an attorney by then.
  - » Because the notes are a summary of what *you* said, the officer should not object to you insisting on a correction of a significant error.

There are also several actions you generally should *not* take at the scene of the accident:

- Do not lie to the police.
  - » This is obvious, of course—but when you are in the heat of the moment, for any of several reasons, you may feel tempted to lie (or at least to shade the truth). Do *not* give in to this temptation, as you could set yourself up for major problems later.
- Do not converse casually about the accident with the police, the other driver, or witnesses.
  - » The other driver (or his/her insurance company adjuster) has an incentive to hear your words as admissions of guilt or an expression that you have not been injured.
  - » Therefore, a statement such as "I am so sorry this happened" can be twisted. Or, a statement that "I'm okay" can later be claimed to be a statement that you were not injured, and therefore any pain you have that showed up later must not have been caused by this accident.
- Do not call your insurance company until you determine whether you want to speak to an attorney first.

» More on this is discussed below.

- Do not agree to speak to the other driver's insurance company or attorney or parents, even if they are "right here on the phone" or "seem really nice and just want to know what happened."

  » Nothing good (for you) can possibly come from those conversations—but a lot of bad can.

JUST SO YOU KNOW

Handling Fender-Benders "Just Between Ourselves"

If you haven't heard these words already, you probably will at some point: "It's just a fender-bender—can't we just handle this between ourselves, rather than wait for the police and get the insurance companies involved?"

That's right, at some point, you will likely be involved in a low-speed accident that causes only minor damage to the cars involved. When that happens, if one of you is obviously at fault, that person may suggest the two of you simply handle the matter between the two of you. Let's assume it is the other driver. He/she offers to let you get an estimate from a repair shop and then hand you a check for the amount of the repair. Should you accept his/her offer?

You may be tempted. After all, given it is a minor accident, unless the cars are blocking traffic the police will assign it a low priority for investigation, so you might be waiting a long time (particularly if it's raining). And maybe you aren't 100% confident you were not at least partially at fault. Maybe you, too, had something to drink. Maybe you don't trust that your insurance rates will not go up, even if you are judged to not be at fault. Etc., etc., etc.

The decision is up to you. But there are three considerations you should weigh before you decide.

- First, you may be technically breaking the law if you do not call the police.

» If there are no injuries and the property damage is minor, you generally do not have to call the police from the scene of the accident.

» However, in every state, the police must be called within a short period of time if the property damage to both cars combined exceeds a specified threshold. That number is zero in Nevada and $250 in Alabama and the District of Columbia. In most states, it ranges from $500 to $1000. (In only eight states does it exceed $1,000.[2])

» Given the high cost of repairs, if there is visible damage to both cars, the cost probably exceeds the threshold.

» In truth, if both parties keep their word, the likelihood the police ever find out is low—but recognize that this is a low-likelihood, high-consequence possibility.

• Second, you will certainly be violating the requirements of your automobile insurance policy.

» Every major insurer requires that you report all accidents to them, usually within 72 hours.

» Again, if both parties keep their word, and if all goes right, the likelihood the insurance company will ever find out is low—but again, this is a low-likelihood, high-consequence possibility.

» If for any reason you later need to reach out to the insurance company (as discussed next), you will have placed yourself in a bad position.

• Third, and perhaps most important, agreeing to such an arrangement constitutes a major act of trust on your part.

» If the other person fails to contact you, or later changes his/her mind (through rethinking whether he/she is at fault, balking at the actual cost to repair your car, or simply refusing your call), you will have few recourses.

So be very careful. If you are tempted to agree, take several steps to raise the odds that the other party will live up to his/her promises:

- First, document the damage to both cars through photographs. That way, there can be no question as to what the damage was, and that you did not add to the damage later through another accident.

- Next, photograph the scene of the accident and the location of the cars relative to each other so that it is clear that he/she hit you, cut you off, etc. (i.e., the fault was truly the other driver's).

- Third, collect the same information from the other driver that was listed earlier in this section. In this way, the other driver knows that you can reach out to his/her insurance company if he/she does not keep his/her promises.

- Fourth, write out and have the other driver sign and date a brief statement admitting the accident was his/her fault.

- Fifth, get in contact with the other driver the very next day to assure yourself that he/she still intends to follow through—and then get busy obtaining the damage estimate. You need to know the true financial situation (and reaffirm the other driver's cooperation in light of the surprisingly large number) before your respective windows expire to notify the two insurance companies.

WHEN AN ACCIDENT INVOLVES INJURIES
· · ·

The converse of the figures I reported earlier is that fully 29% of automotive accidents involve injuries. (For the record, fatalities occur in about 0.5% of accidents.) The specific probability of injuries when the driver is between 20 and 29 years old is about the same.[3]

According to auto industry insurance experts, the average driver will be in about four accidents in his/her lifetime.[4] If you do the math, that means that, on average, 75% of all drivers will be involved in an injury-producing accident at some point in their lives.

Therefore, when injuries are involved, you definitely need to know what to do—and especially, what to do *differently* than in a property-damage only accident. Specifically, you should err on the side of calling 911 for an ambulance (or more than one if necessary) unless you are very sure no one is hurt.

According to government records, the ambulance will take an average of eight and a half minutes to reach the scene if it is in the city, and up to about fifteen minutes in rural areas.[5] A trip to a hospital will typically cost between $200 and $2,000, depending on what services are rendered along the way. Most auto accident policies and many health insurance plans (and potentially *both* if you have both) will at least partially cover the costs.

There are a number of reasons for calling an ambulance, some obvious and some less so, and they vary somewhat based on three situations.

In Situation 1, when you are not the injured person:

- First responders know what they are doing, and you do not.
  - » This is not a good time to rely solely on what you learned in a first-aid class.
  - » Remember especially the advice to not move an injured person. That is because injuries are often internal, and you can do more harm than good if you don't know what you are doing.
  - » While so-called *Good Samaritan laws* can protect you if you accidentally cause harm when making a good-faith effort to provide emergency medical assistance to someone else, why risk taking unnecessary actions you are medically unsure about?
  - » Relatedly, many times people are more injured than they know.
  - » You will not be charged for placing the 911 call. Any charges will go to the person who gets treated.

In Situation 2, when you *are* the injured person:

- Due to the probable onset of shock, you are the worst person to assess the extent of your own injuries.
- In many cases, there will be no charges (or only very low charges) if you ultimately do not need to be transported to the hospital.

- You do not need to worry about the hospital not treating you because you cannot afford it.

  » Under the federal Emergency Medical Treatment and Active Labor Act (EMTALA), everyone has the right to be treated for an emergency medical condition, regardless of their ability to pay.

- If you don't take an ambulance, how else are you going to promptly reach medical treatment?

  » Your car may be undrivable. If it isn't, the law does not permit you to take it from the scene of the accident until the police have finished their investigation, which may take time.

- If you leave the scene of an accident in an ambulance, the police will presume it was medically necessary and therefore not a violation of the law.

  » The judgment of the emergency medical technicians (i.e., the ambulance personnel) that you need to be taken to hospital establishes permission for you to leave the scene.

  » On the other hand, if you leave any other way, the onus will be on you to justify your decision.

- Some attorneys assert that being transported from an accident in an ambulance increases the size of later financial settlements.

  » This is because juries take injuries more seriously when the injured was transported in an ambulance than when they left of their own accord.

In Situation 3, when it is your loved one who is injured:

- Sending your loved one in an ambulance does not mean they must be separated from you.

  » Ambulances almost always permit one passenger to ride along (typically in the front seat unless the victim is a very young child) unless there is no room or the loved one is so distraught that they may impair the treatment of the injured person.

  » Therefore, for example, if it is your child that is injured, you do not have to force your child to endure being alone in order to get him/her to the hospital.

» Further, you can count on the authorities to be very understanding if you leave the scene of the accident because you are accompanying a loved one to the hospital in an ambulance.

Now, if you are to be transported to the hospital, the question arises: Which hospital?

- If you express a preference (or an aversion), the ambulance will follow your guidance, except in unusual circumstances (such as the hospital being temporarily unable to accept more admissions).

- However, if you do not express a preference, you will be allocated by a procedure that factors in a number of considerations other than which hospital is nearest.

  » For example, because a new admission means either new revenue or a burden under EMTALA, some systems deliberately spread their instructions evenly among all the hospitals in the area, regardless of which hospital is closest.

IMMEDIATELY AFTER YOU GET HOME, SHOULD YOU CALL A PLAINTIFF'S ATTORNEY?

· · ·

This section assumes you were *not* charged by the police with anything more than a ticket, and therefore do not need the services of a *criminal* attorney. If you were, stop reading, call *that* attorney, and follow his/her advice.

The next step in the process—*before* you contact either your insurance company or the other driver's insurance company—is to decide whether you want to call an attorney.

- As soon as you get on the phone with either insurance company, everything you say will be on the record.

- That is perfectly fine—most people involved in accidents do not call an attorney.

- But there is universal agreement that if you do want to consider retaining an attorney, your case will be stronger if you do so from the outset, rather than waiting until after you have made statements on the record and the insurance company's behavior convinces you that you need one.

- You must make this decision quickly. Most insurance companies have a short window (e.g., 48 or 72 hours) in which you are required to contact them.

DECIDING WHETHER TO CALL AN ATTORNEY

Plaintiff attorneys like to point out that calling an attorney does not obligate you to retain one. Therefore, they suggest you *always* call. Of course they do—that way, they get the chance to represent the case if it is a good one, and they still have the option to decline the case if it is not.

But what should *you* consider? There are several factors involved, and several questions you will need to ask. If the answers to the following questions result in a reaction of, "I'm still not sure what I want to do," then err on the side of calling—just remember that even after you've spoken to a given attorney, you are not obligated to retain them.

> **QUESTION 1:** "What will it cost me to call an attorney, and what will it cost me to retain them?"

- Virtually every attorney will be willing to speak to you over the phone for free. He/she will ask some qualifying questions, and if the case looks interesting to him/her, he/she will most often be willing to also conduct a more extensive consultation (in person or over the phone) for free before asking you to legally retain him/her.

  » Of note, you do not need to fear that something you say to an attorney before retaining him/her can be obtained by the other side. The attorney-client privilege (under which an attorney cannot share anything you tell him/her) generally begins with the first conversation.

  » Also, the attorney cannot allow himself/herself to be retained by the other side once he/she has that first conversation with you, even if you ultimately do not retain him/her.

- As to attorney fees, once you retain him/her, most but not all plaintiff attorneys will work on a *contingency basis*. That means you do not pay an hourly fee. Instead, the attorney is entitled to a percentage of whatever payments to you ultimately result from his/her work for you (whether those payments result from a lawsuit judgment or from an out-of-court settlement).

  » The percentage typically ranges from 25% to 40%, with 33% being more or less standard. In some cases, the percentage is lower if the payment comes from an out-of-court settlement and higher if it comes from a court judgment; this reflects the greater amount of legal work required to prepare for and conduct a trial.

- Note the contingency fee starts at the first dollar, not at the first dollar over what you could have obtained without the attorney's assistance, as no one factually knows what that amount would have been. Therefore:

  » If the attorney has a 33% contingency fee, you should only retain him/her if you believe the money you will collect would be 50% more than you would have received on your own, since you will only be keeping two-thirds for yourself.

  » Also, be sure you understand whether this particular attorney will want you to pay directly for out-of-pocket expenses (such as court filing fees) as the case proceeds and/or whether the attorney will expect full reimbursement for any out-of-pocket fees before you and he/she split the remaining proceeds based on the contingency percentage.

QUESTION 2: "When should I believe that working with an attorney will indeed result in enough money?"

- While every case is different, of course, the short answers to this question are, (1) when there are injuries and/or pain and suffering involved, and/or (2) when the insurance company you're dealing with has a reputation for poor payouts.

- If the accident involves only property damage, there is usually not enough discrepancy between the insurance company's offer and what you believe is fair to justify involving an attorney.

» Sure, there is some judgment involved in estimating the most appropriate way to repair a car, and the insurance company may well use a stingy judgment.

» But remember, the attorney will want 33% of the entire settlement, not 33% of any *additional* settlement versus what you could have gotten on your own.

» Therefore, only in egregious cases will the attorney be able to obtain enough additional monies to net you additional funds.

• However, there is much more judgment involved when assessing the appropriate medical care to address an injury, and far more judgment involved in assessing compensation for lost wages and/or pain and suffering. The dollars involved can also be much higher. Therefore, the more these are factors in your accident, the more likely it is that you can benefit from retaining an attorney.

• The general rule in the industry seems to be the more serious the injuries, the greater the value of hiring a lawyer.

» If you were in a minor fender bender with little or no injuries, you can probably do without one.

» On the other hand, if you were injured and needed (or think you will need) significant medical treatment, the value of your case rises quickly, and retaining an attorney would probably be a good idea.

• You should also consider the second factor, the insurance company's reputation.

» Insurance companies differ substantially in the degree to which they are seen as being fair in the payments they make for claims. The less fair they are, the more an attorney can be helpful.

» You can find out how well your insurance company or the other driver's insurance company (you *did* collect the identity of the other driver's insurance company back at the scene of the accident, right?) performs on this dimension. J. D. Power performs such ratings. As of this writing, the latest ratings—including the specific rating for settlement fairness—can be found online.[6]

» Be sure to focus on the settlement rating only, not the overall claims satisfaction rating. You are not interested in most of the other factors that go into the overall satisfaction rating. You are only interested in how fair claimants believe the company's payment was.

QUESTION 3: "How much money are we talking about?"

- In looking at the economics of auto accidents, there is an important distinction between the cost of an accident and the amount paid in settlement.

  » While the first is of interest to many parties (and so is studied in depth), the second is the one that is of most interest to you.

  » This matters, because while there is much data available on the first (which is irrelevant to you, so don't get distracted by it), much less data is available on the second.

- It is difficult to find any governmental source data. The best available information seems to come from Martindale-Nolo Research, which serves the legal industry in various ways, and surveyed its readers about personal injury settlements. Their results were as follows:

  » More than 70% of survey respondents received some financial settlement.

  » Of those receiving a settlement, 16% received less than $3,000; 37% received between $3,000 and $10,000; 21% received between $10,000 and $25,000; 10% received between $25,000 and $75,000; and 16% received more than $75,000.[7]

  » However, keep in mind that the readers they surveyed had come to the Martindale-Nolo website to find information about a claim and to look for a lawyer, so this is not necessarily an accurate sample of everyone who has been injured.

- Of course, averages are only a proxy for your real question: "What should *I* expect for my *particular* accident?" The answer, of course, is "It all depends…" However, you might be able to obtain some approximation from the multiple auto accident settlement or personal injury settlement value calculators available on the internet.

QUESTION 4: "I don't like to sue people—will I actually I have to sue that nice old lady?"

- If you're seeking a large settlement (six figures or more), the answer is almost certainly "Yes."

  » Large settlements that are near the top of what an insurance company is willing to pay come only when the insurance company clearly believes you are willing to see the case through to trial. That means being fully prepared to stay with the case through filing a lawsuit, depositions, etc.

  » While each case is different, you and your attorney must maintain a credible threat throughout the process. The insurance company is unlikely to fold at an early stage, so a lawsuit will probably need to be filed.

  » Odds are that the suit will be settled prior to a verdict, but it may only be settled quite late in the process.

- If you're seeking a smaller sum, the answer is probably "Not really."

  » Again, the attorney is only able to negotiate a better settlement than you could if he/she maintains a credible threat. That means you and he/she must give the appearance of being willing to file.

  » However, the odds of going through a full lawsuit are small. The vast majority of such claims are settled out of court. A national TV attorney (see below) recently publicly reported that he reaches settlements in 94% of his cases without going to court.

QUESTION 5: "Will my insurance company get mad and cancel my policy if I retain an attorney?"

- Your insurance company can cancel your policy (going forward, not retroactively; it still has to cover the accident that has already happened) based on your driving record, regardless of whether you retain an attorney or not. The company simply looks at your policy as a balance of the probability (going forward) of how much money will come in through premiums versus the probability of how much money will go out through claims.

- The act of retaining an attorney may ultimately alter the company's calculation, because the attorney has the effect of making your accident more expensive for the insurance company through obtaining a larger payout for you. But that is the point of retaining an attorney to begin with, of course.

DECIDING WHICH ATTORNEY TO CALL

There is no good source of objective information on which to base this decision. However, I believe I can at least provide some helpful guidance.

The first thing to know is that attorneys have specialties, and most of them are irrelevant to your case. You are looking for a *plaintiff's litigation attorney for an individual auto accident.* So, if you have a friend who is an attorney, or your parents have an attorney who has worked with them for many years, these people might be a source for a good referral, but they will most likely not be right for your case. (By the way, if they indicate this is not their specialty, but they could probably handle it, *they will most likely not be right for your case.*)

Next, forget about attorneys whose advertisements on TV refer to diseases or exposures to consumer products. These are *mass tort* attorneys. They are trying to find hundreds or thousands of plaintiffs to bundle into a single class-action case. While they can be excellent plaintiff attorneys, they will not take your case.

You are looking for an attorney who focuses on auto accidents and personal injury claims. They come in three broad flavors:

CATEGORY 1: The very high-end practice

- They have expensive offices and they don't advertise on TV. They only take very large cases involving deaths, very serious injuries, and much pain and suffering. They know the case is likely to take a lot of time and effort (because since the other side has so much to lose, it can be counted on to fight very hard). Therefore, they only get involved when the case is potentially worth hundreds of thousands of dollars or more.

- If your case qualifies for them, these are the ones you want. You find them through asking other types of attorneys in your city who the leading plaintiff attorneys are.

CATEGORY 2: The small practice

- This may be a solo practitioner or single litigator or two within a smaller general practice. Their quality varies widely. If you prefer this type, all I can advise is that you speak to more than one before you decide to retain them and to ask a lot of questions about the following:

  » Their experience, specifically with auto accidents of the same severity as your case, preferably with the same insurance company you will be dealing with

  » The level *and specific names* of resources they will devote to the case (i.e., how much time they will personally devote to the case)

  » Whether they work on contingency, hourly fees, or some blend of the two.

CATEGORY 3: TV attorneys

- You've seen the ads—dozens of them. So what is the reality? Attorneys who advertise on TV fall into two subcategories.

- The first subcategory consists of small, homegrown practices who have been approached by an enterprising ad salesman from the local TV station.

  » Their ads look (and are) cheaply made, and their ads run on cable channels and/or during the lowest-rated times on TV (e.g., after midnight).

  » These attorneys basically fall into the previous category, but they are hoping to make the jump into the big leagues through advertising.

  » If they seem impressive to you, then feel free to give them a call and use the same criteria as suggested above for the previous category.

» But if their ad is cheesy or they come across to you as unimpressive *in the ad,* they will come across equally unimpressive to the insurance company *in person*—and unimpressive means low-threat credibility to the insurance company, and a low settlement offer to you.

- The second subcategory consists of the large, industrialized mega-practices.

  » These are basically settlement mills.

  » They have better-looking ads, and they run them heavily throughout the year. If you have the sense that you have been seeing ads for a particular firm for years, it is almost certainly one of these.

  » These firms are basically in the business of having dozens (or even hundreds) of attorneys efficiently handle large numbers of small- to medium-sized cases for relatively quick settlements.

  » While they may have a small number of higher-powered attorneys on the payroll to pursue a few cases in depth, they do that primarily to maintain some level of credible threat that they *could* actually take a case to court if the insurance company is entirely unreasonable. But their real business is negotiating a moderate settlement with relatively little effort.

  » So, if the personal injury settlement value calculator suggests your case is of moderate value, they may well be appropriate for you. But understand they are not designed for a long, drawn-out battle. If you learn that your case will require such an effort, they are not likely to be right for you.

DEALING WITH TIME LOST FROM WORK
• • •

One final issue to deal with following a car accident is time lost from work, whether due to injuries or simply the administrative burdens of your car repairs.

If you lose wages due to the accident, you must look to the insurance company—not your employer—to compensate you. Whether you will receive any reimbursement will depend on the specifics of the particular insurance policy that is paying out and the laws in your particular state. Both of these factors vary widely.

If you are out of work for any significant time period, I certainly hope your employer lets you return to your job after you've recovered. However, again, each state has different laws regarding your right to return to work, so there is no single answer about what to expect.

ENDNOTES

[1] National Highway Traffic Safety Administration, "Traffic Safety Facts Annual Report Tables," U.S. Department of Transportation, n.d., cdan.nhtsa.gov/tsftables/tsfar.htm. Accessed November 2, 2019.

[2] Joshua Taylor, "What to Do After a Car Accident: Checklist & Tips for Drivers," WalletHub, April 19, 2015, wallethub.com/edu/ci/after-car-accident/12090/#police-fender-bender. Accessed November 2, 2019.

[3] B. C. Tefft, "Rates of Motor Vehicle Crashes, Injuries and Deaths in Relation to Driver Age, United States, 2014–2015," AAA Foundation for Traffic Safety, June 2017, aaafoundation.org/rates-motor-vehicle-crashes-injuries-deaths-relation-driver-age-united-states-2014–2015/.

[4] Des Toups: "How Many Times Will You Crash Your Car? Forbes online. www.forbes.com/sites/moneybuilder/2011/07/27/how-many-times-will-you-crash-your-car/#7d82ab164e62

[5] Andrew M. Seaman: "Be prepared for ambulance wait times" Reuters July 19, 2017. www.reuters.com/article/us-health-emergency-response-times/be-prepared-for-ambulance-wait-times-idUSKBN1A42KQ

[6] "U.S. Auto Claims Satisfaction Study (2019)," J. D. Power, n.d., www.jdpower.com/business/ratings/study/U.S.-Auto-Claims-Satisfaction-Study/10212ENG.

[7] Martindale-Nolo Research, "Personal Injury: How Much Can I Expect to Get?" Lawyers.com, n.d., www.lawyers.com/legal-info/personal-injury/personal-injury-basics/personal-injury-how-much-can-i-expect-to-get.html. Accessed November 7, 2019.

CHAPTER 11

"You're Under Arrest"

AUTHOR'S NOTE

Criminal law is a complex subject, where the specifics matter a great deal and vary by ju-
risdiction (such as federal, state, or local). Therefore, this chapter is simply an orientation
to the subject and should not be construed as constituting legal advice.

Further, I recognize if you are actually arrested, you will be in no position to consult
this chapter. Therefore, you should read it now. You may not remember all the details
when the time comes, but enough should come back to you to be helpful.

Finally, my assumption in writing this chapter is that any arrest you experience is
the result of something largely accidental or incidental to your life—such as drunk driv-
ing, public disorder, small-scale drug possession, etc.—that could involve a felony. (If
you plan to intentionally engage in systematic criminal activity, the descriptions here
may still be useful, but they certainly will be inadequate for your needs. Instead, you
should find and develop a relationship with a highly competent attorney prior to em-
barking on your career—you'll need one.)

A U.S. government study conducted in the 1960s estimated that, on average, American men stood a 50% chance of being arrested at least once in their lifetime. A 2009 update of that study raised the esti-mated likelihood to 60%.[1] A 2019 study showed that, even among college graduates, fully 23% of males and 14% of females had already been ar-rested at least once by age 26.[2]

There are many reasons you might be arrested accidentally or incidentally, ranging from being drunk to getting in a fight to simply being in the wrong place at the wrong time (such as when a protest becomes disorderly, or your roommate is arrested for serious drug possession). Therefore, you need to understand the arrest process, your rights, what to expect, and how to behave so as not to make the situation worse than it already is.

This chapter covers:

- The moment of arrest
- Being processed at the police station/precinct
- The holding cell
- Making *that* call
- "You have the right to an attorney…"
- The interrogation
- The bail-and-release process
- A brief note on what happens afterward

THE MOMENT OF ARREST

· · ·

Despite there being hundreds of crimes one can commit, there are actually only three circumstances under which the police can arrest you:

- The first circumstance is if a warrant has been issued by a judge.
  - » That means the police, the prosecutor, and a relevant judge have jointly determined there is a basis for your arrest. (The basis could be criminal, civil, or the fact that you failed to show up in court when you had been previously ordered to. For this discussion, I will assume the warrant is a criminal one.)
  - » Under this circumstance, when the police locate you, they will announce almost immediately that you are under arrest and usually, but not always, what you are being arrested for.
  - » The police will almost certainly give you the so-called *Miranda warning* ("You have the right to remain silent…") at that time.[3]
  - » You should immediately act as though you have been arrested (see the discussion below).
- The second circumstance is when an officer directly observes that a

crime is being committed at that time, and the officer is confident you are the perpetrator.

» Again, the announcement that you are under arrest will come very quickly, as well the Miranda warning and (probably) the charge, and you should immediately act accordingly.

- The third circumstance comes when an officer is investigating whether you may have committed a crime and interviews you.

» You may not feel you can simply walk away, but this does not mean you have been arrested—at least not yet. You have been *detained*.

If you are detained, you have a choice. How forthcoming you should be during detention depends on whether you have something to hide. On one hand, you are free to refuse to answer questions until you have an attorney present. That is your right, even though you have not been arrested. (Said another way, the Miranda warning that a person is given when arrested does not *give* them that right. It is simply a reminder that he/she already *has* that right.) If you have something to hide, it is probably best to invoke your right to say nothing. However, if you have nothing to hide, remember that if you appear to the officer to be surprisingly uncooperative, that will increase the officer's suspicion that you have something to hide, and this can lead to more questioning and a higher likelihood of arrest.

You can be handcuffed and even taken to a police station while still remaining only under detention (i.e., not under arrest). That is actually good, because you should strongly prefer to remain classified as being under detention only. Detentions do not go on your record but arrests do. So, if you are only detained, if you are ever asked later in life, "Have you ever been arrested?," the correct answer will legitimately be, "No." Further, although there are some narrow circumstances under which it is legal to fingerprint you without arresting you,[4] the police generally do not fingerprint detainees. But they do fingerprint everyone who gets arrested. And, of course, there are many reasons to prefer to not be fingerprinted. For example, there could be other crimes for which your fingerprints would be evidentiary (yes, they can and do check, as we will see later). And even if you have never committed a crime, once your fingerprints are in the system, they are in there forever—so if you ever stray to the wrong side of the law in the future, your fingerprints will already be on file for the police to match with those at a crime scene.

The most important reason to prefer an episode to be deemed a detention is that, even if you are guilty, once some time has passed (sometimes overnight), if the infraction is minor and the perpetrator has behaved well, the police often classify the detention as protective custody and free people without charges.

If the questioning reaches the point where the officer believes he/she has *probable cause* to believe you committed a crime, your detention will become an arrest (complete with the announcement and the Miranda warning). Probable cause is generally defined as "a reasonable amount of suspicion, supported by circumstances sufficiently strong to justify a prudent and cautious person's belief that certain facts are probably true."[5]

At the moment you are officially arrested (not just detained), you should expect to be handcuffed, have your Miranda rights read to you, and have your pockets and body searched for weapons or contraband. You may or may not be told what the charges are, because the requirement to immediately inform you varies by jurisdiction and circumstance.

HOW YOU SHOULD BEHAVE

In you are under either detention or arrest, you should remain calm, courteous, and physically cooperative with the officer—even if you think he/she is being unfair or treating you roughly (short of causing you physical harm, which you should alert him/her to). This is not a good time to shout "Police brutality!" or that your rights are being violated. There is plenty of time to do that later, if you so desire.

Why behave so well? First, bad behavior could result in additional charges regardless of whether you have previously done something wrong or not. As of 2015, 95% of all large police departments reported to the Department of Homeland Security that they had issued, or were planning to issue, body cameras to at least some of their officers.[6] So you should assume there will be objective evidence to convict you of any crimes due to your bad behavior.

Understand, if you are arrested, you will go through a long and unpleasant experience. As I will discuss below, the police have broad discretionary powers in conducting that process to make it shorter and less unpleasant or longer and more unpleasant. Police are human beings. If you start out making an officer angry, how do you think he or she will use that discretion?

Most importantly, remember that being a police officer is a dangerous job. Arrests sometimes turn violent. So if you are behaving badly, the officer will see this as a situation that could turn violent. That will make him/her treat you much more roughly in a physical sense and could prompt him/her to adopt stronger measures.

The instant your status changes to being under arrest, you should immediately and clearly invoke your rights to have an attorney present. (You must be clear. Courts have held that uncertain statements such as "Do you think I need an attorney?" do not constitute you invoking your rights.) As soon as you request an attorney, *you should stop talking until the attorney is present, except for minimal cooperation* such as answering the question, "Do you have anything on your person that might harm me?" when the officer is about to pat you down, or providing your name and address, etc. Demanding that an attorney be present for questioning does not protect you against any voluntary statements you subsequently make being used against you.

JUST SO YOU KNOW
Now is the Time to Identify a Potential Attorney

Given that you are not reading this book in jail, now is the time to identify and record the name and contact information of an attorney you would contact in the event of an arrest.

You do not want to be in jail in the middle of the night and wondering how to find an attorney who will take your call and represent you. And jail is not a good place from which to search for the best price or interview multiple attorneys about their qualifications and track record. Any call that begins with the words, "Hello, Mr. Smith? Of Smith & Jones? I know it's 3:00 a.m. and you don't know me, but I got your name from..." is going to be expensive.

BEING PROCESSED AT THE POLICE STATION

· · ·

The police routine to process or book an arrest is very much the same everywhere in the country, regardless of jurisdiction. If you have ever watched a police drama on television, you will recognize the steps. What may surprise you is how long they take and how long you must wait between each step while the police put other suspects through the same set of steps. You should expect the process at the station to take at least four or five hours. Then, you may be forced to wait in a holding cell until normal business hours for the final phase (bail and release), which itself can take several hours.

STEP 1: They collect some basic information from you and the arresting officer.

- This generally includes your name, contact information, the nature of the alleged crime (including the code section), and other vital statistics. There will be fewer or more questions for you, depending on what is already available through the police citation or account of the incident.

- These questions are not meant as an interrogation. However, remember they can use anything you say at any time against you, so do not get chatty. If they ask any question that seems to you to be more than basic data, remind them that you have invoked your right to have an attorney present for questioning.

STEP 2: They confiscate your personal property and possibly your clothing.

- If they have not already done so, they will confiscate your personal belongings. They may also take your clothes and provide you with a jail uniform. The confiscated items are held until you are released, unless any contraband or evidence is found among them.

- Very importantly, if you were wise enough to carry in your wallet or purse the name and contact information of an attorney, ask for permission to remove it and carry it with you to facilitate your call to the attorney. They may or may not let you. If they do not let you carry it, ask them to write it down for you and make it available later. If you forget to retrieve this information now, there will be far more delay and hassle when you ask them to retrieve the information from your confiscated personal possessions later in the process.

STEP 3: They take your mug shot(s)

- These photos often indicate a suspect's height and include the date and other information related to the arrest. Note these photos are considered public information. Very public. Many papers in medium and small towns publish lists of DUI and drug possession arrests—and believe it or not, some convenience stores even sell magazines that consist entirely of the mug shots taken in their local area over the past week.

STEP 4: They conduct a full-body search.

- The strip search is intended to ensure there are no weapons or drugs brought into the holding cell. Therefore, you will be strip-searched regardless of the nature or severity of the crime in question (even just a traffic violation). It involves removing all your clothes and can involve a body cavity search.

STEP 5: They take your fingerprints and perhaps your DNA.

- An officer will take an impression of your fingerprints. You may also be required to submit a saliva, hair, or other DNA sample. These tests are not covered by the Fifth Amendment protection against self-incrimination, so you do not have the right to refuse them or to force the police to wait for your attorney to be present. The fingerprints and probably your DNA code will be entered into national databases.

STEP 6: They check for other warrants against you.

- Whenever you are arrested, the police check their databases to see if they or other law enforcement agencies have outstanding warrants on you. If you do, you will very probably not be eligible for bail.

STEP 7: They perform a basic health check.

- You will be given a general health screening to make sure you are neither in need of immediate care nor will you be a threat to the officers or other suspects in the holding cell. This could include blood tests and even x-rays.

STEP 8: They interrogate you.

- I have included this step in the list here, but because it is such an important (and unpleasant) step, I will devote an entire section to it below.

STEP 9: They register the charges against you and determine how to set your bail.

- Out of your presence, the police (and the prosecutor if the crime is significant) will make a decision whether to formally file charges against you. This can happen at any point during the steps already listed. If you are lucky, the entire episode may be (almost retrospectively) deemed to have been a detention and not an arrest. If this happens, you will have your personal effects returned to you and you will be free to go.

- If the police proceed with the arrest, they will record the (prospective) charges in the court system,[7] then determine whether bail is required and whether your required bail can be set (and posted) at the station or whether you must appear before a judge to determine bail. If the latter, you will appear before a judge, usually during normal Monday-to-Friday business hours. (That will entail waiting until normal hours, being transported to a courthouse, being placed in another holding cell, and then appearing before a judge.) That hearing will determine whether you are eligible for bail, how much the bail will be, in what form it must be posted (described below), where it must be posted, and where you will be held until bail is posted. As with the previous step, I will devote an entire section to this subject below because this subject is complex.

STEP 10: You post bail and get released.

- Once bail is posted and recorded, you will be released. Your personal articles will be returned to you, and you will be given a set of papers that (among other things) will contain the instructions on when and where to appear at the courthouse for arraignment, as well as an explanation of that process.

STEP 11: You go home and do five things.

- People who have been arrested are generally anxious to do three things: (1) eat a decent meal, (2) get a shower, and (3) go to sleep. If you live alone, feel free to do them in any order. If you have roommates, they will appreciate it if you prioritize the shower.

- Do not forget to do the fourth thing: read those papers you were given, and carefully note when and where you must appear in court. Do not rely on your memory. By the end of the process of arrest, your physical and mental condition will unlikely be such that you can later trust that you understood and remembered the instructions when they were given to you at the station. As we will see later in this chapter, failure to show up for that court date is both a very common problem and a very costly one.

- As for the fifth thing you will need to do: figure out how you are going to handle the fact that word is likely to get around very quickly about your arrest. Whether through others who were present during the arrest sharing the story on social media, or friends and family seeing your name in the local paper, word is likely to spread widely and quickly. It is up to you to decide right away whether you are going to preemptively notify various persons whom you want to hear the story from you first (e.g., your parents, your boss) and what you want your story to be. Further, you need to think through how you are going to handle it when the subject comes up in embarrassing ways among your friends and co-workers. Be aware, once the arrest is memorialized on the internet, it can be there forever for future employers and others to find.

FOR THE LGBTQ COMMUNITY
Processing Based on Birth Gender

In most jurisdictions, transgender persons are processed (including being strip-searched and placed in holding cells) on the basis on their birth gender. While the danger of physical abuse is certainly lower than that of being in long-term incarceration under similar circumstances, the likelihood of humiliation and verbal abuse by other detainees is very high.

THE HOLDING CELL
· · ·

At some point in the process—between some of the steps above and/or while waiting for interrogation and/or while waiting to be formally charged or for bail to be set—you will almost certainly be placed in a holding cell. It is useful to prepare yourself mentally for the experience.

The physical basics of a holding cell are fairly routine, but your experience there will vary widely, depending on location and circumstance. The experience will range from tedious and unpleasant to extremely tedious and extremely unpleasant.

Holding cells vary in size (depending on an area's anticipated demand), but the design principles are always the same. Men are held in a different cell than women, but there is no separation by the type of crime among the arrested individuals (with obvious exceptions, such as potentially violent offenders or persons with communicable diseases).

The cell has solid, bare walls and no windows. There will either be one side open (except for bars) facing the police bullpen or a video surveillance system so the police can monitor the detainees. There will be benches or chairs permanently fastened to a metal rail and an open toilet. There will certainly be no place to lie down, except for the concrete floor. There will probably be no clock. There may be a television permanently tuned to one channel, such as one that advertises bail bondsmen on a continuous loop. The lighting will be harsh, and the temperature will be noticeably cold (regardless of the time of year).

Much of the design is dictated by security and safety considerations. However, the physical design contributes to the misery. The metal bench and harsh lighting are uncomfortable for sleeping. The lack of privacy, poor hygiene of your fellow detainees, and frequent use of the toilet by drunk detainees who are vomiting will make using the toilet quite unpleasant. And the cold air? As miserable as it will be, you should prefer it, as warm air would only increase the ever-present stench. The absence of windows and usual lack of clock deprives you of any sense as to how much time goes by (remember, your watch and cell phone have been confiscated), so it will feel as if time has stopped.

Regarding food, think basic. The menus, raw quality, and source vary dramatically from jurisdiction to jurisdiction, but what they all have in common is the food is intended to meet the minimum required health standard at the least expense possible. The food is usually worse than prison food. Because detainees will be in the holding cell for only a short time, little attention is paid to nutrition, quantity, or preventing unrest due to poor food (which is a consideration in prisons, of course).

Then there are the other detainees. The cell is a fixed size, but the population is not. Therefore, the holding cell could be nearly empty or quite crowded. Crowding is likely on weekends, when more arrests are made and detainees remain throughout the period as most jurisdictions do not conduct arraignments until Monday mornings. In fact, if you have the misfortune of being arrested on a Friday night, you may experience ever more crowding over the next two days.

Many detainees will stink upon arrival. Some detainees may not have bathed for some time, but no one (including yourself) will bathe in the holding cell, so body odor will be rampant. Others (e.g., drunks or drug users) may vomit, urinate, or defecate. The police may remove the worst of these after the damage is done, but the odor will linger.

Physical danger is rarely a problem. Most of the detainees are there for minor crimes. The police quarantine persons whom they perceive as potentially violent, and they monitor the behavior of the detainees. However, there could well be persons who are angry, sullen, and physically intimidating. They could be nasty and even enjoy hassling you just to pass the time (e.g., "I'm going to find you out there when this is all over"). Everyone's irritability increases the longer they are held.

You will likely talk to one or more of any apparently compatible detainees. You won't be able to help it. The holding cell is the ultimate boring environment, and detention lasts for an interminably long time. As the two of you search for something in common to break the ice, one of you will ask, "What are you in for?" *Be careful!* Avoid getting into any discussion of the events that led up to your arrest. Remember that you are not entitled to any expectation of privacy. That is important, because most of the people within earshot (including your new friend) are looking for a way to curry favor with the police and/or prosecutor (after all, by definition, they are waiting to be charged with a crime). They would love to be able to trade damning information about someone else's case for leniency in theirs.

MAKING *THAT* CALL
• • •

First, the bad news: in many jurisdictions, you do not have the *right* to make a phone call. Now the good news: if you have behaved well and the police are not worried that you will abuse the call to ask an accomplice to destroy evidence, they almost always let you make a call—in fact, several calls if necessary. (In most jurisdictions, the police have discretion to allow you to make any number of calls.) Therefore, you do not need to panic if the person you try to call doesn't answer when you call. And you can call an attorney, as well as your loved one to let them know what has happened, as well as your boss to tell her you won't make it to work. Ask the officer if you can call a specific list of people. Don't abuse the privilege—remember, it is *privilege, not a right.*

So how does society reconcile the fact that you have a right to an attorney but not the right to make a call? How are you supposed to reach an attorney? The answer is that if you demand an attorney be present and the police choose to not permit you to make a call, they will make one on your behalf to the attorney of your choosing.

Before you make the call, be prepared. The person(s) you call will need to know the address of where you are being held. (The officer will tell you.) They may need to know where you left your car or other personal property. (The arresting officer may know.) For reasons of helping you to get bail (as I will discuss below), they will need to know what crime you are being charged with and the monetary amount of bail (if any) for that crime listed on the bail schedule and what types of bail are accepted in this jurisdiction. (An officer at the station will almost always know. Your being polite will improve the chances that he/she will tell you.) And if the particular place you are being held permits it, they will need to know whether you need a change of clothes due to falling, vomiting, or how cold the holding cell is. If you must appear before a judge for a bail hearing, they will need to know where to post bail (if bail is granted, as discussed below) and where you will be released.

A few jurisdictions have rules governing how quickly you must be allowed to make a call, but most do not. So, while the large majority of police are willing to be helpful (unless you are making their lives difficult), they will be helpful at their convenience, not yours. You may face an extended wait before receiving that privilege—and the more fuss you make about that, the longer your wait is likely to be.

"YOU HAVE THE RIGHT TO AN ATTORNEY..."

• • •

"You have the right to have an attorney present during questioning. If you cannot afford one, one will be appointed for you." It sounds so simple, but in fact, there is a lot to think about in those phrases.

First, do you want an attorney? If the crime you are being charged with is major, the answer is definitely yes. You need the police to not be allowed to ask you questions while you are alone. You need protection during inter-rogation so you are not asked questions you shouldn't answer and not give answers you shouldn't give, and an attorney can help reduce the size and conditions of bail.

But criminal defense lawyers are not cheap. In rural areas, they typically charge $100 to $200 per hour (although cheaper ones can be found). In large cities, that rate can be $200 to $400 per hour. On average, across the country, the soup-to-nuts services of a criminal defense attorney range from $3,500 to $4,500,[8] with there being a wide variation depending on the seriousness of the crime and the complexity of the case. For example, one illustrative attorney charges $750 to $2,000 for misdemeanor possession of marijuana, but the rate is between $750 and $10,000 for possession of a controlled substance, depending on the client's criminal history and the amount of the substance involved in the arrest.

Therefore, if the crime you are being charged with is a minor misdemeanor, the answer of whether to call an attorney is less clear. In fact, about 80% of suspects waive their rights to remain silent or have an attorney present during questioning. (However, do not be lulled into a false sense of security by this statistic—most of those suspects then end up confessing, as we will see below.)

When might you choose to not call an attorney? Pretend that your situation is as follows:

- You are clearly guilty and you know the police have incontrovertible evidence.

- There was no obvious flaw in the arrest process that an attorney could use to get the charges dismissed or reduced.

- The bail schedule suggests you will not need to post bail.

- The penalty is a fine of moderate size (not jail time).

In this case, you will plead guilty, and the value to be added by an attorney may not be much. Demanding an attorney will cost you significant money and may delay the process, because if the police plan to interrogate you, they cannot do so before your attorney arrives. So you have a choice to make. If you decide not to call an attorney, you can inform the officer that you have changed your mind (because you *did* invoke your right to one back at the arrest site, right?) and you are willing to state, on the record, that you are revoking your privilege.

Assuming your situation is one in which you do want an attorney, which attorney should you want: the best, the cheapest, or the one who will get there fastest? When you place a call to an attorney, he/she may insist you retain him/her for not just the day of the arrest but for the whole criminal process. So your call may decide the quality of your representation throughout the whole process. Depending on your priorities and the severity of the crime involved, you might make different choices about who is the right attorney for you.

Let us assume you call an attorney. You will need to wait for him/her to arrive. On television, a suspect demands to have an attorney present, and then the attorney instantly and magically appears in the next scene. That is not how it happens in real life. It may be hours before you are permitted to make the call to an attorney. Then the attorney does not live next door to the police station and may be busy. So you should count on it taking some time for him/her to arrive. That means you will have to discipline yourself for several hours to maintain your silence without the assistance of an attorney. Once your attorney arrives, you will be permitted to meet with him/her in private. One of the first things he/she will ask you is, "What have you already said?"

JUST SO YOU KNOW
"If You Cannot Afford An Attorney..."

You've heard the phrase on TV crime shows: "If you cannot afford an attorney, one will be appointed for you." You will be surprised to learn that this is not actually true—yet. If you ask for an attorney but do not have the resources to retain one, you will go through the initial arrest process without one, most likely including the process of setting bail.

The determination that you cannot afford an attorney and subsequent appointment of one for you comes only when you appear before a judge during your *arraignment*, which occurs either at the end of the arrest process for major cases or at a later date for minor cases.

The only exception that will be made to the normal arrest process is that you will not go through formal questioning yet. Because the police cannot conduct an interrogation without an attorney present (if you have demanded one), you will go through the initial arrest process without being interrogated. This will not affect your bail, because, as I will discuss below, bail is based on the nature of the charges and whether you present a danger to anyone, not on the likelihood of your being guilty.

However, you will not have escaped interrogation, just merely delayed it. Once the court appoints an attorney for you, the police will insist on questioning you—with your attorney present.

THE INTERROGATION
· · ·

If you are being questioned while still under detention, you should assume the police suspect you have something to hide. If you are being interrogated after you have been arrested, you should assume the police believe you are guilty. Particularly in the second case, the police think that the purpose of this interrogation is to gather additional evidence against you and to have you implicate any others who might be involved. They will be genuinely surprised if the interrogation exonerates you.

In theory, the interrogation process is intended to be objective, and I certainly do not mean any disrespect to the police. However, police officers and detectives are human beings, subject to the same biases as the rest of us. Consider the following: (1) they would not have arrested you if they didn't already believe you are guilty; (2) they feel good about themselves and get rewarded if they solve crimes—if you confess or provide evidence against yourself, that is a victory for them; and (3) they recognize your natural bias will be to present only those arguments and facts that suggest you are innocent, so they want to level the playing field.

Therefore, regardless of whether or not you have something to hide, you need to understand and be mentally prepared for the interrogation process, because it is *designed* to be problematic for you.

For the purposes of this section, let us assume that you have waived your right to an attorney. We make this assumption, first, because (as mentioned earlier) 80% of suspects waive this right. Second, you need to understand what an interrogation is like without an attorney so that if you actually retain one, you can understand what the attorney will be doing when he/she attempts to disrupt the interrogator's process.

The most important thing you need to understand and remember is that your one and only trump card in this process is that you can invoke your right to an attorney at any time. That's right—even during the interrogation, even if you have previously waived your right to one, you can demand to have an attorney present. If you do, the interrogation must stop immediately, right then and there, until your attorney arrives. Don't worry that you are going back on your word to the officer. He/she is not your friend. Do not let the officer interrupt you when you start to invoke the right (as he/she has been taught to do, which we will see). Assert your right if you need to.

So, what is the process like? The most popular interrogation technique in the United States was developed in the 1950s by John Reid, who was a psychologist, a polygraph expert, and a police officer. The Reid technique was designed to psychologically manipulate people to confess. It is a biased process. Studies have linked it to potential false confessions so much so that, in 2017, one of the largest police-consulting firms in the country (which had previously trained hundreds of thousands of police in the method) announced it would no longer teach the method and would only use the method to educate police on the risk of false confessions.[9] Despite this, the Reid technique is still the de facto process in most police departments, so it is the technique you should expect.

You will be taken to a special room. It will be much smaller than you have seen on television. It will be barely large enough to accommodate you and two detectives. The only furniture will be a small metal table and just the right number of chairs. (The room will be larger if you have an attorney present.) Your chair will be uncomfortable. The walls will be blank except for possibly a large one-way mirror. You will most likely see one or more cameras recording you. Each of these design elements is specifically intended to raise your anxiety.

The technique itself begins with a phase called the Fact Analysis, followed by the Behavior Analysis interview, then followed by Reid's nine steps of interrogation. The first two phases are not confrontational but are used by the police to establish baselines from which to push you later and judge your responses. For example, they will observe your facial gestures when you are trying to recall something versus when you are lying. They want to see how you unconsciously behave when they ask you something uncomfortable. During these phases, the interrogators are sizing you up to guide your manipulation through the nine steps.

The Reid technique treats interrogation as an accusatory process in which the questioner tells you the evidence clearly shows you committed the crime in question. It is generally conducted as a monologue rather than a question-and-answer session.

It is critical you understand that whether or not the police use the Reid technique, the police are allowed to lie to you (except for a few specific prohibitions). That's right. They can tell you they have evidence they actually do not have. They can say someone has identified you. They can say your accomplice has already implicated you. Do not accept their statements at face value, and do not rely on their statements in your decision-making during the interrogation.

The Reid technique's nine steps of interrogation are as follows:[10]

STEP 1: Direct confrontation.

- Advise the suspect the evidence has led the police to the individual as a suspect. Offer the person an early opportunity to explain why the offense took place.

STEP 2: Try to shift the blame away from the suspect to some other person or set of circumstances that prompted the suspect to commit the crime.

- Develop themes with reasons that psychologically justify or excuse the crime. Themes may be developed or changed to find one to which the accused is most responsive.

STEP 3: Minimize the frequency of suspect denials.

STEP 4: Dismiss objections.

- At this point, the accused will give a reason for why he or she did not or could not commit the crime. Try to use this to move toward an acknowledgment of what they did.

STEP 5: Reinforce sincerity to ensure that the suspect is receptive.

STEP 6: Move the theme of the discussion toward offering alternatives

- If the suspect cries at this point, infer guilt.

STEP 7: Pose an alternative question, giving two choices for what happened, one more socially acceptable than the other.

- The suspect is expected to choose the easier option, but whichever alternative the suspect chooses, guilt is admitted. (There is always a third option for the suspect, which is to maintain he/she did not commit the crime.)

STEP 8: Lead the suspect to repeat the admission of guilt in front of witnesses and develop corroborating information to establish the validity of the confession.

STEP 9: Document the suspect's confession and have him or her prepare a statement (audio, video, or written).

When the Reid technique is followed in its classic form, the questioner comes across as understanding, patient, and non-demeaning. He or she wants to gradually make you more comfortable with telling the truth. The technique is for him or her to first imagine and then offer various psychological justifications for the crime of which you've been accused, leading you to correct the details of his/her theory and thereby gradually make a full confession.

However, some police use a number of hostile variants of the technique. For example, two questioners may adopt the classic "good cop/bad cop" ploy, where one is deliberately nasty toward you and the other acts as your defender, as studies show that people often open up to those who are acting to protect them. Or, they may be particularly heavy-handed in their application of Steps 1, 3, and 4.

Regardless of the variation the police employ, you must remain mentally strong if you wish to not incriminate yourself. Frankly, the odds are not with you. Studies have shown that between 42% and 55% of all suspects confess during interrogation.[11] Assuming that the propensity to confess is lower when an attorney is present, one must imagine that the portion of suspects without an attorney who confess is even higher.

What if it gets hard to mentally stand your ground? Remember your trump card. Assert your right to have an attorney present. (If you do not actually intend to have an attorney, you can then revoke that right later, after you have rested.)

THE BAIL-AND-RELEASE PROCESS
• • •

In the United States, as in most countries, the accused is legally innocent until proven guilty in a court of law, and so society believes it generally unjust for the accused to be held in custody prior to being formally charged and convicted of a crime. At the same time, however, the police and prosecutors have a strong interest in the accused showing up for various court dates, including his/her trial. To ensure that, the court can demand the accused deposit money or other valuables with the court that will be returned only if the accused shows up for all required court dates. That deposit is called *bail*.

The most important fact to know about bail is that if you do not show up for court, the person who posted the bail (referred to as the *surety*) will probably lose the full amount of the bail. This is true even if the particular form of the bail (discussed later) does not require the full amount be deposited with court up front. Importantly, showing up for court means that you make *all* of the court dates until the case is closed, not just the first court date. The liability in a bail arrangement extends that long, and any monies deposited with court will be held that long.

The process begins at the station where you are being held. Once the police (and possibly the prosecutor) decide to file charges, an officer consults a schedule that (1) specifies whether bail is required, (2) specifies whether bail can be administered at the station or whether a judge *must* be involved, and (3) if the station can administer the bail, what the amount and form of the bail must be.

If the bail process takes place at the station, it will do so almost immediately, even in the middle of the night. Also, the amount of bail may shock you, but it will likely be one you can handle. For example, In Houston, one study found the median bail amount for misdemeanors was $2,800. In Las Vegas, as of the writing of this book, the bail amount for most misdemeanors was $1,000. Bail for DUI first offenses was $2,000 and second offense was $3,000.[12]

However, in general, across the country, bail is set separately for each crime of which you are accused. To be released, you must pay the bail for each of these crimes. It is not simply a matter of paying the largest one, and there are no discounts for multiple bails.

The form of the bail will be fairly simple. In fact, many jurisdictions even allow the use of credit cards. That is good, because you want a small number and a form of payment that is quick so you can get out and go home.

Some bail situations cannot be handled at the station. Further, the police have the discretion to force a bail hearing they could normally handle at the station to take place in front of a judge. An example of this would be if the particular circumstances of the crime or the accused lead the police to believe a larger bail would be advisable (e.g., the accused has a history of not showing up in court).

If the crime or circumstance requires a bail hearing before a judge, the situation is much more complicated and costlier in a number of ways.

First, if the hearing will take place at the judge's courtroom, that usually means waiting until normal Monday-through-Friday business hours (although a minority of jurisdictions have night court). It also means being transported to the courthouse.

Then there is the matter of setting bail. If your case requires a judge, expect the amount to be a large number. The precise amount varies dramatically by jurisdiction (e.g., one study found the median bail in New York was $5,000, while it was $20,000 in Pennsylvania and $50,000 in California).[13] Bail also varies dramatically by type of crime. For example, in Southern California, bail for assault typically starts at $25,000 and goes up from there, to over $1 million under certain circumstances.[14]

Because the intent of bail is not punishment, but is limited to ensuring the accused returns to court and that the community is not endangered, many of the factual elements of your alleged crime will not be considered in the bail discussion. Nor will the likelihood of your being convicted be considered. Rather, the judge will focus on five factors: (1) the seriousness of the charge; (2) your prior history with the law and pattern of showing up for court in prior situations; (3) how strong your ties are to the community (e.g., do you have a job you would be reluctant to give up, do you have relatives living in the area you would be reluctant to leave behind); (4) whether there is any indication you were caught preparing to leave the area, such as having a large amount of cash and a passport; and (5) whether there is any perceived risk to anyone else if you are released.

For obvious reasons, the prosecutor will be there to argue for higher bail or even that you be remanded without bail (i.e., continue to be held in custody). Your attorney will argue for less bail or even that you be *released under your own recognizance* (or *ROR*), meaning that no bail will be required at all and the court trusts you to show up. This is one instance where an attorney can add real value. Arguments as to why you are really a good person and therefore less bail is needed have more weight coming from an attorney than if you try to make the argument yourself.

What are the typical outcomes with respect to bail being required? A 2009 study concluded about 20% of detainees were released ROR (i.e., without a bail requirement). At the other end of the spectrum, about 10% of detainees were denied bail. Of the 70% for whom bail was required, about half found a way to pay it and were released, while the other half could not pay their bail and remained in custody until their case was adjudicated.[15]

Once bail has been established, the court (or the officer in charge at the station if bail is handled there) determines which *forms* of bail will be acceptable (e.g., all in cash from you personally, or part cash and part promise by your mother). Sometimes the allowed form(s) of bail is predetermined by the standard schedule or by the amount of bail the judge decides on. Other times, the judge can hold a separate discussion about the form of the bail.

Allowed forms of bail vary on two dimensions. The first concerns who is going to be the surety (i.e., the person financially responsible for the obligations of the bail agreement)? That person can be you, or sometimes a relative or friend, or sometimes even a group of relatives or friends, or sometimes a professional bail bondsman, whom I describe below. The primary criteria from the court's perspective are (1) will the surety be available, able, and ready to meet the obligation, and (2) how does this particular surety have the influence over you to ensure you will appear?

The second dimension concerns how the immediate financial obligation will be met. There are several forms of bail, as detailed below.

The simplest form of bail (but often most difficult to afford) is a *cash bond*. It is required in about 10% of bail cases. In a cash bond situation, the surety has to deposit with the court the full amount of the bail before you get released.

A *percentage bond* (sometimes called a *deposit bond*) requires that some percentage be deposited in cash (most commonly 10%), and the surety signs a legal contract agreeing they will pay the remainder if you do not show up. This form is used in about 10% of bail cases.

In both cash and percentage bonds, there can be a variant for fulfilling the cash portion of the requirement. This is called a *property bond,* and it works very much like a pawn shop. The surety posts the title to some property (e.g., a car, or real estate) that the court holds until the case is closed.

A *commercial bond* involves a professional bail bondsman. This is used in about 70% of bail cases. An independent business (i.e., the bail bondsman) that is pre-registered with the court provides the court with a guarantee that he/she will pay the bail if you fail to show up for court. (Note that because of his/her registered relationship with the court, he/she does not actually have to deposit any cash with the court.) To be willing to do this, the bondsman charges you a nonrefundable fee, which is usually 10% to 15% of the bail amount.

There are two drawbacks to the bail bondsman approach that you should be aware of. First, unlike when you post the bail with the court, you do *not* get back the fee the bail bondsman charges you. Therefore, the 10% is an irrevocable expense to you, not a temporary use of your cash. Second, the bail bondsman is not really absorbing the risk if you fail to show up in court. The bail bondsman will not be willing to issue the bail bond without getting the same kind of guarantees (such as a signed indebtedness contract) from your relatives that the surety would have had to give the court under a percentage bond.

So why would anyone ever go to a bail bondsman? Because (1) if the portion of cash you would have to come up with under a percentage bond exceeds 10%, using him involves less cash out of pocket up front, and (2) he may be willing to sign a contract with persons whom the court would not.

One other point about the bail-and-release process is worth noting. Courts, particularly federal courts, often set conditions on your release other than just posting bail. For example, pretrial supervision, drug testing, mental health evaluations, travel restrictions, and electronic monitoring are all common conditions.

JUST SO YOU KNOW
The Facts on Skipping Bail

In the news, and particularly in Hollywood, we are often exposed to stories about defendants skipping or jumping bail. How often does it happen? Is it generally a good or bad idea?

The most definitive study on the subject[16] estimated that 23% of felony defendants had bench warrants issued against them for failure to appear (FTA) at a required court date. However, this figure may be misleading out of context, as the same study indicated that 94% of those charged with FTA subsequently appeared in court within a year.

I say this may be misleading because explanations of those figures diverge wildly, depending on the view of the commentator.

- On one hand, proponents of less onerous bail make the point that there are many non-culpable reasons why defendants miss court dates (forgetfulness, homelessness, inability to find transport, etc.). They point out that studies have shown the propensity to no-show for personal medical appointments also runs between 20% and 30%. Given that few people have an incentive to run out on a medical visit, these advocates suggest that forgetfulness etc. accounts for the vast majority of FTAs.

- On the other hand, advocates of tougher bail laws claim that defendants subsequently appear in court as the result of being arrested for a different crime, and the warrant search described earlier in this chapter resulted in their appearance. Therefore, they say, the suspects should not be given credit for later appearances.

So what is the true skip rate? No one knows, but perhaps we can gain some insight by looking at the incidence of forfeiture of bail monies, which one article claimed hovers in the range of 5%.

It appears that bail jumping is a bad idea. The act itself represents a betrayal of the trust of the surety (or the guarantor to your bail bondsman). That person must know you very well to have volunteered to be the surety, and he/she will be quite angry given what may now happen to him/her financially. He/she probably knows how the police can find you.

Given the 94% figure above, it would also appear that the strategy usually fails—and the penalty for that failed strategy is high. Bail jumping is a separate crime in itself (even if you are later proven innocent of the original crime). For example, for serious skip attempts, the state of Georgia can seize your bail, impose fines between $1,000 and $5,000, or sentence you to between one year and five years in prison. Or do all three.

WHAT HAPPENS AFTERWARD
· · ·

It is beyond the scope of this book to describe all the steps, paths, and possible outcomes of the criminal proceedings against you. But there are a few basics you should know:

- Your first ordered appointment at the court will most likely be your *arraignment.* This is when the court formally reads you the charges against you and you enter a plea (which can be changed later). However, you or your attorney may well have met with the prosecutor prior to that time to try to convince him/her to drop the charges or to negotiate a plea deal, in which you agree to plead guilty to the charge (or a lesser charge) in return for a lesser penalty than you might receive if you go to trial.

- The length of the adjudication process is usually shorter than you might expect, given what you often see on television. For example, in the state of California,[17] approximately 60% of misdemeanor cases are cleared within 30 days, and 80% are cleared within 120 days. In the case of felonies, 45% are cleared within 30 days, 70% within 90 days, and about 80% within a year.

- Finally, what are your odds of conviction? While that depends entirely on the circumstances and facts surrounding your case, some figures from California may be instructive. In the case of misdemeanors, 99% were resolved without a trial, with 63% resulting in convictions and 36% resulting in dismissals etc. In the case of felonies, 97% were resolved without a trial. Of those cases, 65% resulted in a felony conviction, 15% resulted in conviction for a misdemeanor only, and 20% resulted in dismissals etc. In the relatively rare case (i.e., 3% of total cases) where a trial occurred, 77% resulted in felony convictions, 8% resulted in conviction for a misdemeanor only, and 15% resulted in an acquittal or dismissal, etc.

~

If you are arrested, you can be guaranteed an unpleasant process. You will most likely incur expensive attorney fees and be deprived of the use of a sum of your money for some time (or worse yet, incur bail bondsman fees). And the statistics indicate you will most likely be found guilty. It seems you should try hard to avoid arrest. Most police are not anxious to arrest you if it is not really necessary—it is a hassle for them, too. If you have accidentally or incidentally done something wrong, respectful behavior toward the police can be your best friend.

ENDNOTES

1 See Douglas Belkin, "More Job Seekers Scramble to Erase Their Criminal Past," *Wall Street Journal*, November 11, 2009, www.wsj.com/articles/SB125789494126242343. Accessed July 17, 2019.

2 Rand Corporation Press Announcement, "Younger Americans Much More Likely to Have Been Arrested than Previous Generations; Increase Is Largest Among Whites and Women," February 25, 2019, www.rand.org/news/press/2019/02/25.html.

3 While the exact wording may vary, the warning generally consists of the following: "You have the right to remain silent. Anything you say can be used against you in court. You have the right to have an attorney present during questioning. If you cannot afford one, one will be appointed for you."

4 U.S. Department of Justice, Justice Manual, Criminal Resource Manual, CRM 1–499, CRM 201–299, "251. Fingerprinting—Search and Seizure," 2018, www.justice.gov/jm/criminal-resource-manual-251-fingerprinting-search-and-seizure. Accessed July 21, 2019.

5 See J. G. Handler, *Ballentine's Law Dictionary, Legal Assistant Edition* (Albany, NY: Delmar, 1994), 431.

6 Major Cities Chiefs and Major County Sheriffs, *Technology Needs—Body Worn Cameras* (N.p.p.: Lafayette Group, 2015), assets.bwbx.io/documents/users/iqjWHBFdfxIU/rvnT.EAJQwK4/v0.

7 You will not be *formally* charged until your arraignment, as discussed below.

8 "How Much Does a Defense Attorney Cost?" Thumbtack, September 11, 2019, www.thumbtack.com/p/criminal-defense-attorney-cost#complexity-of-the-case. Accessed July 25 2019.

[9] Radley Balko, "Big changes may be coming to police interrogations," *Washington Post*, March 10, 2017, www.washingtonpost.com/news/the-watch/wp/2017/03/10/big-changes-may-be-coming-to-police-interrogations/?noredirect=on&utm_term=.7f84da22f5a1. Accessed July 31, 2019

[10] David E. Zulawski and Douglas E. Wicklander, *Practical Aspects of Interview and Interrogation* (Ann Arbor: CRC Press, 2001).

[11] Julia Layton, "How Police Interrogation Works," How Stuff Works, n.d., people.howstuffworks.com/police-interrogation.htm. Accessed July 30, 2019

[12] Shawn, "Average Bail Amounts in Las Vegas, NV," Al Star Bail Bonds, November 14, 2014, allstarbailbondslv.com/blog/standard-bail-amounts. Accessed July 28, 2019.

[13] Patrick Liu, Ryan Nunn, and Jay Shambaugh; "The Economics of Bail and Pre-trial Detention" The Hamilton Project. Brookings Institution. December 2018. www.hamiltonproject.org/assets/files/BailFineReform_EA_121818_6PM.pdf

[14] Mike Herbert, "6 Common California Crimes and Their Bail Amount," Herbert Bail Bonds, June 26, 2018, herbertbailbonds.com/6-common-california-crimes-and-their-bail-amount. Accessed July 28, 2019.

[15] Patrick Liu, Ryan Nunn, and Jay Shambaugh; "The Economics of Bail and Pre-trial Detention" The Hamilton Project. Brookings Institution. December 2018. www.hamiltonproject.org/assets/files/BailFineReform_EA_121818_6PM.pdf

[16] Thomas H. Cohen and Brian A. Reaves, "State Court Processing Statistics, 1990–2004: Pretrial Release of Felony Defendants in State Courts," Bureau of Justice Statistics, U.S. Department of Justice, November 2007, www.bjs.gov/content/pub/pdf/prfdsc.pdf.

[17] Judicial Council of California, 2017 *Court Statistical Report: Statewide Caseload Trends*, 2006–2007 Through 2015–2016 (San Francisco: Judicial Council of California, 2017), www.courts.ca.gov/documents/2017-Court-Statistics-Report.pdf.

CHAPTER 12

Dealing With Mental Health Issues

Mental health issues are a widespread and potentially dire phenomenon for recent college graduates. As I will discuss, young adulthood is the peak time for the manifestation of clinically described mental illness. It is also a time of high incidence of substance addiction and suicide, both of which are clearly mental health issues, but they only partially overlap the clinically defined incidence of mental illness. The net result of this is that if your circle of close friends is larger than six, the odds of you or one of your friends being afflicted by significant mental health issues in just the next year is over 50%.

Therefore, this chapter discusses:

- Clinically-defined mental illness
- Substance abuse and addiction
- Suicidal tendencies
- Taking care of your own mental health.

CLINICALLY-DEFINED MENTAL ILLNESS

• • •

The National Institute of Mental Health estimated in 2017 that some 26% of young adults (ages 18 to 25) experienced some level of mental illness (defined as a "mental, behavioral, or emotional disorder"), which was the highest for any adult age group. When it measured severe mental illness—defined as "a mental, behavioral, or emotional disorder resulting in serious functional impairment, which substantially interferes with or limits one or more major life activities"—it found 7.5% of young adults were afflicted, which again was the highest prevalence among the age groups it studied. Despite this higher prevalence, proportionately fewer young adults received treatment than their older counterparts.[1]

The most common forms of mental illness that affect young adults are described below.

- Major depression

  » This is defined as "a period of at least two weeks when a person experienced a depressed mood or loss of interest or pleasure in daily activities, and had a majority of specified symptoms, such as problems with sleep, eating, energy, concentration, or self-worth."

  » Major depression strikes about 30% of young adults (ages 18 to 29) each year, with higher rates among women than men. Again, the key issue is impairment. 64% of episodes result in severe impairment.

  » Treatment consists primarily of a combination of medications (principally antidepressants) and psychotherapy, while smaller numbers are treated by only one of these methods rather than both simultaneously. More worrisome, victims receive no treatment in some 35% of episodes.[2]

- Anxiety disorders

  » These manifest themselves in excessive anxiety and behavioral disturbances. Several of the most common forms of anxiety disorders are:[3]

    › Panic disorder, which involves a sense of imminent disaster or paralyzing terror.

> › Phobias, including fear of objects, fear of the judgment of others, and fear of social situations.

> › Obsessive-compulsive disorders, which include stressful thoughts and a powerful urge to perform repetitive acts (e.g., handwashing).

> › Post-traumatic stress disorders (PTSD), which are usually related to a horrible or frightening event that an individual has witnessed or experienced.

» Anxiety disorders affect about 22% of the population in the 18 to 29 age range each year, with a higher incidence among women than men.

» The key issue here is the degree of impairment of the individual's ability to function in his/her everyday life. 23% of those who suffer an anxiety disorder (or about 5% of the total population) are seriously impaired, and another 34% (or more than 7% of the total population) are moderately impaired.[4]

» Anxiety disorders are generally considered treatable with medications (such as antidepressants, buspirone, and, in limited circumstances for acute cases, benzodiazepines) and cognitive behavioral therapy (a form of psychotherapy).[5]

• Other mood disorders

» Also known as affective disorders or depressive disorders, these involve individuals experiencing significant mood changes involving depression or elation. The primary types of mood disorders are as follows:

> › Bipolar disorder, also known as manic-depression, involves significant mood swings from euphoria to depression or despair.

> › Persistent depression disorder involves mild long-term depression.

> › Seasonal affective disorder (SAD) involves severe depression related to lack of daylight. (Later in this chapter we will discuss the importance of sunlight.)

• Schizophrenic disorders

» These are highly complex conditions. Symptoms include delusions, thought disorders, hallucinations, withdrawal, and lack of motivation.

To locate treatment services in your area, you can call the federal government's Substance Abuse and Mental Health Services Administration (SAMHSA). It operates a 24/7 treatment referral helpline, at: 1-800-662-HELP (4357).

SUBSTANCE ABUSE AND ADDICTION
• • •

Use of alcohol, marijuana, and illicit drugs among young adults is clearly widespread. Research shows that 55% of young adults (aged 18 to 25) regularly consume alcohol,[6] 38% (aged 18 to 30) have used marijuana in the past year, and 19% percent (aged 18 to 30) have used illicit drugs other than marijuana in the past year.[7]

Your author does not presume to offer comment on those activities. Rather, this section focuses only on the subset of that usage that can be said to directly affect your mental health—that is, substance abuse or addiction.

In 2013, the American Psychological Association dropped the terms *substance abuse* and *substance dependence* in favor of *substance use disorder*. Substance use disorder is now the medical term for addiction.

According to government statistics,[8] among young adults (aged 18 to 25), alcohol continues to be the drug most used to such as degree as to be classified as a *use disorder*. Specifically, 10% of all young adults fit into this category. (However, more broadly, fully 28% engage in binge drinking, which many in the health community consider a use disorder, even if it is not so classified in government surveys).

The second-most frequent category is prescription stimulants (e.g., Ritalin and Adderall), involving 6.5% of all young adults, followed by marijuana at 5.9%, prescription pain medications at 5.5%, and LSD at 3.5%. Cocaine usage (which is not distinguished from a use disorder) is 1.5%, and other harsh drugs (such as heroin and methamphetamines) are each below 1%.

At what point does a friend's or family member's usage cross the line into substance use disorder? There are no definitive measures, but there are often some relatively straightforward outward indications the person has lost the ability to control their own usage and its effects. These include:

- Unreliability at work or school, including sharp declines in performance or attendance.

- Significant declines in physical attributes, either health-wise (e.g., weight changes, red eyes, energy levels) or care about appearance (e.g., sudden lack of interest in grooming or clothing cleanliness or care).

- Secretiveness that is suggestive of deliberately hiding something.

- A rise in money issues, such as sudden needs to borrow, stealing, or sudden reliance on credit cards in order to hoard cash.[9]

Even more important than your ability to spot issues among friends is your ability to monitor yourself and recognize whether you have begun to lose control, because if you wait until the symptoms are recognizable to others, you are likely already in trouble. Ask yourself:

- Do you feel you have to use the substance regularly, or do you even just have urges so intense that they block out other thoughts?

- Do you find you need higher quantities of the substance to obtain the desired effect?

- Do you take more than you intended beforehand?

- Do you continue to use the substance even after it has begun to cause collateral problems in your reliability and/or relationships?

- Have you tried to take a break from the substance for a specified period of time, but found an excuse why it was okay to cut that time short?

- Do you experience any withdrawal symptoms when you go for a period without using the substance?[10]

Any of these could be a strong indication you are moving toward a substance use disorder. Multiple indications suggest you have already crossed over. And remember, the phrase substance use disorder is simply a medical euphemism for addiction.

Is addiction curable? Many treatment centers advertise in ways that suggest they always succeed. The real answer, according to the federal government, appears to be, "Yes, it is curable, sort of, much of the time." Specifically, the National Institute on Drug Abuse (NIDA) described substance abuse as a chronic disease that—like heart disease or asthma (NIDA's analogies, not mine)—can be controlled. It rejects the word *cured*, but reports, "Addiction *can* be managed successfully. Treatment enables people to counteract addiction's disruptive effects on their brain and behavior and regain control of their lives." Quantitatively, NIDA indicates that 40% to 60% of substance addicts—once treated properly—do not relapse, even over long periods of time. Further, it indicates that relapse does not mean the case is hopeless. It describes relapse as part of the process for some people and an indication that treatment needs to be resumed, modified, or changed to a new regime.[11]

The specific treatment varies, based on the substance in question, but usually combines medicinal treatment with behavioral therapy or counseling. Medications are available that help in detoxification from alcohol, opioids, nicotine, and certain other drugs, but there are currently no such medications for stimulants or cannabis. Further, it warns that detoxification outside of a full treatment program generally fails to prevent relapse.[12]

If you or a loved one or a friend is facing substance addiction, and you do not know of any resources to help, a good place to start is the Substance Abuse and Mental Health Services Administration (SAMHSA) mentioned earlier. It operates a 24/7 treatment referral helpline, at 1-800-662-HELP (4357) that is confidential, free, and operated in English and Spanish for individuals, friends, and family members facing mental and/or substance use disorders. It can provide referrals to local treatment facilities and support groups as well as free publications and other information.

SUICIDAL TENDENCIES
• • •

Suicidal thoughts are very common among young adults. In 2018, 11% of persons between 18 and 25 reported having had suicidal thoughts in the past year.[13] While only a portion of these persons will progress toward actual attempts on their own lives (as discussed below), the mere contemplation of such a course indicates a degree of despair that is problematic in and of itself. Further, in the general population, contemplation leads to attempts about 13% of the time, and in young adults, the incidence is even higher at about 17%.[14]

Suicide attempts have statistically low odds of success (i.e., death). In 2017, only about 3% of attempts resulted in death. But that dramatically understates their physical harm. That same year, 55% of suicide attempts required medical attention, and of those, 71% (representing 39% of attempts) required overnight (or longer) hospitalization.[15]

Not surprisingly, some of the warning signs a person may be contemplating suicide bear a strong resemblance to indications of depression. They include sleeping too much or too little, significant weight gain or loss, avoiding social interactions with others, dramatic mood swings, and excessive alcohol or drug consumption. Others are relatively obvious and specifically indicative of suicidal thoughts: talking about feeling hopeless, trapped, or alone, saying they have no reason to go on living, making a will or giving away personal possessions, or talking about suicide as a way out.

The National Alliance on Mental Illness (NAMI) flags the following as indications suicidal action may be imminent: mood shift from despair to calm, putting their affairs in order, giving away possessions, saying goodbyes to friends and family, or planning or looking to acquire a means to kill oneself, such as a firearm or potentially lethal drugs (e.g., a large quantity of sedatives).[16]

Should you or a friend exhibit such symptoms, it is time to act immediately, because (in the general population) 36% of those who engaged in suicide planning then made an attempt. (Of course, there were also attempts that were not preceded by planning.[17])

Various experts provide relatively similar suggestions on how to best proceed with your friend if they are exhibiting such symptoms. If the danger is not immediate, the experts say to begin with an open, but non-judgmental conversation about your concerns. Don't be afraid to ask if they are thinking about suicide. Be ready to explain the basis of your concerns, because they are likely to ask. Don't minimize their problems, and don't attempt to shame them into changing their mind. It does not matter whether *you* think their problems are small or fixable—what matters is that *they don't*. Listen and show your support. You can also encourage them to seek help from a professional. They may feel so overwhelmed that they will need you to help them find a healthcare provider, make a phone call to a helpline, or go with them to their first appointment.

If you know of no suicide helpline, you can call the National Suicide Prevention Lifeline at 1-800-273-8255). Trained counselors are available 24/7.[18]

Finally, you need to know that, if a person who has attempted suicide before exhibits signs that he/she is again considering such action, there is high cause for alarm. Studies have shown that about 30% of first attempters try again, at least once, and the efficacy of their attempts is much higher. Whereas the estimated "success" rates of suicide attempts overall is small at 3%, approximately 23% of repeat attempters eventually succeed (figures are not available as to specific rates for second attempters versus third attempters, etc.[19]) According to a *New York Times* article, the highest likelihood of additional attempts lies in the first three months after the first attempt.[20]

FOR THE LGBTQ COMMUNITY
Suicide Is Far More Prevalent Than Average

As worrisome as the above figures are for the general population, suicide is a far more prevalent issue in the LGBTQ community than in the population at large.

Lesbian, gay, and bisexual youth are four times more likely to attempt suicide than their straight counterparts. Transgender adults are 12 times more likely to attempt suicide than their straight counterparts.[21]

If you or a loved one is struggling with suicidal tendencies, and you would be more comfortable speaking with a counselor who brings an LGBTQ perspective to suicide prevention, you can call the Trevor Lifeline 24/7 at 1-866-488-7386.

TAKING CARE OF
YOUR OWN MENTAL HEALTH
• • •

Mental health is broader than just avoiding the specific difficulties described above. It also involves being able to fully experience and build upon what your life has to offer. That requires more than the absence of malady—it requires an assertively positive approach to mental health.

Mental health is frequently described as a state of psychological well-being in which an individual has achieved a satisfactory integration of one's instinctual drives acceptable to those involved in your social and professional environment. While mental health is important at every stage in life, it assumes a particularly important role when an individual is going through a major transition, such as your transition from college life to the professional world.

To be mentally healthy, you must be constantly aware of your mental health status, constantly working to maintain and enhance your mental health, and constantly prepared to act and seek help when necessary.

To achieve this, first recognize that the dimensions of your new world add up to a recipe for the potential creation of stress, anxiety, lack of confidence, uncertainty, depression, lost sleep, poor diet, and lack of time for the exercise you used to enjoy so greatly.

Next, recognize that serious psychological stress is prevalent, not rare. 4% of adults have experienced serious psychological distress in the past 30 days. While that might sound like a small proportion, it is consistent with close to half of the population experiencing such levels of stress over the course of a year.

If your mental health is important (and clearly it is), what can you do to help yourself be mentally healthy? Some simple steps are listed below. [22] At first glance, you may wonder if these simple steps can really make a difference. The answer is yes, and if practiced on a regular basis, these steps can help you maintain and enhance your mental health.

- Value yourself.
  - » Treat yourself with respect and kindness. Do not constantly criticize

yourself. Enrich your life with hobbies, projects, and personal growth.

- Take care of your body.
  - » Proper diet, exercise, adequate sleep, and hydration are essential.
- Surround yourself with good people.
  - » Strong social and family connections provide support networks. Strengthen and expand the scope of these networks.
- Volunteer.
  - » Volunteer your time and resources. When you share your time and resources with others, particularly those in need, you will experience a very rewarding sense of satisfaction.
- Quiet your mind.
  - » Your mind, like an engine, cannot be constantly running at top speed. Relaxation, exercise, prayer, and meditation can have a calming and restorative effect.
- Set realistic goals.
  - » Decide what you want to achieve, the steps you will need to take to achieve your goal, and establish a realistic time line for your efforts. Unrealistic and unachievable goals can and will be a source of frustration that will affect your mental well-being.
- Avoid monotony.
  - » While routines are necessary, do not let them dominate your life. Alter your routines and try new activities. Such changes will have a rejuvenating effect.
- Avoid excessive alcohol.
  - » If you are going to drink alcohol, do so only in moderation. Alcohol can easily become the go-to crutch when you are faced with stress or anxiety. Tobacco in any form should be avoided.

The preceding steps can help you maintain and enhance your mental health. But heed this additional caveat: *if you sense you need mental health help, seek it.* Seeking help is a sign of good judgment and strength, not weakness.

There is an aid to mental health that you probably haven't thought about even though you see it almost every day: sunlight. Sunlight improves your mood and focus by increasing serotonin levels in your body. Sunlight also enhances your sleep, promotes bone growth, helps strengthen your immune system, and can lower blood pressure and promote weight loss.

There is another interesting and simple perspective worth considering. It is based on the work of Tim Herrera, heath editor of the *New York Times*. [23]

- Solitude can be good.
  - » Our lives have become increasingly hectic. Recent college graduates beginning the next phase of their lives can find themselves pulled in many directions. The demands of your professional role, proving yourself, advancing professionally, developing new social relationships, trying to be physically fit. Your schedule will be hectic.
  - » Choosing, even disciplining yourself to spend some time alone, can help every aspect of your mental health. Solitude can help bring your thoughts, concerns, and emotions into perspective.
- Just do nothing at all.
  - » Do not let your level of activity and a never-ending to-do list be self-perceived as your level of commitment or status. Sometimes idleness can be a mental health asset.
- Cultivate casual friendships.
  - » Low-stakes relationships can benefit your sense of well-being and connectedness. Such relationships can include a wide range of contacts: individuals you encounter going to and from work, your barber or hairdresser, neighbors, or a favorite store clerk.
- Learn to enjoy today.
  - » *Planning* for the future is wise—but *worrying* about the future rarely, if ever, helps your state of mind.
- Love your guilty pleasures.
  - » Junk food, low-grade action movies, listening to golden oldies, etc.—all in moderation, of course—can help you deal with stress.

- Accept compliments.
  - » Learn to accept and appreciate praise and compliments—they strengthen your foundation.
- Embrace repeats.
  - » We tend to be attracted to new experiences, and new experiences are enriching. But so is repetition. There is a degree of comfort in repetition.
- Learn from regrets.
  - » We frequently try to avoid thinking about past mistakes, missed opportunities, or failed relationships. It is healthier to view such instances as learning opportunities.

～

Mental health issues are far more prevalent among young adults than most understand. Whether or not such issues rise to the level among your friends or yourself that they require professional attention, it is worth your time and effort to monitor each other's well-being. You don't want to wake up years from now and only then recognize that your life or your loved ones' lives could have been so much richer if only you had acted sooner.

ENDNOTES

1 "Mental Illness," National Institute of Mental Health, February 2019, www.nimh.nih.gov/health/statistics/mental-illness.shtml#part_154785.

2 "Major Depression," National Institute of Mental Health, February 2019, www.nimh.nih.gov/health/statistics/major-depression.shtml.

3 Tim Newman, "What is mental health?" Medical News Today, August 24, 2017, www.medicalnewstoday.com/articles/154543.php. Accessed January 3, 2020.

4 "Any Anxiety Disorder," National Institute of Mental Health, November 2017, www.nimh.nih.gov/health/statistics/any-anxiety-disorder.shtml.

5 "General Anxiety Disorder," Mayo Clinic, n.d., www.mayoclinic.org/diseases-conditions/generalized-anxiety-disorder/diagnosis-treatment/drc-20361045.

6 Elinore McCance-Katz, "The National Survey on Drug Use and Health: 2018," Substance Use and Mental Health Services Administration, n.d., www.samhsa.gov/data/sites/default/files/cbhsq-reports/Assistant-Secretary-nsduh2018_presentation.pdf.

7 John E. Schulenberg et al., "Monitoring the Future: National Survey Results on Drug Use, 1975–2018," Volume 2: "College Students and Adults Ages 19¬–60," National Institute on Drug Abuse, National Institutes of Health, July 2019, www.monitoringthefuture.org//pubs/monographs/mtf-v012_2018.pdf.

8 See note 2.

9 "Drug addiction (substance use disorder)," Mayo Clinic, n.d., www.mayoclinic.org/diseases-conditions/drug-addiction/symptoms-causes/syc-20365112.

10 "Drug addiction (substance use disorder)," Mayo Clinic, n.d., www.mayoclinic.org/diseases-conditions/drug-addiction/symptoms-causes/syc-20365112.

11 "Drugs, Brains, and Behavior: The Science of Addiction," National Institute of Drug Abuse, n.d., www.drugabuse.gov/publications/drugs-brains-behavior-science-addiction/treatment-recovery.

12 "Drugs, Brains, and Behavior: The Science of Addiction," National Institute of Drug Abuse, n.d., www.drugabuse.gov/publications/drugs-brains-behavior-science-addiction/treatment-recovery.

13 "Suicidal Thoughts and Suicide Attempts," Suicide Prevention Resource Center, n.d., www.sprc.org/scope/attempts.

14 "Suicidal Thoughts and Suicide Attempts," Suicide Prevention Resource Center, n.d., www.sprc.org/scope/attempts.

15 "Suicidal Thoughts and Suicide Attempts," Suicide Prevention Resource Center, n.d., www.sprc.org/scope/attempts.

16 April Kahn, "What You Should Know About Suicide," Healthline, April 30, 2019, www.healthline.com/health/suicide-and-suicidal-behavior.

17 See "Suicidal Thoughts and Suicide Attempts," Suicide Prevention Resource Center, n.d., www.sprc.org/scope/attempts.

18 National Suicide Prevention Helpline suicidepreventionlifeline.org/

19 "Attempters' Longterm Survival," Harvard School of Public Health, n.d., www.hsph.harvard.edu/means-matter/means-matter/survival/.

[20] Jane Brody, "After a Suicide Attempt, the Risk of Another Try," *New York Times*, November 7, 2016, www.nytimes.com/2016/11/08/well/live/after-a-suicide-attempt-the-risk-of-another-try.html.

[21] "Mental Health by the Numbers," National Alliance on Mental Illness, n.d., www.nami.org/learn-more/mental-health-by-the-numbers.

[22] "Ten Things You Can Do for Your Mental Health," University of Michigan University Health Service, n.d., www.uhs.umich.edu/tenthings. Accessed January 3, 2020.

[23] Tim Herrera, "8 Ways to Be Kinder to Yourself in 2020," *New York Times*, December 24, 2019, www.nytimes.com/2019/12/24/smarter-living/8-ways-to-be-kinder-to-yourself-in-2020.html.

PART IV

Life as a Young Adult

CHAPTER 13

Love and Marriage

There is about to be an explosion of marriages among you and your friends. In 2018, only 9% of persons aged 21 were married. Among those aged 25, that percentage jumped to 25%. So, if trends continue, *at least* another 16% of current 21-year-olds will marry in the next four years. Then, in the following five years, *another* 29% will marry. By age 30, over half of the population will be married.[1]

Further, the path to marriage generally leads through living together. According to the Centers for Disease Control, 75% of women will live with a lover outside of marriage (referred to as cohabiting) before they turn 30. We can assume the portions for men are roughly similar. Among cohabiters of all ages, over a three-year period, 40% get married, 32% continue cohabiting, and 27% break up.[2]

You already know about the love and romance side of relationships. But what do you know about the legal and financial side of a path to living together and marrying? There is much you need to know.

LIVING TOGETHER

• • •

In Chapter 2, I described the legal entanglements associated with living with another person. Specifically, I explored the impact of one (or the other) person signing the lease versus both signing as joint tenants, and the legal consequences you might bear if your roommate commits any crimes while the two of you are living together.

But there is more to know if the two of you are engaged in cohabitation, which we will define as a cross-gender or same-gender couple living together in a sexual relationship without being married. (Should you want or need to look up either statistics or laws relating to cohabitation, please note that much of the historical research and some of the current wording of some laws define cohabitation in cross-gender terms only. It appears many have not caught up to the realities of modern life.)

For example, cohabitation is still technically illegal in three states (Michigan, Mississippi, and North Carolina), although these laws appear to be rarely enforced. More broadly though, because marital status discrimination is not prohibited in the housing sector in more than half of U.S. states, landlords can reject unmarried couples due to their relationship status.[3]

For most couples, the real issues come from the intermingling of finances. Living together is usually less expensive than living separately, but how are the two of you going to share the expenses? Roommates who are not romantically involved have an easier time coming to an agreement, because there is no ambiguity around what's yours, what's mine, and what's ours. Couples tend to make more joint purchases, and sorting out who gets what if there is a breakup is harder. Furthermore, there can be disagreements over how to split expenses (e.g., 50/50, proportional to income, or pool your resources and pay jointly). If you follow the last alternative, what will the rules be later if you break up? This matters because, as we saw in the paragraph above, a significant portion of couples do break up.

Some attorneys recommend that a couple create a written *cohabitation agreement*, which is a legal contract that specifies what a couple has agreed to regarding the above-listed issues. Most states (but not all) legally recognize such contracts as legally enforceable if they are in writing and signed by both parties.[4] That said, while I have found no statistics, I believe such formal agreements are relatively uncommon.

GETTING ENGAGED
. . .

Couples who plan to marry typically get engaged well in advance of the actual wedding. One study found the average engagement period to be 13.6 months.[5] The same study concluded, at the time of the engagement, about 70% of couples had dated for more than two years, about 15% of couples had dated for between one and two years, and 15% had dated for less than a year.

At the time of the engagement, it is still the overwhelming custom for the future bride to receive an engagement ring. According to a 2019 study, 97% of couples exchange rings at the time of engagement. On average, the rings cost $5,900 which is surprisingly less than the figure that was reported when the survey was conducted two years earlier. In fact, several other surveys showed the same thing: spending has been declining.[6] Of those buying an engagement ring, 86% of couples chose a diamond as the center stone.

BREAKING AN ENGAGEMENT

Not all engagements result in weddings. According to a study that polled 1,000 people, 20% of all engagements are called off before the wedding. About 40% of the persons involved in such breakups blame the other person, about 40% blame both parties, and less than 10% blame themselves.[7] (Yes, I know those figures do not add to 100%. I do not know who accounts for the missing figure—perhaps third parties, such as prospective in-laws.)

The good news is that, according to the same study, most people are later happy that the engagement was broken. 83% report that they do not regret the breakup.

When an engagement is broken, two legal issues arise: (1) who ends up with the engagement ring, and (2) whether the jilted party can sue.

Who gets the ring? It's a legitimate question, considering the amount of money spent of the ring.

If the recipient of the ring (or his/her family) paid for the ring, the recipient keeps it. However, in most cases, it is the donor who paid for the ring. In those cases, if it comes down to being settled by the courts, the answer depends on where you live:

- In most states, an engagement ring is not considered an outright gift. It is considered a *conditional gift*, which means you must fulfill a future condition (i.e., actually get married) before the ring is truly yours.

- However, some state courts can make exceptions to this doctrine if the ring was given on a gift-giving occasion, such as Christmas, a birthday, or Valentine's day.

- But here is where things get interesting. Even though most states agree that the ring is a conditional gift, they do not agree on who ends up with it in the case of a broken engagement.

- In most states, it is the giver of the ring. However, a handful of states adopt a more contractual view of the conditional gift. Under their view, when the engagement contract is broken by the ring's recipient, the ring should be restored to the giver. However, if the contract is broken by the giver, then the recipient should keep the ring so as not to reward the giver for breach of contract.

- And then there is the state of Montana. That state, alone in the country, simply says a gift is a gift. The recipient gets to keep it.[8]

After it is clear which party ends up with the ring, the question arises as to what to do with it. While you might want to turn it into another piece of jewelry or save it to give to the next love of your life (not advised), most people think of selling it. And that is where the bad news comes in. Various experts place the price you can expect to receive for a diamond at resale at between 20% and 40% of retail price.[9]

The second legal issue that arises when an engagement is broken concerns whether the jilted party can sue the one who broke off the engagement. While you might be tempted to react by declaring, "In this day and age? Of course not!" you would not be completely correct:

- A long time ago, women in general had the right to sue when an engagement promise was broken, under a theory that the woman's prospects for finding another suitable human were diminished. The laws allowing this were referred to as *breach of promise laws*.

- While the notion of jilted parties being damaged has changed, about half the states still allow for different kinds of breach-of-promise lawsuits. In these states, a promise to marry is considered legally enforceable, so long as the promise meets the tests of a valid contract. The breaking off of the engagement is therefore examined as a potential breach of contract.

- In a breach-of-contract lawsuit, the plaintiff must demonstrate he/she has incurred damages, which could include (1) financial losses, such as money spent in preparation for the wedding, moving expenses, etc., and (2) compensatory damages for injuries to health or emotional state. Further, if the perpetrator had malicious intent or was violent or engaged in fraud, punitive damages may be assessed. (Moreover, if fraud was involved, action can be taken in states without such statutes.[10])

- It appears such suits are rare, but they are filed occasionally.[11]

GETTING MARRIED: PROCESS, RIGHTS, BENEFITS, AND RESPONSIBILITIES
• • •

Getting married involves a number of issues across several categories. In this section, we will cover the following topics in turn:

- Prenuptial and postnuptial agreements

- The legal requirements for, and legal process, of getting married

- Marriage rights and benefits

- Financial responsibilities

- The wedding itself and the honeymoon

- Joint finances

PRENUPTIAL AND POSTNUPTIAL AGREEMENTS

A prenuptial agreement (referred to in some states as an antenuptial agreement or premarital agreement) is a written contract between two persons before their marriage for the purpose of specifying how financial and other matters will be handled if and when the marriage ends.

All fifty states recognize the validity of prenups, so long as you follow the specific rules of that state in establishing it.[12] In general, these requirements include that it must be in writing, it must be entered into voluntarily by both parties, it must be based on full disclosure (meaning that neither side hid their true financial condition), it must be fair (or at least not egregiously unfair), and it must be validly executed (which includes having both signatures notarized in most states).[13]

Prenups are mostly used when one partner brings substantially more financial assets to the marriage than the other. They are also more common when one partner has children from a prior relationship. While some advocates (mostly attorneys who could earn fees if you retain them to write a prenup) assert that such contracts are becoming more common and that more couples would benefit from such contracts, only about 5% of married couples have a prenup in place.[14]

State laws dictate what subjects can be included in a prenup, but typical provisions include property and other asset and debt splits in the case of divorce, spousal support (alimony) in the case of divorce, and agreements about what (if anything) a spouse will inherit in the case of death. In some states, the agreement can even specify child support and custody, although these provisions are not permitted in all states.[15] Other less common provisions include ownership of present and future cryogenically stored embryos, ownership of intellectual property, and pet ownership. Some prenups contain expiration dates (known as sunset clauses).

A prenuptial agreement does not come cheap. It has been estimated the average prenup costs $2,500. However, the range is wide. If finances are straightforward and the couple agrees on all the major provisions before calling an attorney, the cost can be less than $1,000. However, if your finances are complicated, the two of you have different views and want separate attorneys, and you haggle for a long time, the cost can be multiples of the average figure.[16] And that does not include any potential harm that comes from the suspicion that can grow between the future new-lyweds during negotiations. Attorneys who have an incentive to promote the use of prenups like to point out how such an agreement can potentially make the future marriage stronger by increasing communication and knowledge. However, I found no factual analyses of the portion of couples who found the process to be positive rather than negative.

A postnuptial agreement is conceptually similar to a prenup, except that it is negotiated and signed at some point after the marriage takes place. In some states, a postnup offers different options than a prenup as to the topics that can be covered. Sometimes a postnup is created to amend a pre-nup. At other times it is a response to a particular event, such as to con-vince a spouse to remain in a marriage after the other has cheated. Postnups can be treated similarly to prenups in the courts, although courts often pay particular attention as to whether one spouse might have exer-cised undue influence over the other in convincing him/her to sign.[17]

THE LEGAL REQUIREMENTS FOR, AND LEGAL PROCESS OF, GETTING MARRIED

Marriage is the legal union of two people. Afterward, the couple is treated as a single entity for many financial and legal purposes. In most states, a couple becomes married when they obtain a marriage license, take part in a ceremony, and sign a certificate of marriage. In some states, a couple can create a legal marriage without any of these three conditions, by living to-gether for a significant period of time (for which *no* state provides a specific definition), holding themselves out to be a married couple, and intending to be married. This type of marriage, which is legally recognized in most states, is called *common-law marriage*.[18]

As of June 2015, as the result of a Supreme Court decision, marriage be-came legally recognized and available to same-sex couples in all fifty states.

In order to get married, both parties must meet certain requirements, which vary slightly from state to state. Both must have reached the age of consent in their state. They cannot be too closely related (from a genetic standpoint). They must both have the required mental capacity to under-stand the consequences of their getting married. They must be sober. Some states require they both have recently taken and passed blood tests. And neither person can be currently married to someone else.

The couple must then obtain a marriage license (which lasts only for a period of time specified by the issuing state) from a county clerk's office. A ceremony by an authorized person (sometimes referred to as an officiant) is required, although there are generally no specific requirements as to what the ceremony must include, other than an acknowledgment by each person that they are entering the marriage. Further, the standards regarding who may qualify to perform the ceremony are often very low, so it is quick and easy for a friend or loved one to become an authorized officiant. The certificate is then signed by the officiant and the couple and filed at the county clerk's office.[19]

MARRIAGE RIGHTS AND BENEFITS

Married couples enjoy a range of legal rights and benefits, including:

- Income tax benefits.
  - » Federal and state income taxes can be lower when a couple files a joint return rather than two people filing separate returns.
- Estate planning benefits.
  - » Upon the death of one spouse, an unlimited amount of property can pass to the other spouse without incurring estate taxes.
- Social Security, Medicare, and government disability benefits.
  - » To some degree, these benefits cross over between spouses.
- Employee benefits at work.
  - » Many employers offer benefits to the spouses of employees.
- Decision-making rights.
  - » Such matters as medical decisions can be made by one spouse when the other spouse cannot make them for himself/herself.
- Financial support.
  - » This right/benefit may even continue after divorce.

- Family pricing for many consumer items.
  » This includes, for example, insurance and cellular phone service.

FINANCIAL RESPONSIBILITIES

The above benefits come at a price, though. Although there is some variation by state (as with everything else in this book), when a couple marries, they generally share financial responsibility for the household, are jointly responsible for most debts and expenses, have usually equal shares in income and property acquired during the marriage, and bear permanent financial responsibility for any children.

THE WEDDING ITSELF AND THE HONEYMOON

Whole books and yearlong magazine subscriptions have been devoted to planning weddings. Further, given the legal requirements for a wedding are minimal, but there are no maximums, it would be impossible to condense into a single section all you need to know about the subject.

That said, I can provide you with some knowledge about norms and averages, just to help you think about the nature and scale of undertaking you might want.

Before you get to the wedding, you might choose to have a bachelorette or bachelor party. The average cost per participant of such parties/trips is $708 and $1,044 respectively.[20] Most often, the participants themselves pick up the cost. And you may want to let them do that, because you are about to incur some major expenses yourself.

The average U.S. couple in 2019 spent an estimated $38,700 on their wedding. Of that figure, the ceremony and the reception accounted for about $29,000—because the venue accounted for $9,000; catering, $6,700; the band or DJ, another $3,900; photography, $2,400; flowers, $1,800: the wedding dress, $1,700; and décor, $1,400. Then came the invitations, cake and desserts, and an officiant at roughly $500 each.

Regionally, New York City weddings were more ($50,000 on average) while midwestern weddings (such as Cleveland) were less ($22,000 on average).[21] As large as those figures are, they do not include several common extras, such as a rehearsal dinner or gifts for bridesmaids and groomsmen.

How costs are split can vary widely based on specific cases, but on average, couples pay for 41%, with the parents of the bride picking up 44% and the parents of the groom contributing 14% (not counting the honeymoon).[22]

On top of the cost of the wedding comes the honeymoon. The average couple spends seven to nine days on a honeymoon, at a cost between $4,000 and $5,000.[23]

Surprisingly, destination weddings on average are cheaper than hometown weddings, because the higher cost per participant (including the couple covering part of the costs of guests attending) turn out to be more than off-set by the smaller average number of guests. In 2016, the average cost of a destination wedding was 80% of the average cost of a hometown wedding.[24] And, of course, the location of the wedding and the honeymoon may be combined, resulting in some savings.

The real bargain comes from eloping, just the two of you and a romantic setting. Apparently, on average, eloping couples spend only $3,000,[25] and there is little distinction between the wedding and the honeymoon.

Now, of course, these are averages. You could spend much more or much less. These simply provide points of discussion with your partner. But start those discussions soon. The average couple spends 13 to 18 months planning their wedding. Given that we learned above that the average engagement lasts only 13.7 months, planning can occupy 100% of the time you are engaged.[26]

JOINT FINANCES

Money is one of the two leading causes of difficulties in marriages (the other being sex). Therefore, quickly finding a way to constructively work together on money issues is central to your marriage succeeding.

The task starts when the relationship between you and your partner first gets serious. Each of you should observe how the other handles money. Is one person frugal while the other spends generously? Does one of you have a poor credit rating or regularly need to borrow money from parents or friends (or their partner)? Can you find sufficient evidence that your prospective partner has the same attitude toward savings that you do? Is one of you very meticulous with keeping track of spending while the other seems to give it little mind? These are all signs the two of you may be incompatible when it comes to finances. That doesn't mean that a marriage cannot work, but it means this is likely to be an area of difficulty.

Then, ideally, you will have a conversation. It may come after you start living together, or if you do not live together, it should come as you begin to discuss marriage and well before there is a formal engagement. Both sides need to be willing to open up completely about their current financial condition, their income, their debts, their income prospects for the future, and their financial aspirations. If you are not comfortable being completely open, then you are not yet ready to seriously consider marriage.

Think about it for a second—the two of you are going to be jointly battling a mountain of expenses together in the coming years. Right now, there is student debt. Then there will be wedding expenses. Then there will be the cost of a down payment on a home. Then there will likely be the cost of raising kids. Then come the kids' college expenses and supporting them after college. And all the while, you are supposed to be saving for retirement. Neither of you can handle all of that while having your spouse tugging in a different direction because he/she and you did not get on the same page at the beginning. Being uncomfortable does not mean you have to break up as a couple—but it does mean you are not yet ready to commit to getting married.

Once you are engaged, it is time to address some more specific issues:

- Given your joint incomes, how will you generally allocate funds between housing, boring day-to-day expenses, entertainment and fun, etc., versus paying down debt and/or saving?
- Which of the four general strategies for managing the day-to-day spending will you follow?
  » The keep-separate-accounts model, where one partner is chosen to pay each type of expense.
  » The share-and-manage-everything-as-a-couple model.
  » The one-person-takes-the-lead-on-managing-the-money-and-gives-the-other-one-an-allowance model.

» The share-most-responsibilities-but-keep-some-things-private model.[27]

- How meticulously will you track expenditures and reconcile them against the promises and framework established by your answers to the above questions?

- What will your reaction be if the other partner fails to adhere to various parts of the plan? What kinds of failures would likely cause big issues between the two of you?

Once you are married, take the time to stay on top of your plan and adjust it as necessary. There is a saying in the military that "no battle plan survives the first engagement with the enemy." The situation is the same in the finances of a marriage. Things go wrong. Unplanned expenses crop up. People get laid off from their jobs.

Your financial situation will inevitably change—sometimes for better, sometimes for worse—over time. However, if you have a history of working together constructively and openly, you will successfully adjust. If you have never discussed some subjects or are not able to be honest while still being unemotional, you will be one of the couples who identify money as a leading cause of difficulty in your marriage.

ENDNOTES

1 Andy Kiersz, "Here's when you're probably getting married," Business Insider, February 6, 2019, www.businessinsider.com/average-marriage-age-united-states-2019–2. Accessed December 18, 2019.

2 Emanuella Grinberg, "CDC says more women opting for cohabitation before marriage," WTVR.com, April 4, 2013, wtvr.com/2013/04/04/cdc-says-more-women-opting-for-cohabitation-before-marriage. Accessed December 18, 2019.

3 Meagan Day, "'Living in sin' is still illegal in several U.S. states," Timeline, April 9, 2015, timeline.com/living-in-sin-is-still-illegal-in-several-u-s-states-d1fc799bf97d. Accessed December 18, 2019.

4 "Cohabitation Agreements," FindLaw, n.d., family.findlaw.com/living-together/nonmarital-agreement-living-together-contracts.html. Accessed December 18, 2019.

5 Maddy Sims, "Here's the Average Length of Engagement for Couples," The Knot, n.d., www.theknot.com/content/too-long-to-be-engaged. Accessed December 18, 2019.

6 Michelle Graff, "The Average Amount Spent on an Engagement Ring Is . . ." National Jeweler, November 6, 2019, www.nationaljeweler.com/independents/retail-surveys/8245-the-average-amount-spent-on-an-engagement-ring-is. Accessed December 18, 2019.

7 Diana Bruk, "20 % of All Weddings are Called Off—Here's Why," BestLife, May 15, 2018, bestlifeonline.com/engagements-called-off-break-up-stories. Accessed December 18, 2019.

8 Melissa Heinig, "Returning an Engagement Ring," Nolo, n.d., www.nolo.com/legal-encyclopedia/returning-engagement-ring-30198.html. Accessed December 18, 2019.

9 "How to Determine the Resale Value of a Diamond," Jewelry Notes, n.d., www.jewelrynotes.com/how-to-determine-the-resale-value-of-a-diamond. Accessed December 18, 2019.

10 Kourosh Akhbari, "Damages for Breach of Promise to Marry," LegalMatch, March 11, 2018, www.legalmatch.com/law-library/article/damages-for-breach-of-promise-to-marry.html. Accessed December 18, 2019.

11 "The Legal Consequences of Leaving Someone at the Altar," Minnesota Bride, August 22, 2019, mnbride.com/expert-wedding-advice/legal-consequences-leaving-someone-altar. Accessed December 18, 2019.

12 "What You Need to Know About Prenuptial Agreements," Nationwide, n.d., www.nationwide.com/prenuptial-agreement-basics.jsp. Accessed December 19, 2019.

13 "Everything You Need to Know About Postnuptial Agreements," LegalNature, n.d., www.legalnature.com/guides/everything-you-need-to-know-about-postnuptial-agreements. Accessed December 19, 2019.

14 Jeffrey Broobin, "A Harvard Law School Takes a Look at Prenuptial Agreements," StreetDirectory, n.d., www.streetdirectory.com/travel_guide/13993/legal_matters/a_harvard_law_school_takes_a_look_at_prenuptial_agreements.html. Accessed December 19, 2019.

[15] "Everything You Need to Know About Postnuptial Agreements," LegalNature, n.d., www.legalnature.com/guides/everything-you-need-to-know-about-postnuptial-agreements. Accessed December 19, 2019.

[16] Hillary Hoffower, "You don't need to be rich to get a prenup—here's how much you should expect to pay," Business Insider, October 20, 2018, www.businessinsider.com/how-much-does-prenup-cost-2018–10. Accessed December 19, 2019.

[17] "Prenuptial Agreements vs. Postnuptial Agreements: The Pros and Cons of Each," Michael A. Robbins, n.d., www.michaelarobbins.com/Blog/Prenuptial-Agreements-vs-Postnuptial-Agreements-The-Pros-and-Cons-of-Each.shtml. Accessed December 19, 2019.

[18] "Getting Married: An Overview," Nolo, February 17, 2016, www.nolo.com/legal-encyclopedia/getting-married-overview-29966.html. Accessed December 19, 2019.

[19] "Marriage Requirements, Licenses, and Ceremonies FAQ," Nolo, n.d., www.nolo.com/legal-encyclopedia/marriage-requirements-licenses-ceremonies-faq.html. Accessed December 19, 2019.

[20] Maggie Seaver, "How Much Does It Cost to Attend a Bachelorette Party? Less than a Bachelor Party, Survey Says," RealSimple, September 11, 2019, www.realsimple.com/weddings/budget/bachelorette-party-cost. Accessed December 19, 2019.

[21] Hillary Hoffower, "More couples are taking on debt to have Instagram-worthy weddings. Here's how much it costs to get married in the US," Business Insider, July 26, 2019, www.businessinsider.com/how-much-does-it-cost-to-get-married-average-wedding-2019–7. Accessed December 19, 2019.

[22] Sims, "Here's the Average Length of Engagement for Couples," The Knot, www.theknot.com/content/too-long-to-be-engaged. Accessed December 18, 2019.

[23] Kim P, "Study: Average Honeymoon Cost," CreditDonkey, November 5, 2019, www.creditdonkey.com/average-honeymoon-cost.html. Accessed December 19, 2019.

[24] "Why elopements and destination weddings cost less," CapitalOne, n.d., www.capitalone.com/bank/money-management/saving-wedding/destination-wedding-costs. Accessed December 19, 2019.

[25] "How Much Does the Average Elopement Cost," Elopetonola, October 31, 2019, www.elopetonola.com/why-elope-in-nola/how-much-does-the-average-elopement-cost. Accessed December 19, 2019.

[26] Emily Barge, "How Long Does It Take to Plan a Wedding?" Pop the Knot, May 22, 2017, www.poptheknot.com/long-take-plan-wedding. Accessed December 19, 2019.

[27] "Should you manage money jointly or separately?" Money Advice Service, n.d., www.moneyadviceservice.org.uk/en/articles/should-we-manage-money-jointly-or-separately. Accessed December 19, 2019.

CHAPTER 14

Purchasing Your First Home

While buying a home might seem to be unrealistic when you first graduate (or at least seem decades away), about a quarter of all persons in the United States purchase their first home by age 25, and about a third do so by age 30.[1] Among college graduates, the percentage is presumably even higher.

If you have never bought a home, it can seem like a very complicated process. This chapter will walk you through all the steps so you can approach buying your first home with confidence, including:

- How much you can afford to spend on a home, according to the lenders
- Finding the right home
- How much to offer
- What you need to know about the contract
- What happens between the contract and the closing
- The closing

HOW MUCH YOU CAN AFFORD TO SPEND ON A HOME, ACCORDING TO THE LENDERS

• • •

Almost all first homes are purchased with a combination of *down payment* (i.e., cash you pay out of your own pocket at the time of the purchase) and a mortgage (which is a loan in which you pledge the home you are buying as *collateral* for the loan—which means the lender can foreclose on the home and take it away from you if you do not make the required payments). How expensive a home you can buy depends on the sum of the two.

Let's start with the mortgage, because if you cannot get a mortgage, you probably cannot buy a home. Assuming you have a reasonably steady income and a credit score above 570, you can probably qualify for a mortgage loan of some size. Exactly how large a mortgage depends on how much other debt you have and whether your mortgage is a conventional loan or a loan through the Federal Housing Authority (*FHA*). FHA loans are very popular with first-time homebuyers, and they have more generous lending terms (lower required qualifications and a willingness to lend more money to a given borrower than conventional loans). However, because most borrowers use conventional loans, I will explain that one first, and then explain what is different with an FHA loan. So, don't be depressed if your calculations under the conventional loan rules suggest you cannot afford a home. The FHA loans are much more lenient, although that lenience comes at a price, as we will see later.

CONVENTIONAL LOANS

To qualify for a conventional loan, most lenders require you to have two years of solid employment history, an ability to verify your income (e.g., through a W-2), and a minimum credit score over 640[2] (although many lenders use a minimum figure of 700 and 740 or higher to qualify for their best rates).

As to how much they are willing to lend, most use some slight variance of the so-called "28/36 rule" I mentioned in Chapter 5. They like to see your housing costs stay below 28% of your take-home pay, and the sum of housing costs plus other debt payments stay below 36% of your take-home pay.

Like all rules, slight variations occur. If you have little debt other than the

prospective mortgage, you can often exceed the 28% by a couple of percentage points. If your other debts consume much more than 8% of your
income, the lender might set a ceiling on the mortgage that is far below
28%, so that your combined number stays a few percentage points below
the normal 36% combined number.

Understand that the 28% limit has to cover more than just your mortgage payment. It has to cover *all* of the financial costs of housing. Therefore, it also has to cover real estate taxes, homeowner's insurance, and
any condo or homeowner association fees.[3] These will each absorb a portion of the 28%. Of note, the 28% does not need to cover home maintenance and repairs etc.

So, to illustrate, let's work a numerical example. Before we do so, though, if
you have a phobia about numbers, don't panic over what you are about to
read. There are mortgage calculators available on the internet that can help
you avoid most of the math we are about to do. I include it all here because
I believe it is helpful to most first-time buyers to understand the logic that
lies behind the rules and the results, particularly since your home will
probably be the single largest item in your budget each month. But, again,
if this section gets too uncomfortable, know that you can skip it and seek
out an internet mortgage calculator instead. Here goes:

- Pretend your annual income (salary plus bonus plus commissions etc.)
  is $50,000. Multiply that by 28%, and the formula says you can spend
  $14,000 a year on housing. Now subtract about 45% ($6,300) to cover
  real estate taxes and paying down the balance on the loan itself. (I will
  explain later in the chapter where this comes from, but for now, it is
  good enough for estimation purposes.) The resulting figure is $7,700
  per year. According to the formula, that is approximately the amount of
  money you can afford to spend on interest payments alone.

- Next, simply Google "mortgage interest rates." As of this writing, the
  interest rate on a 30-year fixed-rate conventional mortgage seems to
  average about 3.5%. So, divide $7,700 (the amount you can afford to
  pay) by the interest rate (3.5%), and you see you can afford a
  maximum conventional mortgage of about $220,000.

  » That does not mean you should take out a mortgage that large, of course. Also, note that if interest rates change, even a little, the $220,000 figure will change quite a lot.

- Now, the down payment can also be a constraint. So how much do you have in savings for a down payment? With a conventional loan, it is important that you have indeed saved the money, as conventional loans generally do not allow you to rely on a last-minute gift for the down payment.

- Not all of your home-related savings are available for the down payment. First, you need to set aside about $5,000 for something known as closing costs (which I will describe in detail later-you may not need all of that, but it is a useful estimate for the moment.). Conventional lenders like you to keep enough in savings to handle two to three months of mortgage payments, just in case your income is interrupted. To broadly estimate how much that would be, take the interest rate you used in the calculations (3.5% in our example) and add 1.5% to it (to cover the principal portion of the loan and real estate taxes). Multiply the resulting figure (5%) by the mortgage amount you calculated above: $220,000 x 5% = $11,000. Now divide $11,000 by 12 to get a monthly payment figure ($916), and multiply that figure by three to cover three months ($2,750). That amount must also be set aside, so your new total is $5,000 + $2,750 = $7,750.

- The remaining money in your home savings can be used for the down payment, unless you are buying a house in need of immediate repairs or refurbishment. Conventional loans require a down payment of at least 5% of the purchase price, but most conventional lenders want the down payment to be 20%. If the down payment is less than that, you will be required to purchase something called *private mortgage insurance* (PMI), which costs about 0.5% of the mortgage amount each year for a conventional loan.[4]

- If your available funds for a down payment are less than a quarter of the maximum mortgage you calculated above (because the 20% down payment would then be a quarter the size of the 80% mortgage), then your down payment may become the binding constraint on how much you can spend on the house. In fact, you will need to go back and recalculate the maximum size of the mortgage. To return to the example from above, the $7,700 annual payment only covered the interest, so you divided it by 3.5% to yield a maximum mortgage of $220,000. Now, you must divide it by 4.0%, which covers the interest of 3.5% and the private mortgage insurance of 0.5%. Therefore, the maximum mortgage is now only $192,500. That, plus your available down payment, yields the maximum amount you can afford to spend on the house, according to the conventional loan formulas.

- There is another constraint if your available funds for a down payment are quite small. The minimum percentage the down payment can be under any conventional loan is 5%. So divide your available funds by 5%. If the resulting number is less than the one you just calculated in the prior paragraph, then this smaller number is the maximum you can afford under the formula.

FHA LOANS

The federal government believes owning a house is good for its citizens. Therefore, it created a program that enables persons to qualify more easily for loans. If you are purchasing a home that costs less than $314,000 anywhere (or up to $726,000 in the highest cost areas; the limit varies by where you are in the country), you may be able to obtain an FHA loan. The biggest benefits of an FHA loan over a conventional loan are:

- These loans do not follow the "28/36 rule" mentioned above. Instead, they use the "35/48 rule," and that means one can afford a more expensive house, which we will calculate below.

- They usually require you to have been in your job for less time.

- They allow for lower credit scores (as low as 580).

- They allow for an even lower down payment (as little as 3.5% of the purchase price).[5]

The drawback is that FHA loans require that you purchase a different type of private mortgage insurance, one that is more expensive than the PMI for conventional loans. There is an up-front fee of 1.75% of the loan amount (which reduces your available down payment) and an annual fee of 1.3% of the loan amount (instead of about 0.5%). Further, in a conventional loan, even if you need PMI at first, you can cancel it when you have paid off part of the principal of the loan. That is not true with an FHA loan—you are stuck with the PMI until you sell the house or pay off the loan.[6]

Therefore, FHA loans are more expensive per dollar of home purchased, and that is why most people still prefer conventional loans if they have the 20% down payment available.

Now, how much more loan can you obtain under an FHA loan than a conventional loan? Remember in the example above, the mortgage was limited to $192,500 after PMI was included.

- Under the FHA program, the $50,000 borrower income is multiplied by 35% to produce maximum affordable housing payments of $17,500.

- Subtract the same $6,300 from the $17,500 that was previously subtracted from the $14,000 figure we used earlier.

- The result ($11,200) is divided by 4.8%, not 4.0%, in order to reflect the higher PMI payment (i.e., 1.3% versus 0.5%).

- That means the new maximum mortgage is $233,333.

- However, the amount of down payment you have available is reduced by $4,083, because of the up-front PMI payment you must make.

Now that you know how much you *can* spend, it is time to think about how much you want to spend. The limits (particularly the FHA limits) can leave you "house poor," meaning that your housing expenses are high enough that they crowd out your ability to afford everything else in your life. For example, the FHA limits—particularly the combined house and debt service ratio of 48%—will definitely leave you in violation of the budgeting rules described in earlier chapters.

To avoid being "house poor," I suggest you select a lower maximum price than the lenders say you can afford, and look at houses in that lower price range. And remember: Just as I warned you in the chapter on your first housing situation, if you look at more expensive houses, you will prefer the expensive houses.

FINDING THE RIGHT HOME

$\bullet \quad \bullet \quad \bullet$

Your first step is to get oriented to the housing market without feeling obliged to any particular real estate agent. You can accomplish this by looking online first. Every city has at least one real estate firm that has an online presence that accesses the so-called *multiple listing service* (which you will often see referred to only by its acronym, MLS). That means you can go to the website of one firm and see every house in the city that is listed by all the firms. Most of these sites do not require you to enter any contact information, so you can browse anonymously.

Once you believe you understand the market, know which areas you want to (or are willing to) live in, and know whether you can find homes that *generally* meet your requirements in those areas while staying within your budget, you are ready to get serious and find a professional, licensed, real estate agent. If you cannot find houses online that at least appear to come close to your requirements and budget in your desired areas, you need to go back and do some more online research. You will be wasting both your and your agent's time to start his/her work until you can narrow the search within some reasonable parameters.

I believe that first-time home buyers are better off working with a professional, licensed real estate agent than trying to do everything on their own. (Of note, you will sometimes hear the terms "real estate agent" and "Realtor" used interchangeably. Technically, "Realtor" is a trademark referring to someone who is a registered member of the National Association of Realtors. For reasons I won't bore you with, not all real estate agents are Realtors, and not all Realtors are real estate agents. For our purposes, the key is simply that you find a professional, ethical, licensed, expert to assist you, whether they happen to be called a "real estate agent" or a "Realtor"). Why do I advise utilizing a professional? Because although this chapter can help orient you, real estate transactions are large, complicated, and highly specific to local laws. Further, every real estate market has many wrinkles that professional real estate agents will know that most locals will not, such as whether there are plans for new construction that might alter traffic patterns or whether a particular neighborhood is known for being good for families etc.

Working with an agent does not cost you anything under normal circumstances. The sales commission (typically 5% to 6%)[7] is paid entirely by the seller, and it does not change based on whether you approach the seller directly or whether you work with an agent. (The only thing that changes is that, if you have an agent, the commission is split between the seller's agent and your agent, whereas if you do not have an agent, the same commission goes entirely to the seller's agent.)

How do you choose the right agent? Sometimes friends or family provide referrals, but the fact that a friend had a good experience does not mean the agent is right for you.

If you do not have a source of referral, concentrate on finding which realty company has the highest market share in the specific areas you are interested in. If you cannot find this out directly, just look for which company has the most signs posted in front of houses that are for sale in the area in which you're interested in finding a home. Then go to the company's office and ask to speak to the *broker in charge*, not an agent. (The broker oversees the work of the individual agents.) Explain that you are potentially interested in purchasing a house, and briefly explain what you are looking for (including your price range). Ask him/her to match you with his/her best agent who happens to have a temporary gap in activity. That way, you'll get a very good agent who will have the time to pay attention to your needs.

When you meet with the agent, share with him/her the calculations behind your estimate of what you can afford. He/she can then adjust the estimate based on local conditions (such as higher/lower real estate taxes, homeowner association fees, etc.). Explain to him/her what you are looking for, and let the agent get to work.

Then, ask your agent if it would be a good idea for you to get *pre-approved* by a lender for a mortgage up to a certain amount before you start the process of looking at homes. (To be precise, the lender is not pre-approving the ultimate mortgage itself—that cannot be done until a specific house has been chosen and appraised. Rather, the lender is committing that the loan will not be turned down due to any factors that are specific to you.) Being pre-approved eliminates any danger that you will make an offer on a house you cannot afford, and it strengthens your offer in the eyes of the seller because it removes the potential for one of his/her biggest nightmares. Every seller fears turning down several offers from other buyers in favor of one who ultimately cancels the contract because he/she cannot get a mortgage.

Okay, now it's time to go see some homes! And, once you find one you like, to make an offer.

HOW MUCH TO OFFER
· · ·

Everyone—particularly first-time homebuyers—experiences real anxiety when it comes time to make an offer on the home you want. No one wants to pay too much, but you (or worse, your spouse) may become emotionally attached to a particular home and will be crushed if you don't get it. How do you handle the tradeoff?

For starters, you need to understand that for all the help your agent has given you throughout the search process, when it comes time to make an offer, he/she will be biased toward you making a higher offer. Agents only get paid when the deal closes, so he/she prefers offers that have a higher likelihood of being accepted—that is, a higher offer. So be ready for a warning from your agent that "you do not want to offend the seller with a low offer, because the seller will not want to negotiate with you," or even a statement that your agent "would be embarrassed to present such a low offer."

Do not be persuaded by such emotional appeals. Do your homework, and you will make the right offer. A right offer will not offend the seller (even if it is low) unless the seller is irrational. And an irrational seller will be unreasonable in every other aspect of the deal, so you might as well find that out now.

So, what homework do you need to do? First, find out if the home's listing price is aggressive (low) or rich (high). You can do this via several free online sites that provide an estimate of the value based on *comparables* (i.e., based on prices that other people have recently paid for similar homes in the same area as the home you're considering). These sites include Zillow, Trulia, and Redfin.[8] Once you check more than one site, you will have a very good idea. The value of doing this homework is that it tells you what signals the seller is already receiving from his/her own agent about expectations.

Next, ask your agent how long this house has been on the market (the data is contained in the listing itself), and compare it to how long similar homes take to sell in your market. For example, as of December 2019, the national average was 68 days, but in San Jose, California, the average was only 36 days. If your agent does not have this information for your market, you can find out from sites such as Zillow.[9] The longer a home has been on the market relative to the average, the more flexible the seller should be. Be sure your agent checks to see the *real* length of time a home has been for sale—i.e., there is a practice in the industry of taking a slow-moving home off the market for a short time and then re-entering the listing, which officially causes the clock to start over.

Further, ask your agent if the home is *unique in a positive way* (meaning that it should attract an unusually large number of buyers relative to the average home), *average*, or *unique in a negative way*. For example, the upscale sections of Atlanta and some other southern markets tend to have very traditional tastes in architecture. If a home has more contemporary elements in its exterior design, the home will be considered unique in a negative way and be harder than average to sell. This may or may not have been picked up in the computerized analyses of the comparables you consulted.

Next, look for whether there are indications about the seller's mind-set. If the listing says "motivated seller" or whispers among the real estate community use that word, the seller is very anxious for any offer.

Finally, think about the strength of the non-price elements of your potential offer. For example, first-time homebuyers can have an advantage over a current homeowner, who sometimes must make the offer dependent on selling his/her own house before he/she can complete the transaction (this is called a *contingent offer*.) Or, maybe you can be flexible about how quickly or slowly the sale must close. Or, if you have already been pre-approved by a financial institution for a mortgage amount, you can make your offer contingent only on the home being appraised, rather than on your being approved for a mortgage. All of these items can make a somewhat lower offer more attractive.

Enough about the house. It is also time to be honest about the emotional state of your partner and yourself. How much do you care if you lose this house unless you pay full price? If you don't care very much, you can be much more aggressive in negotiations. I'm familiar with a couple who looked at houses for a few weeks, then announced they had "narrowed down the number of candidates to 29." They had a hard time finally choosing which house to actually make an offer on, but they were in a good position to be very demanding in their negotiations, because they had 28 alternatives if the seller wasn't willing to negotiate.

There is no magic algorithm for translating the above information into the precise offer to make, and there are no statistics to provide reference points. But the above facts will probably make it clear how aggressive you can be. And your agent can be helpful here (if you counter his/her own biases).

As you put together your offer, note there are more items you can negotiate about than just the raw figure of the purchase price. For example, a house sale involves a number of so-called *closing costs*. These are various fees that must be paid to several parties at the time the final sale takes place, including appraisers, the title insurance company, and the closing attorney. Collectively, these can be as much as 2% to 5% of the purchase price itself. For many of them, there is no set rule on whether the buyer or the seller will pay those fees. Another potential item is a one-year home warranty. These are insurance contracts that cost about $450 to $600 that will reimburse you if an appliance breaks, there is a plumbing problem, etc. Another item is the closing date. The sooner you close, the sooner the seller gets his money (and you start paying). Is there any reason why the seller would value a shorter or longer closing time? Your author once received a terrific deal on a house because the seller had a tax issue that had to be settled by the end of the year. It was a real scramble to achieve, but it cut 10% off of the purchase price of the house.

WHAT YOU NEED TO KNOW
ABOUT THE CONTRACT
• • •

The way you formally make an offer is by filling out a contract to purchase the house, signing it, and submitting it to the seller (through your real estate agent, if one is involved). The seller may accept it, reject it, or scratch out the part he/she disagrees with (such as the price) and substitute his/her counterproposal, initialing the change.

Typical contracts for house sales are available for free on the internet. It is worthwhile to download one or two at the outset of the house-hunting process, just to familiarize yourself with the terms and provisions. *However, be sure you also read the actual contract you are signing when you make an actual offer—word for word.* There are dozens of variations of every provision in these contracts, and sometimes those variations have major consequences.

Several provisions bear particular attention:

- Earnest money.

  » To ensure that buyers do not arbitrarily back out of contracts, the buyer makes a deposit (usually with the seller's agent) that the seller can keep if the buyer backs out for any reason other than those specified in the continencies section (see below). The amount of the deposit is not specified by law, but there are local norms. Nationally, the average earnest money is 1% to 2% of the purchase price, but it can be quite a bit higher.[10]

  » If the sale closes successfully, the deposit is applied as part of the down payment.

  » If the sale fails for one of the specified contingencies, the money is returned to the buyer.

  » If the sale fails for any other reason, the seller keeps the earnest money (or the buyer and seller fight about it in court).

- Contingencies.

  » At the time a contract is signed, certain events that are necessary to complete the sale may have not yet occurred. For example, what if the mortgage company were to refuse to lend enough money to enable you to purchase this house because the company does not believe the house is worth the price? What if you were to find out that the house is in far worse condition than was apparent, such as a termite infestation?

» To protect yourself in signing the contract, the purchaser always lists the items that must be satisfied before he/she will complete the sale. Be sure to list the following:[11]

› Financing contingencies—the sale is conditioned upon you receiving final approval for a mortgage in the amount you need to proceed.

› Appraisal contingencies—the sale is conditioned upon an appraiser saying the house is worth the purchase price.

› Inspection contingencies—the sale is conditioned upon the house being found in good condition by a home inspector.

› Title insurance contingencies—the sale is conditioned upon an insurer being willing to guaranty that no one else claims that they, instead of the seller, actually own the home or have a claim that would force you (the buyer) to pay them.

• Closing date and requirements.

» You want to require the sale to take place late enough that you can be prepared, but not so late that you are frustrated and waiting around to move in.

• Whether the buyer or the seller has to cover various closing costs.

» Be sure you understand and approve of the contract's specification regarding who will pay which of these fees.

WHAT HAPPENS BETWEEN THE CONTRACT AND THE CLOSING

• • •

Once the contract has been agreed to and signed by both parties, there are a number of administrative tasks to be completed before the *closing* (i.e., the official sale) can take place. Many of them are straightforward. However, two processes deserve particular attention—obtaining a home inspection, and applying for a mortgage.

OBTAINING A HOME INSPECTION

As mentioned above, your contract should specify that you have a certain number of days to have the home inspected and that you have the option to void the contract if you are not satisfied with the inspector's findings.

Unless you have been a general contractor that has actually built a house from scratch, do not perform the inspection yourself. Hire a professional. You do not have the skill necessary to assess all the various structural, roofing, plumbing, electrical, insulation, heating and other systems that together form a house, not to mention the landscaping, the rain runoff patterns in the yard, and so on.

The national average for professional home inspections is $329, although the amount varies by home size and location.[12]

If the inspector is thorough, he/she will identify a long list of deficiencies in the home. Do not despair. Every house has deficiencies, and the inspector's job is to point them out. This does not necessarily mean you should void the contract, unless he/she finds something catastrophic. More likely, you will require the seller to fix the defective items before closing or adjust your price offer accordingly.

APPLYING FOR A MORTGAGE

If you were not already pre-approved for a mortgage amount that enables you to purchase this particular house, the contract usually commits you to make an application within a certain time after the home inspection and obtain approval within another specified time. You need to get started right away, as the application often involves more paperwork than you expect, and paperwork will be necessary from third parties who may or may not take longer than you expect.

Mortgage loans (conventional or FHA) vary on two dimensions. The first dimension is how the interest rate is calculated.

- A *fixed-rate mortgage* is one in which the interest rate is set for the length of the loan. For example, I referred above to a 3.5% loan. That loan will charge 3.5% interest on the outstanding balance every year until the loan is paid off.

- An *adjustable-rate mortgage* (ARM) has one interest rate for an initial period (typically a bit lower than the prevailing fixed rate), and then the interest rate changes every once in a while, based on whether interest rates in the economy have risen or fallen since the loan was taken out. For example, a "10/1 ARM" is a mortgage whose initial rate is locked for 10 years, then the rate can change every 1 year after that (within certain pre-negotiated limits, which can be small or, during certain periods, quite large).

- These days, more than 90% of borrowers choose a fixed-rate loan.[13] When interest rates are higher, ARMs become more popular.

The second dimension along which mortgages vary is the duration of the mortgage—that is, how long it will take to pay off the mortgage. About 90% of borrowers go with a 30-year mortgage.[14] The second-most popular duration is a 15-year mortgage. To understand the difference, you need to understand how a mortgage works:

- Mortgages are structured so the payment remains the same each month over the life of the mortgage.

  » At first that seems strange, because (1) in the first month of the mortgage, you still owe the full amount of the mortgage, so the interest is being charged on the full amount, but (2) by the last month of the mortgage, you have already paid off almost the entire balance, so your interest charges should be small.

  » Well, some genius figured out a long time ago a formula that enabled all of that to happen.

  » The monthly payment is set to a somewhat higher amount than necessary to just cover the interest charge in the first month. (In fact, this amount has a different name. It is called the *mortgage constant*, as opposed to the mortgage rate.) That way, you pay down a little bit of the loan.

  » Then the second month, you owe a little less money in interest, because you just paid off a little bit of the loan the prior month. So the interest charge is a little less, even though the rate is still the same. If the total payment remains the same, you pay off slightly more of the loan amount the second month than you did the third month.

» And so on. By the thirtieth year of the mortgage, you owe very little of the loan balance and are still paying a little interest. Most of your later payments go toward eliminating the last of the balance.

- On a 30-year loan, the mortgage constant (when interest rates are 3.92%) is 5.67% annually. That is 1.76% higher than the actual interest rate of 3.92%. On the $220,000 loan I described at the outset of the chapter, that would equate to about $3,860 in principal payments the first year.

  » By the way, $3,860 is the majority of the $6,300 we deducted from our illustrative borrower's $14,000 that could be spent on housing to discover how much interest he/she could afford. The other $2,400 consisted of property taxes on a $240,000 house, because nationally, property taxes average about 1% of the property's value.[15]

- However, on a 15-year loan with the same interest rate, the mortgage constant is 8.83%, or 3.2% higher than the 30-year loan. This equates to about another $7,040 of principal payments that first year. The higher loan constant translates into a lower allowable mortgage. That is why 90% of borrowers choose the 30-year option.

THE CLOSING

· · ·

Completing a house purchase actually consists of several separate but inter-related transactions: the bank lending you the mortgage money, you combining the mortgage money with your down payment (and the earnest money you deposited earlier) to actually purchase the home from the seller, and you legally pledging the home as collateral to the lender. All of these take place in a single meeting referred to as the closing. The meeting is usually run by a closing attorney.

There are many different documents to be signed in the meeting, and the attorney will explain each of them to you. However, the document you should make the most effort to understand in detail is the *settlement statement*. This statement lays out how all of the money flows to and from the seller and buyer. It can be confusing because:

- Taxes may be paid *in advance* or *in arrears*.
  - » Imagine that you purchase a home on March 31, 2021. Imagine that one property tax authority (e.g., the county) forced the previous homeowner to pay all of the county taxes for 2021 before January 1, 2021. This is called paying taxes in advance.
  - » As the buyer, you would owe the seller a reimbursement for the portion of the taxes that correspond to your period of ownership from April 1 through December 31, 2021.
  - » Imagine, though, that the city requires 2021 taxes to only be paid in December 2021. This is called paying taxes in arrears. Then you would pay the city not only for the time you owned the house but also for the time between January 1, 2021 and March 31, 2021, when the previous owner held the house.
  - » In that case, at closing, the seller should reimburse you (in advance) for the portion of the tax bill associated with his ownership.

- You must pay for a title insurance policy for the benefit of the lender and for a separate title insurance policy for you, *unless* you say you do not want a separate policy. Many people refuse such homeowner title insurance policies.

- Interest on your mortgage is charged from the day of the closing. That means a partial month's payment will be due at the end of the month. However, some lenders want that payment now, but others do not. Some lenders even want to set the date of the month that later payments will be made to be something other than the first of the month, so the number of days in the partial month will not equal the actual number of days left in the month, etc.

- Some lenders want you to put money *in escrow* (i.e., put money aside now to cover expenses that will come due in the future), for example to cover real estate taxes that will come due in the future.

If you do not understand a charge on the settlement statement, be sure to question it, and be willing to make the closing attorney (or his assistant) take you through the calculation in detail. Based on your author's personal experience, the settlement statement frequently contains errors that will not be found if you do not question the charges. I have been through many closings over the years—and more than 75% of the draft settlement statements contained errors that would not have been found without my scrutiny.

ENDNOTES

[1] Joshua M. Brown, "Homeownership Rates by Age Group," The Reformed Broker, March 11, 2015, thereformedbroker.com/2015/03/11/homeownership-rates-by-age-group. Accessed December 16, 2019.

[2] "Conventional Loan Requirements and Guidelines for 2019," The Lenders Network, n.d., thelendersnetwork.com/conventional-loan-requirements. Accessed December 15, 2019.

[3] "The 28/36 Rule: How It Affects Your Mortgage Approval," Million Acres, December 21, 2019, www.fool.com/millionacres/real-estate-financing/mortgages/2836-rule-how-it-affects-your-mortgage-approval. Accessed December 14, 2019.

[4] "Conventional Loan Requirements and Guidelines for 2019," The Lenders Network, n.d., thelendersnetwork.com/conventional-loan-requirements. Accessed December 15, 2019.

[5] Sarah Davis, "How to Qualify for an FHA Loan," Money Under 30, April 15, 2019, www.moneyunder30.com/qualify-fha-loan. Accessed December 15, 2019.

[6] Sarah Davis, "With New Fees, Credit Requirements, FHA Loans Are More Expensive but Still Accessible," Money Under 30, April 7, 2019, www.moneyunder30.com/new-fha-loan-fees-requirements. Accessed December 15, 2019.

[7] "How Real Estate Commission Works," Redfin, n.d., www.redfin.com/guides/how-much-is-real-estate-agent-commission-buyer-seller. Accessed December 15, 2019.

[8] Rob Berger, "10 Home Value Websites to Lookup the Value of Your Home (and your neighbor's home)," DoughRoller, December 12, 2019, www.doughroller.net/tools-resources/9-great-alternatives-to-zillow-to-lookup-the-value-of-your-home-and-your-neighbors-home. Accessed December 15, 2019.

9 "What Is the Average Time to Sell a House?" Zillow, n.d., www.zillow.com/sellers-guide/average-time-to-sell-a-house. Accessed December 15, 2019.

10 Margaret Heidenry, "8 Earnest-Money Deposit Mistakes Home Buyers Live to Regret," Realtor.com, February 21, 2017, www.realtor.com/advice/finance/earnest-money-deposit-mistakes-buyers-make. Accessed December 16. 2019.

11 "Home Contingencies to Consider Before You Buy," FindLaw, n.d., realestate.findlaw.com/buying-a-home/contingencies-to-consider-before-you-buy.html. Accessed December 16, 2019.

12 "How Much Does a Home Inspection Cost?" HomeAdvisor, n.d., www.homeadvisor.com/cost/inspectors-and-appraisers/hire-a-home-inspector. Accessed December 16, 2019.

13 Michele Lerner, "Adjustable-rate mortgages are making a comeback. But are these loans right for you?" *Washington Post*, May 2, 2019, www.washingtonpost.com/realestate/adjustable-rate-mortgages-are-making-a-comeback-but-are-these-loans-right-for-you/2019/05/01/1c0e3bea-443f-11e9-aaf8–4512a6fe3439_story.html. Accessed December 16, 2019.

14 Christina Majaski, "30-Year vs. 15-Year Mortgage: What's the Difference?" Investopedia, May 7, 2019, www.investopedia.com/articles/personal-finance/042015/comparison-30year-vs-15year-mortgage.asp. Accessed December 16, 2019.

15 Jean Folger, "The 10 Best States for Property Taxes—and Why," Investopedia, December 6, 2019, www.investopedia.com/articles/personal-finance/102015/7-best-states-property-taxes-and-why.asp. Accessed December 16, 2019.

CHAPTER 15

Having Children

More than 50% of women have a child before age 30. (We can assume the portion for men is about the same.) There are hundreds if not thousands of books that provide excellent advice on parenting, so I will not attempt to compete with them in a single chapter here. Instead, this chapter focuses on your decision to have a child, or two, or... and on whether this is the right time to do so.

I do not intend to discourage anyone from having children, or to encourage delay. In fact, I strongly believe that children are wonderful—and the overwhelming portion of parents agree. In a national survey of parents with children aged zero to five, 91% of respondents said that parenting was their greatest joy, and 70% agreed with the statement that their life started when they became a parent.[1]

But children are also expensive, burdensome, and unrelenting. And more couples are deciding to either delay having children or to forego children all together. In fact, the most commonly used measure of fertility (the number of births for every one thousand women of childbearing age) was at a record low in 2017. The total fertility rate (which estimates how many children women will have based on current patterns) fell to 1.8 in 2017—that is, below the 2.1 rate which is required to maintain the current population level.

The United States is now almost on par with the low rates in the rest of the developed world.[2] Most of the decline seems to be because couples are delaying having children and deciding to have fewer than their parents did, rather than choosing to be childless for life. In a survey of 20- to 45-year-olds, about half of the respondents were already parents. Another 21% said they wanted children, and 17% said they weren't sure; only 12% said they did not want children at all.[3]

You deserve to know the medical statistics, the legal responsibilities, the financial costs, and the emotional impact children will have on your relationship with your partner. And if you are considering being a single parent or adoption as your route to parenthood, you deserve to understand what is different in those situations. Therefore, this chapter will help answer a variety of questions you and your potential parenting partner may have, including:

- Are there surprising legal consequences of having a child?

- What does it cost to have a child?

- Will having a baby adversely impact your relationship with your partner?

- Are there downsides of waiting until later to have children?

- What are the odds of getting pregnant once you decide to try?

- Once a pregnancy occurs, what are the odds of a healthy baby being born, and what are the risks to the mother?

- If we have trouble getting pregnant, should you consider IVF?

- How much time can you take off work, and will you get paid for that time?

- Should you consider adoption?

ARE THERE SURPRISING LEGAL CONSEQUENCES OF HAVING A CHILD?

• • •

The short answer, if you think about it, is that your legal responsibilities are exactly what you would imagine they would be, but it is certainly worth taking some time to think about it.

Specifically, parents must meet their child's basic needs (food, clothing, housing, medical care, and education) and carry out their parental duties in a way that serves the child's best interests. They have a financial duty to support their child until he/she reaches the age of 18 or graduates from high school or has special needs. Further, parents must serve a child's emotional and physical needs and protect the child from abuse.

In return, parents have several legal rights, including the right to physical custody, the right to legal custody (meaning the ability to make major decisions about the child's health, education, and religious upbringing), and gift and inheritance rights.[4]

Importantly, those responsibilities hold for each parent, whether or not they are married at the time of the child's birth or divorce later on. However, in such cases, the courts often get involved in dividing the rights and responsibilities between the disagreeing parents.

WHAT DOES IT COST?

· · ·

Child-rearing costs a lot more than most people think. Surveys have shown potential parents tend to underestimate the cost of having a child by about half. Here are the facts:

- Let's start with the birth itself. The average bill for doctors' fees and hospital charges runs around $9,700 for a normal delivery, and roughly $2,500 more for a cesarean section.[5] Fortunately, most couples have medical insurance that covers most of those costs.

- Then comes the baby's first year. According to a 2010 U.S. government report, the average middle-income family will spend roughly $12,000 that year. By age two, that number rises to more than $12,500 per year. However, it appears those figures do not include day care, which can add thousands more.

- What is the cost for an entire childhood? According to the U.S. government, the average cost from birth to the child's 18th birthday is

$233,000 for a middle-income household. For upper-income families, the cost is estimated at $372,000. And that does not include college.[6] Add $83,000 for a public college or $187,000 for a private college.[7] And remember, in Chapter 1 we saw that 70% of college graduates were still financially dependent on their parents two years later.

- Finally, is a second child less expensive than the first one? Logic would suggest it is, and the U.S. government report on the subject asserts that it is. The report says that each child costs roughly 25% less to raise than his/her next older sibling.[8] However, Googling the question reveals that most bloggers disagree.

WILL HAVING A BABY ADVERSELY IMPACT YOUR RELATIONSHIP WITH YOUR PARTNER?

• • •

Unfortunately, the conclusive answer is yes. The subject has been formally studied for the last 30 years, and the studies consistently show that the relationship between partners suffers at least somewhat after children join the household.

The fuller story is that satisfaction with marriage declines in the first few years of marriage, even without kids. If the decline is too steep, divorce often occurs. The studies show that the arrival of kids causes the rate of decline in satisfaction to be approximately twice as steep as it would otherwise be, and if the pregnancy was unplanned, the decline is even steeper.[9]

The causes appear to be largely centered on a crowding-out effect. The amount of time and attention the partners can devote to each other drops as the time devoted to the kids increases. Meanwhile, the time the partners do get to spend alone gets devoted in part to the planning needed to care for the kids. And as we saw earlier, children are quite expensive, which crowds out discretionary funds for luxuries, exotic vacations etc.

Here is a surprise, though. According to several studies, having children statistically *decreases* the likelihood of divorce by as much (according to at least one estimate) as 40%. It seems that, while the presence of children may lower satisfaction with the spouse, the kids themselves present a more than offsetting incentive to stay in the relationship. Or maybe the rate of decline in marital satisfaction is faster, but that just means it reaches a still-acceptable (rather than unacceptable) steady state more quickly.

Of course, outcomes are typically rosier if the children are healthy. Some children have challenging physical or mental health conditions that impose extreme stress on the parents. For these couples, the divorce rate is higher, rather than lower, than those for childless couples.

ARE THERE DOWNSIDES OF WAITING TO HAVE CHILDREN?
• • •

As indicated in the introduction to this chapter, many couples are waiting until later to have children. The average age when women have their first child is now 28 (up from 24 in 1970). In fact, in 2016, the birth rate for women between 30 and 34 was slightly higher than for women between 25 and 29.[10]

While there are clear reasons for waiting (among them the chance to save money in advance of the birth), there are medical consequences associated with waiting. These include reduced fertility (so getting pregnant is harder), a higher risk of complications for the mother, and a greater incidence of birth defects.[11]

WHAT ARE THE ODDS OF GETTING PREGNANT ONCE YOU DECIDE TO TRY?
• • •

The odds that a couple *can* have a child are encouraging. Only about 9% of men and 11% of women (of the relevant ages) experience fertility problems. Even some of these succeed, because fully 90% of couples who have tried steadily have become pregnant within two years (in fact, about 86% have become pregnant within one year[12]). However, these statistics will change as you age. Women in their 30s are about half as fertile as women in their 20s.

More tactically, the odds a couple will succeed in any given month are about 20%. Therefore, in healthy couples in their 20s, the odds of conceiving are 40% to 60% within three months.

And what about the odds of being surprised by twins, or even triplets? When the baby is conceived naturally (i.e., through intercourse), the odds are low. Specifically, the odds of having twins are about 3.3%, while odds of having triplets are about 0.1%.[13] When a baby is conceived via in vitro fertilization (covered in the section below), the odds are much higher.

WHAT ARE THE ODDS OF A HEALTHY BABY BEING BORN, AND WHAT ARE THE RISKS TO THE MOTHER?

· · ·

Once a pregnancy is discovered, the odds are about 80% that the fetus will survive the first 20 weeks of pregnancy (out of an average duration of 37 weeks from conception to birth). A baby who is lost during the first 20 weeks is termed a miscarriage.

New research, however, suggests the *total* portion of pregnancies that result in miscarriages is higher, about 50%. This higher rate is due to previously-uncounted miscarriages that occur before the woman ever knows she is pregnant. However, if this figure is accurate, then the odds a woman gets pregnant are also higher than what has been reported, as many unrecognized pregnancies and miscarriages occur, and therefore are never reported. The figures in this chapter reflect known rates of pregnancy, etc.

A baby who dies in a mother's womb after the 20th week (or at the moment of birth) is termed stillborn. Fortunately, stillbirths are relatively rare in the United States, occurring in only about 1% of pregnancies.[14]

How many times have you heard prospective parents reply to the question about any preferences as to the baby's gender with the phrase, "We don't care—we just want the baby to be healthy"? Thankfully, in the United States, 96% to 97% of all babies are born healthy.[15] And 99.4% of babies survive their first year.[16]

Included in these survival figures is a condition that has received a lot of attention in recent years, making it every parent's worst nightmare: sudden infant death syndrome (SIDS). Fortunately, although it is a tragedy, it is statistically quite rare, occurring in only about three one-hundredths of 1% of babies.[17]

While childbearing entails risk to the mother, statistically the odds are encouraging. Maternal mortality in the United States, while rising (partly due to the increased use of cesarean sections, which carries some additional risk), is only two one-hundredths of 1%.[18]

IF YOU HAVE TROUBLE GETTING PREGNANT, SHOULD YOU CONSIDER IVF?

• • •

In vitro fertilization (IVF) is a procedure that consists of removing eggs from the mother, combining them with sperm from the father in an external container, and implanting the resulting embryo back into the mother. The procedure has been conducted about eight million times since it was first used with humans in 1977 (after which the resulting baby was born in 1978.) It is common in the United States, producing approximately 100,000 babies each year.

The procedure is generally considered safe for the mother, although some side effects can occur. Some studies have suggested that IVF carries slightly higher odds of birth defects (approximately one additional percentage point). However, critics point out that the mothers who undergo IVF are typically older than average, and that fact alone might explain the difference. Further, more recently, a technique known as *preimplantation genetic screening* has been employed to ensure the embryo is genetically healthy before it is placed into the mother's womb, thereby reducing the odds of birth defects. This will likely improve the birth defect statistics as use of the technique spreads. That same screening produces a side benefit for those parents who want it—they can choose the gender of the embryos that are implanted, thereby choosing the gender of the child.

For women under the age of 35, IVF has a 54% chance of success per cycle, defined as a single time that multiple eggs are retrieved from the woman's ovaries. Therefore, about half of all couples must go through multiple cycles in order to have a child. One study found the average couple goes through 2.7 cycles, but this result is driven by the fact that most women who undergo IVF are older, and success rates decline with age.[19]

The average cost for one IVF cycle is about $12,000, not including the cost of medications, which will likely be between $1,500 and $3,000 per cycle. Then there are incidentals, such as monitoring. One study tracked the total cost and found the average couple spent $19,234 on their first cycle and an average of $6,955 for additional cycles.[20] More recently, variations of IVF have been introduced that are less expensive. These include approaches called *mini-IVF*, *micro-IVF*, and *IUI treatment*. However, these are not as widely applicable as conventional IVF.

There is one other aspect of IVF you should know about from the outset. Statistically, the odds of having twins is over 12%, or nearly four times the likelihood than when a baby is conceived naturally.[21] However, this does not happen entirely by accident. The doctor (and you) control how many fertilized eggs to implant into the mother's body. Adding more eggs raises the chances that one will survive to become a baby, but it also raises the chances that more than one will survive to produce fraternal (not identical) twins.

HOW MUCH TIME CAN YOU TAKE OFF WORK, AND WILL YOU GET PAID FOR THAT TIME?

• • •

According to the *Economist* magazine, the United States is one of only two countries in the world with no statutory national policy of paid maternity leave[22] (the other being Papua New Guinea).

The federal government regulates a minimum standard that must be met by most companies, but certain states have regulated more generous provisions.

Let's review the federal government requirements. If you work for a company with 15 or more employees and your company offers paid sick leave, then by law, your boss must treat pregnancy and childbirth like any other short-term disability. In practice, that usually means the mother is entitled to 6 to 8 weeks of paid time off. However, note the two caveats: the company must have at least 15 employees, and it must have a policy of offering paid sick leave. Otherwise, this law does not apply. And because it is based on a disability standard, it does not apply to adoptions, or to the father, or to the non-pregnant spouse in a same-sex couple.

If the above does not apply to your situation, then you may fall under the Family and Medical Leave Act of 1993 (FMLA), which applies to companies that have 50 or more employees. This law enables one or both parents to go on maternity or family leave after the birth or adoption of a child. Additionally, FMLA defines parents as biological, adoptive, step, or foster parents who stood *in loco parentis* ("in the place of a parent"), including same-sex parents and spouses. Under this law, legal parents are protected for up to 12 weeks of unpaid leave. It ensures the job security of parents/employees, but it does not protect employees who go on paid leave with their employers.

Many states have supplemented these federal regulations with far more extensive maternity leave benefits, including expanding paid or flexible sick time, expanding access for workers in smaller companies or with less time on the job, and pregnancy accommodations.[23]

Beyond this, in 2019, about 40% of employers offered paid parental leave, which is up from only 25% just four years earlier.[24] Therefore, the real answer to the question is, "It depends on who you work for."

SHOULD YOU CONSIDER ADOPTION?

• • •

There are many reasons to consider adopting a child. Most of them are personal to you and your situation, and thus they lie beyond the scope of this book. Further, adoption is a complex subject, governed mainly by state laws, which makes definitive statements impossible.

However, most people have significant misconceptions about the prevalence and the process of adoptions. Therefore, this section provides some facts that may help you to decide whether you want to investigate the subject in more detail.

First, when someone says adoption, most of us think of adoptions involving a mother giving up her newborn baby to an unrelated couple. In fact, this is only a surprisingly small portion of the adoption universe. The latest comprehensive study of adoptions is a report by the National Council on Adoptions titled "Adoption by the Numbers," published in 2017 and based on data from 2014. It indicates that while there were 110,373 total adoptions that year in the United States, 41,023 (or 37%) were related, or kinship, adoptions (for example, when a spouse adopted the children from his/her spouse's previous relationship). Only 69,350 were unrelated adoptions, and the majority of those were adoptions of children from the foster care system. Only 18,329 adoptions consisted of infant adoptions.

To put that in context, there were 18,329 infant adoptions out of the 3,985,000 babies born in the United States that year—which means that less than one-half of 1% of babies were given up for adoption. Further, the notion that unwed mothers often give up their babies for adoption is wrong—in reality, 99% of unwed mothers elect to raise the child themselves. Further, most mothers giving up their baby for adoption do not fit the "unwed teen mother" stereotype. Many women who choose adoption are older and already have other children. Many are married when they decide to place their baby for adoption. Most have completed high school, and nearly half have completed college.[25]

Other countries are often mentioned as a source of candidates for baby (not newborn) adoptions, but this practice is also infrequent. International adoptions fell from a peak of almost 23,000 in 2004 to just under 6,000 in 2014, a drop of 74%. Therefore, domestic infant adoptions outnumbered international adoptions be three to one. Furthermore, the number of international adoptions has declined even further since then, due to increasing governmental restrictions.[26]

How does a couple find a healthy baby to adopt? The largest source is private adoption agencies, which appear to account for about 75% of such adoptions. Almost all of the others are independent adoptions (sometimes called private adoptions). These are adoptions arranged between the birth mother and the adoptive parent(s). Public agencies are rarely involved in newborn situations.

As suggested by the figures above, the linchpin in an independent adoption is finding a prospective mother who wants to give up her baby for adoption. An adoption attorney then assists with the arrangements and the negotiations between the birth mother and the adoptive parent(s). These negotiations can include birth mother self-care responsibilities, reimbursements by the adoptive parents, involvement by the birth mother in the child's life, etc.

Working with an adoption agency involves signing up with an agency, specifying any restrictions you want to place on which children you are willing to adopt, and waiting for a match between your requirements and those that a birth mother places on what adoptive families she is willing to place her child with. How restrictive you are is plays a major role in how long you have to wait for a match.

A recent annual survey by *Adoptive Family Magazine* placed the average cost of a domestic infant adoption through an adoption agency at $43,000. It indicated that 62% of adoptive families found a match within a year, and 82% were matched within two years. It also reported that the results associated with working with an adoption attorney instead of an adoption agency were remarkably similar in terms of both cost and time.[27]

There is one final point that you should be aware of if you pursue adoption. The birth mother does not legally sign the so-called *termination of parental rights* (TPR) until after the baby is born. In some states, she even has the right to change her mind for another 30 days after she signs the TPR, even though the child has been with the adoptive parents for some time.[28]

～

In some respects, this chapter may make you feel pessimistic about the prospect of having children. That is not my intent. I count myself among the 91% of parents who consider parenting to be their greatest joy. But I am also committed to providing you with the facts, so that you can make the best decision for yourself and be fully prepared for both the wonderful and difficult outcomes resulting from that decision.

ENDNOTES

[1] "National Parent Survey Overview and Key Insights," Zero to Three, June 6, 2016, www.zerotothree.org/resources/1424-national-parent-survey-overview-and-key-insights. Accessed December 3, 2019.

[2] Claire Cain Miller, "Americans Are Having Fewer Babies. They Told Us Why," *New York Times*, July 5, 2018, /www.nytimes.com/2018/07/05/upshot/americans-are-having-fewer-babies-they-told-us-why.html. Accessed December 3, 2019.

[3] Miller, "Americans Are Having Fewer Babies," /www.nytimes.com/2018/07/05/upshot/americans-are-having-fewer-babies-they-told-us-why.html. Accessed December 3, 2019.

[4] Kristina Otterstrom, "The Legal Rights and Responsibilities of a Parent," Lawyers.com, n.d., www.lawyers.com/legal-info/family-law/children/the-legal-rights-and-responsibilities-of-a-parent.html. Accessed December 6, 2019.

[5] Diane Harris, "The Cost of Raising a Baby," Parenting, n.d., www.parenting.com/pregnancy/planning/the-cost-of-raising-a-baby. Accessed December 4, 2019.

[6] Mark Lino, "The Cost of Raising a Child," U.S. Department of Agriculture, March 8, 2017, www.usda.gov/media/blog/2017/01/13/cost-raising-child. Accessed December 4, 2019.

[7] "Got young kids? 6 ways to manage costs," Fidelity, February 20, 2019, www.fidelity.com/learning-center/personal-finance/college-planning/managing-costs-raising-child. Accessed December 4, 2019.

[8] Lino, "The Cost of Raising a Child," www.usda.gov/media/blog/2017/01/13/cost-raising-child. Accessed December 4, 2019.

[9] "Decades of Studies Show What Happens to Marriages After Having Kids," Fortune, May 9, 2016, fortune.com/2016/05/09/mothers-marriage-parenthood. Accessed December 4, 2019.

[10] Maria LaMagna, "More American women are having babies in their 30s than their 20s," Market Watch, October 16, 2018, www.marketwatch.com/story/american-women-are-having-babies-later-and-are-still-conflicted-about-it-2017-05-19. Accessed December 4, 2019.

[11] "Having a Baby After Age 35: How Aging Affects Fertility and Pregnancy," American College of Obstetricians and Gynecologists, July 2018, www.acog.org/Patients/FAQs/Having-a-Baby-After-Age-35-How-Aging-Affects-Fertility-and-Pregnancy?IsMobileSet=false. Accessed December 4, 2019.

[12] "How Common is infertility?" National Institute of Child Health and Human Development, n.d., www.nichd.nih.gov/health/topics/infertility/conditioninfo/common. Accessed December 4, 2019.

[13] "National Center for Health Statistics: Multiple Births," Centers for Disease Control and Prevention, n.d., www.cdc.gov/nchs/fastats/multiple.htm. Accessed December 3, 2019.

[14] "What Is Stillbirth?" Centers for Disease Control and Prevention, n.d., www.cdc.gov/ncbddd/stillbirth/facts.html. Accessed December 4., 2019.

[15] "General Population Risk for Birth Defects," Emory University School of Medicine, n.d., genetics.emory.edu/documents/resources/Emory_Human_Genetics_General_Population_Risk_for_Birth_Defects.PDF. Accessed December 4, 2019.

[16] "Reproductive Health: Infant Mortality," Centers for Disease Control and Prevention, n.d., www.cdc.gov/reproductivehealth/maternalinfanthealth/infantmortality.htm. Accessed December 4, 2019.

[17] "Sudden Unexpected Infant Death and Sudden Infant Death Syndrome: Data and Statistics," Centers for Disease Control and Prevention, n.d., www.cdc.gov/sids/data.htm. Accessed December 3, 2019.

[18] Suzanne Delbanco et al., "The Rising U.S. Maternal Mortality Rate Demands Actions from Employers," *Harvard Business Review*, June 28, 2019, hbr.org/2019/06/the-rising-u-s-maternal-mortality-rate-demands-action-from-employers. Accessed December 3, 2019.

[19] Rachel Gurevich, "The Chances for IVF Pregnancy and Success," Very Well Family, November 9, 2018, www.verywellfamily.com/what-are-the-chances-for-ivf-success-1960213. Accessed December 7, 2019.

[20] Rachel Gurevich, "How Much Does IVF Really Cost?" Very Well Family, March 20, 2019, www.verywellfamily.com/how-much-does-ivf-cost-1960212. Accessed December 7, 2019.

[21] "How to increase your odds," Healthline, n.d., www.healthline.com/health/pregnancy/chances-of-having-twins#increasing-the-odds. Accessed December 4, 2019.

[22] "The World in 2020," *Economist Magazine*, December 27, 2019, 40.

[23] Wikipedia, s.v. "Maternity leave in the United States," December 30, 2019, en.wikipedia.org/wiki/Maternity_leave_in_the_United_States. Accessed December 4, 2019.

[24] Anne Stych, "40% of employers now offer paid parental leave," Bizwomen, February 4, 2019, www.bizjournals.com/bizwomen/news/latest-news/2019/02/40-%-of-employers-nowoffer-paid-parental.html?page=all. Accessed December 6, 2019.

[25] "A Comprehensive Tour Through Modern Adoption," American Adoptions, n.d., www.americanadoptions.com/adoption/adoption_overview. Accessed December 7, 2019.

[26] Jo Jones and Paul Placek, "Adoption: By the Numbers," National Council for Adoption, February 15, 2017, www.adoptioncouncil.org/publications/2017/02/adoption-by-the-numbers. Accessed December 6, 2019.

[27] Dawn Davenport, "Adoption in the US 2018: How Many? How Much? How Long Do They Take?" April 30, 2018, Creating a Family, creatingafamily.org/adoption-category/adoption-blog/adoption-cost-length-time. Accessed December 7, 2019.

[28] Julianna Mendelsohn, "What If the Birth Mother Changes Her Mind?" Adoption.org, n.d., adoption.org/birth-mother-changes-mind. Accessed December 7, 2019.

CHAPTER 16

A Primer on Divorce

Researchers estimate that 41% of all first marriages in the United States end in divorce, and that the average age of couples going through their first divorce is 30. Said another way, roughly 20% of all the marriages that occur in people's teens and 20s have ended by age 30.

While most of us know one or more young couples who have divorced, the process and the experience of every couple is unique. So, extrapolating from the reports of your friends or parents about what the rules and procedures are may not paint an accurate picture of what to expect. This chapter provides an overview of the legal processes and issues involved, to give you a broader framework within which to place your own prospective situation.

Importantly, the specific laws around each aspect and stage of divorce vary from state to state. Therefore, if you reach the point of actively considering divorce, be sure to consult your state's laws and processes before proceeding.

A survey of divorce professionals cited the following as the main cause of divorce in the cases they had handled. First was basic incompatibility at 43%, which was followed by infidelity at 28% and money issues at 22%.

Emotional or physical abuse was cited only 6% of the time, and both parenting issues and substance abuse were cited less than 1% each.[1]

Given the preponderance of the first three issues, it is worth considering the question of whether marriage counseling might have helped many of the couples. There is some evidence the answer is yes, *if* they begin the process before reaching the point of no return.

Prior to the 1980s, couples counseling had a relatively low success rate of about 50%. It therefore gathered the reputation as being not very effective. Research was conducted, and as a consequence, counseling practices were changed to a new paradigm called *emotionally focused therapy,* which is now roughly 75% effective, as measured by a scientific instrument called the Dyadic Adjustment Scale. The major positive outcome is the reduction in complaints (relationship stress) between partners. And, the improvement has been shown to continue for at least two years after the counseling concludes. Success has been tested in high-stress situations such as military couples, parents of chronically ill children, and infertile couples.

Further, the 25% of couples who did not see improvement were not entirely random. They were concentrated in couples who had abusive relationships, where one or both partners engaged in substance abuse and were not actively managing the addiction, or couples who had already made the decision to separate.[2]

Should you reach the point of considering divorce, you will need to understand several topics in advance.

- Separation versus divorce
- Contested versus uncontested divorce
- The divorce process
- How financial and child custody/support issues are typically handled by the courts in a divorce
- An important note about fault in a divorce

SEPARATION VERSUS DIVORCE

. . .

If you know someone who has been through a divorce, it is likely you were aware they went through a first stage referred to *separation*. In fact, there are two forms of separation, and they have different legal constructs and consequences.

Some couples just need some time apart. If so, one might move away from the home for a period of time. This is known as an *informal separation* or *trial separation*. It is not necessarily a first step toward an inevitable divorce. Some marriage counselors estimated that 50% of their clients who have engaged in a trial separation have reconciled. The odds appear better if both parties explicitly discuss the reasons for the separation, agree on the ground rules, and use the time to think about repairing the relationship rather than stoking their anger and plotting their next move in the divorce process. Dating other people during an informal separation has decidedly negative effects on the likelihood of reconciliation.

The courts are not involved in informal separations. However, that does not mean there are no legal consequences to an informal separation. In some states, even the date of an informal separation can influence the way property is divided, calculations of spousal and child support, and other issues. If there are major changes in either of your financial situations, such as a large bonus or losing your job, it could affect the final settlement. Other states do not recognize informal separation dates at all.[3]

Dating while informally separated can also be a tricky legal issue, not to mention a tricky emotional issue with both your spouse and your new love interest. States vary with respect to their legal views on adultery and its impact on financial settlements.

Some attorneys recommend you and your spouse draw up a written agreement that governs the arrangements while you are informally separated, in order to avoid additional conflicts when the two of you have genuinely different understandings of the rules of the road. However, they also warn the informal separation agreement can turn into a formal separation agreement, and/or guide elements of the permanent divorce settlement. The agreement can be used by the court to determine such things as spousal support arrangements and even child custody details. For example, if you agree to shared custody during an informal separation period, it will be difficult to convince a judge that you deserve sole custody later, absent some major changes in behavior or circumstance of your soon-to-be-former spouse.[4]

Formal *legal separations* aren't very common. In a legal separation, a court issues an order that mandates the rights and duties of a couple while they are still married but living apart. They usually are sought when the partners cannot agree on the terms and conditions while waiting for the divorce to proceed. As with informal separations, the legal consequences of dating while formally separated vary by state.

In both informal and formal separations, the couple is still legally married, and as a consequence:

- Healthcare and other benefits continue, including certain social security benefits that terminate with a divorce.

- Legal separation does not change marital status; therefore, neither partner is free to marry someone else.

- Spouses are still considered next-of-kin and can still make medical and financial decisions for the other.

- Spouses may still be responsible for the debt of the other spouse in a legal separation.

- Legal separation preserves each spouse's legal rights to property benefits upon the death of the other.[5]

CONTESTED VERSUS UNCONTESTED DIVORCE
· · ·

An *uncontested divorce* is one in which the two parties form a written agreement that covers all of the issues involved in the dissolution of the marriage and brings that signed agreement to court. The major issues that must be covered in a divorce agreement (or in a judge's decision, in the case of a contested divorce) are asset and debt division between the parties, spousal support (if any), child support requirements, and child custody/visitation rights. Each of these issues is discussed below.

If the court finds the agreement acceptable, and is confident that neither side was coerced into the agreement, the court can approve the document and issue the divorce order. However, the judge is not required to accept the terms of the document. For example, if there are children involved, the judge will separately consider whether the terms agreed to by the parents are in the best interests of the children. If a judge disapproves of the terms of the document, he/she can send the parties back to the negotiation table and/or order a hearing or trial.

In a *contested divorce*, the two parties cannot agree on one or more significant issues in the terms of the divorce. In this case, a trial has to be held before a judge to determine the ultimate resolution. Another form of contested divorce occurs when one of the parties disagrees that a divorce should take place at all. However, this may be best thought of as a delaying or negotiating tactic by one party, as all states have some form of a no-fault divorce such that either party can eventually obtain a divorce over the objections of the other party.

There are three significant differences between an uncontested and a contested divorce.

- First, uncontested divorces are generally less expensive.
  - » If the split is amicable and there are no children involved, some states allow couples to engage in a do-it-yourself approach without involving attorneys. That can cost less than $500. In fact, in Wyoming, the filing fee is apparently only $70.
  - » The necessary documents can be obtained online. Most of the time though, it is wise to involve attorneys. Most attorneys charge by the hour, but the average attorney's fee for an uncontested divorce is about $1,000 per side. For contested divorces, the average is $2,500.
  - » Frankly though, these figures can be misleading. What drives up the cost of a divorce is the time the two sides spend arguing. The phrase *noncontested* refers strictly to what takes place officially at the courthouse. Negotiations in a noncontested divorce can be as acrimonious and protracted as those that take place before and

during a contested divorce. That is why some sources place the average cost of a divorce at $15,000 per side once they figure in the cost of accountants, property appraisers, etc.[6] There are particularly egregious cases where each side has spent over $1 million.

- Second, and related, uncontested divorces generally take less time.

  » Every state has a minimum time it takes to obtain a divorce.

  » First, each state (except Washington, South Dakota, and Alaska) has a residency requirement, which specifies how long you must have lived there before you can file a divorce.

  » Then, how long a couple must be separated before filing for divorce in some states depends on whether the divorce is considered a *fault divorce* or a *no-fault divorce*.

    › While these terms sound similar, they are not identical. One can have a no-fault contested divorce, and though rare, one can have a fault uncontested divorce.[7]

    › This distinction affects timing because many states impose a period in which the spouses must live apart before they can file for a no-fault divorce, but there is no such delay to file for a fault divorce. (More on the distinctions between fault and no-fault divorces below.)

  » But the real difference in the speed of divorce comes from the process time.

    › The statutory minimum process times in an uncontested divorce vary from 14 days (Nevada and Oklahoma) to six months (several states),[8] or even longer if children are involved.

    › But in a contested divorce, the process is lengthened by delays in the court's own calendar—that is, delays in hearings held before the judge, delays waiting for a trial date, and further delays while the judge considers the evidence and writes a decision. One survey placed the average process time at eighteen months.[9]

- Finally, a judge's ruling in a contested divorce, under certain circumstances, can be appealed to a higher court. By contrast, in an uncontested divorce, both parties have agreed to the settlement, so the terms of the divorce are generally not appealable (the exception is that, in some states, if the circumstances of one or both of the parties change substantially, a party may petition to have the terms modified[10]).

THE DIVORCE PROCESS ITSELF
• • •

Broadly speaking, the divorce process consists of seven steps.[11]

STEP 1: The couple separates.

- It does not matter whether they separate formally or informally in most states.
- However, the date of the separation begins the fulfillment of the time requirement described in the previous section.

STEP 2: One partner or the other files a legal petition asking the court to terminate the marriage.

- The petition indicates that one or the other spouse meets the residency requirement and specifies the reason for the divorce.
- All states allow for a no-fault divorce.

STEP 3: The petitioning spouse provides a copy of the paperwork to the other spouse (often referred to as serving the papers) and files proof of service with the court.

- If the papers are not served, or if the proof of service is not given to the court, the process stalls.
- The spouse receiving the papers is then required to acknowledge to the court that he/she has indeed been served.

STEP 4: One spouse or the other may request a temporary order from the judge.

- This can occur at the same time as the filing or soon thereafter.

- A temporary order sets in place legal arrangements during the divorce process. For example, if one spouse is financially dependent on the other, but the two have not agreed on what support will be provided during the process, the dependent spouse might apply for a temporary support order. Or, one spouse may want to prevent the other from selling property. Or, there may need to be orders concerning support and visitation of the children.

- If a temporary order is requested, the court schedules a hearing, collects evidence or testimony from both sides, and issues whatever order the judge deems appropriate.

STEP 5: The parties attempt to negotiate a settlement.

- Note that while the terms may be similar to those previously agreed to by the parties in an informal or formal separation agreement, this is a separate legal agreement—a permanent one.

- The parties are not obliged to agree in the permanent settlement to the terms they agreed to previously, although the earlier agreement can establish some precedents. After all, during the negotiations, information may have been discovered that alters one or the other spouse's views about what is fair.

STEP 6: If the parties agree on a settlement, they file it with the court. However, if the parties cannot agree, a trial process takes place.

- This is a full-blown trial, often involving depositions, discovery requests, motions before the court, witnesses, and many of the other elements of a classic trial.

- As noted above, it can extend for a long time and involve much expense.

STEP 7: The judge issues the *order of dissolution* that ends the marriage and spells out certain rights and obligations.

- These could include the couple's custodial responsibility and parenting time, child and spousal support, and the division of assets and debts.

- If the parties agreed on a settlement, the filing spouse's attorney drafts the judgment and obtains the respondent's attorney's consent before submitting it to the judge. However, if there was a divorce trial, the judge will write the final order.

HOW THE BIG ISSUES IN A DIVORCE ARE TYPICALLY ADDRESSED

· · ·

There are usually four sets of issues that must be addressed in a divorce. While every case is different, there are some common conventions, norms, and formulas that are typically employed. The four sets of issues are dividing assets and liabilities (i.e., debts), spousal support (i.e., alimony), custody of the children, and child support payments

DIVIDING ASSETS AND LIABILITIES

Most people who have never been through a divorce assume that their state is a so-called *community property state,* in which all of the property acquired during the marriage is considered joint property, and it is divided up evenly (50/50) between the spouses upon divorce, as are the debts incurred. In fact, only nine states are technically community property states: Arizona, California, Idaho, Louisiana, Nevada, New Mexico, Texas, Washington, and Wisconsin. Even in these states, a prenuptial agreement can trump the community property treatment of assets.[12]

The other 41 states are so-called *common law states* that rely on the principle of *equitable distribution.* The idea is that property ownership is inherently unequal due to various factors such as education, earnings level, age, and health. And some property might be in one spouse's name rather than in the name of both spouses. Therefore, the distribution should be fair, but not necessarily equal. Judges, for example, may require one spouse use their separate property (explained in the next paragraph) to make a settlement fair to both spouses.

In both community property and equitable distribution states, it is essential to understand what are and are not marital assets or marital liabilities.

Marital assets refers to all property (such as houses, stocks, property, cars, insurance, etc.) acquired during the marriage, regardless of ownership or who holds the title to it. However, in many states, there are exceptions for assets acquired before marriage, assets acquired by inheritance, gifts to one individual, or assets that derived directly from another asset that was held by one of the partners before the marriage (such as cash from the sale of a house that one spouse owned before the marriage), and, of course, any other asset that both spouses agree is separate property.

The consequence of this designation is that the property is not split between the two parties in a divorce. For example:

- Imagine that a divorcing couple (Bill and Jane) have $125,000 of assets, and the judge's decision is to split the marital assets evenly.

- However, $25,000 of the total $125,000 is separate property owned by Jane (from before the marriage).

- In this case, Bill is entitled to $50,000 of assets and Jane is entitled to $75,000 of assets—being $50,000 in marital assets and $25,000 in separate assets.[13]

Marital liabilities (also called marital debt) are the debts incurred during the marriage. Typically, the debts that one spouse brings into the marriage remain the responsibility of that spouse. During a divorce, marrital debts must be divided according to who is responsible for repaying the debt. But be careful. Although the judge's decision can bind the divorcing parties, the judge does not have the power to obligate a lender to release one of the two parties if both signed the loan. If both spouses co-signed for a debt, the lender may not accept that only one party is now responsible for the debt. Rather, both spouses will probably be held to *joint and several liability* for the debt (i.e., both are individually responsible for the entire debt), even if only one spouse enjoyed the benefit. This practice is analogous to the treatment of premarital assets.

If the couple filed joint tax returns, the IRS holds both spouses to joint and several liability for taxes.[14]

For persons under age 30, the handling of student debts may be particularly important in a divorce settlement, and it can be complex. Although the tendency is for each spouse to be responsible for his or her own student debt, a judge can sometimes assign partial or even full responsibility for a student loan of one spouse to be repaid by the other spouse. Local laws on this vary wildly—it often depends on whether the debt led to a larger income, which enabled both parties to enjoy a higher standard of living.

Note that regardless of the judge's actions, the point of view of the lender is that the name on the student loan is the one that matters. That is, if the debt is in your name, it is you that the lender will look to for repayment. If your ex-spouse agrees (or is ordered) to partially cover your student loans as part of the divorce settlement and then reneges, the lender will come after you for repayment, and it is your credit rating that will get hit.

Further complicating the situation is that most student loans through a private lender (which many are) require a co-signer. For married couples, that co-signer is often the spouse. If you co-signed a loan, both names are on the loan. Now, some private student loans offer co-signer release, which could be a smart move in divorce. Otherwise, you may need to look into refinancing the loan with a new loan, one that is only signed by the former student, and for which the spouse (or former spouse) is not a co-signer.[15]

JUST SO YOU KNOW
Providing False Financial Information During a Divorce

In all contested divorces and some uncontested divorces, both partners are required to sign a *financial affidavit* that discloses all assets, liabilities, income, and expenses, so that the other spouse—and, if necessary, the judge—sees the full financial picture of both spouses when assessing what is a fair settlement.

However, there is a common practice in which the spouse with greater resources hides assets or income from the other spouse, or exaggerates the amount of their expenses or indebtedness.

No one knows exactly how often this occurs during divorce, but surveys indicate that about a third of spouses admit to hiding their true financial situation from their partner during their marriage.[16]

Providing false financial information during a divorce is illegal, and the court has wide discretion in penalizing a party found to have engaged in such practices, including monetary penalties, changing the divorce settlement, and even incarceration.

Should you suspect your spouse is hiding assets (or providing other false information), you should engage an attorney (if you have not already done so) and describe the basis of your suspicion. There are well-known practices for this kind of behavior, and well-accepted ways to test the likelihood of a spouse hiding information even prior to any specific hiding spots being found. And even if you cannot find the hidden assets (or other false information) prior to the divorce settlement, should you find indications later, that can be the basis for asking the court to reopen the settlement agreement.[17]

SPOUSAL SUPPORT (ALIMONY)

In uncontested divorces, any spousal support—called *alimony*—is set at whatever the two parties can agree to, as long as the judge does not consider one party to have been coerced into the agreement.

In contested divorces, alimony is determined by the judge. However, the judge does not have complete discretion. Every state has laws dictating what factors must be considered. In principle, alimony is awarded only when one spouse is unable to meet their needs (broadly defined) without financial assistance, and the other spouse can afford to pay it. Spousal support may be temporary, to allow a former spouse time to get back into the job market or raise the children. In some cases (usually involving older people), it can be permanent if a spouse will likely never become self-supporting due to age or disability.[18]

In setting the amount of alimony to be paid, the courts look at what the reasonable expenses are for each of the spouses, what income each could expect to have if no alimony is ordered, and whether an alimony award would enable each to maintain "the standard of living established during the marriage."

If there isn't enough money for both parties to re-establish something close to their marital standard of living, then most judges will set the level of alimony where the divorcing parties share the pain equally.

However, recognize that alimony—and property distribution—is a separate issue from child support. The ex-spouse with whom the children reside may also collect income from the other ex-spouse for child support payments (described below). However, the two income amounts are computed separately by the courts.

CUSTODY ISSUES

Of all the issues in divorce, child custody is both the most emotional and the most complex. Therefore, consider the points covered here to be only an introduction to the subject.

Even in an uncontested divorce, judges in every state must decide custody based on the best interests of the child.[19] The best interests laws require the courts to focus on the child's needs and not the parent's needs. The law requires courts to give custody to the parent who can best meet the child's needs. That being said, while they are entitled to do so, judges are not likely to intervene in a joint agreement between the two parents unless there is some specific reason that causes him/her concern.

In contested divorces, the judge alone makes the custody decision. However, according to at least one article,[20] true battles over custody are the exception, not the norm. The article states that in just over half of custody decisions, both parents agree that the mother should become the custodial parent. (It implies that most others result in some form of *joint custody*, as described below). It states that 91% of custody decisions did not require the family court to decide, and only 4% of custody cases required going to trial before primary custody was decided.

Joint custody takes one of three forms: *joint physical custody* (children spend a substantial amount of time with each parent), *joint legal custody* (parents share decision-making on medical, educational, and religious questions involving the children), and *both joint legal and joint physical custody*. In some states, the courts are required to award joint custody except where the children's best interests—or a parent's health or safety—would be compromised. Many other states expressly allow the courts to order joint custody, even if one parent objects to such an arrangement.[21]

FOR THE LGBTQ COMMUNITY
LGBTQ Custody Discrimination

In some states, a parent's sexual orientation cannot in and of itself prevent a parent from having custody of or visitation with his/her child. In others, it can.

However, even in those states where such discrimination is banned, LGBTQ parents may be denied custody or visitation. This is because judges have discretion when considering the best interests of the child. If the judge is prejudiced, they may find other reasons to deny custody or visitation. If you have any concerns, be sure to seek attorney representation that is specifically qualified on this issue, because you may well end up having to appeal the offending judge's opinion to a higher court.[22]

CHILD SUPPORT PAYMENTS

Since 1992, the Child Support Enforcement Act has required all states to implement child support guidelines. However, the states are permitted to use any of three different (but not wholly different) systems for determining the level of child support and which spouse has to contribute how much.

Forty states use the *incomes shares* model, which develops an estimate of the cost to raise a child in that particular jurisdiction. It then apportions that cost between the parents based on their respective incomes. It also adjusts the actual payments made from one spouse to the other based on the percentage of time the child spends in one home versus the other, under the theory that the parent in whose home the child physically spends time is the one who is directly laying out cash to third parties (e.g., for food at the supermarket) in support of the child.

Seven states use the *percentage of income* model. It looks at the non-custodial parent's income and mandates that a certain percentage of that parent's income be turned over to the custodial parent for child support. The percentage can be a flat percentage or one that is adjusted for various factors (for example, in Texas, the amount is 20% of the parent's net resources for one child, graduating up to 40% for five children.)

Three states use the so-called *Melson formula*. It is a more complex version of the incomes shares model, as it also considers the two parents' financial needs.[23]

Individual state variations include working from gross pay versus net (i.e., after income tax) pay; the degree to which other child support obligations exist (e.g., to children of another marriage); and whether the child is a special-needs child.

AN IMPORTANT NOTE ON "FAULT" IN A DIVORCE
· · ·

Earlier in this chapter I mentioned that, separately from whether a divorce is contested or not, there is a distinction between whether the divorce is a *no-fault* divorce or a *fault* divorce. In the latter case, one spouse is held more responsible for the failure of the marriage than the other. Being held at fault has a number of potential consequences.

Not every state permits fault divorces, but about two-thirds do. The traditional grounds for granting a fault divorce include cruelty, adultery (see the comments about dating while being separated), desertion (also called abandonment), substance addiction, undisclosed inability, and confinement in prison for an extended length of time.

Both sides can be guilty of the grounds for granting a fault divorce. A long time ago, that would result in the absurd result that neither side could obtain a divorce. Today, the court decides who is less at fault and who is more at fault, and then grants the divorce to the less faulty party under a doctrine of comparative rectitude.

Why this matters is that fault can be a factor in the judge's decisions with respect to dividing property and in awarding alimony.[24] This is not to say that the judge deliberately biases the distribution and/or alimony as punishment for bad behavior, but rather that the judge may alter the settlement to compensate for bad acts that affected the family's finances. For example, a spouse's gambling may have depleted the family assets. Or, one spouse may have diverted income or assets while romancing another party. Or, one spouse's crime could have resulted in government seizure of jointly owned property.

However, like all aspects of a divorce before a judge, there are standards for making a claim that bad behavior should affect a settlement. Specifically, the economic impact of the behavior must be demonstrable, significant, and within the court's ability to reach a reasonable estimate of a fair adjustment to make.

ENDNOTES

1 "Survey: Certified Divorce Financial Analyst (CDFA) Professionals Reveal the Leading Causes of Divorce," Institute for Divorce Financial Analysts, n.d., institutedfa.com/Leading-Causes-Divorce. Accessed December 8, 2019.

2 Dianne Grande, "Couples Therapy: Does It Really Work?" Psychology Today, December 6, 2017, www.psychologytoday.com/us/blog/in-it-together/201712/couples-therapy-does-it-really-work. Accessed December 8, 2019.

3 Shawn Leamon, "Informal Separation: A way to save your marriage, or just delaying the inevitable? (Recommended)," Divorce and Your Money, May 17, 2017, divorceandyourmoney.com/blogs/informal-separation. Accessed December 8, 2019.

4 Leamon, "Informal Separation," divorceandyourmoney.com/blogs/informal-separation. Accessed December 8, 2019.

5 "Legal Separation vs. Divorce," Find Law, n.d., family.findlaw.com/divorce/legal-separation-vs-divorce.html. Accessed December 8, 2019.

6 Terin Miller, "How Much Does a Divorce Cost on Average in 2019?" The Street, March 8, 2019, www.thestreet.com/personal-finance/education/how-much-does-divorce-cost-14882536. Accessed December 8, 2019.

7 "How to File for an Uncontested or No Fault Divorce," Rocket Lawyer, n.d., www.rocketlawyer.com/article/how-to-file-for-an-uncontested-or-no-fault-divorce.rl. Accessed December 8, 2019.

8 "How Long Does It Take to Get Divorced?" Divorce Writer, n.d., www.divorcewriter.com/how-long-does-divorce-take. Accessed December 8, 2019.

9 Jason Crowley, "How Long Does It Take to Get a Divorce," Survive Divorce, November 6, 2019, www.survivedivorce.com/how-long-does-divorce-take. Accessed December 8, 2019.

[10] "Contested vs. Uncontested Divorce," Justia, n.d., www.justia.com/family/divorce/the-divorce-process/contested-vs-uncontested-divorce. Accessed December 8, 2019.

[11] "What Happens in a Divorce: An Overview of the Basic Divorce Process," Nolo, n.d., www.alllaw.com/articles/family/divorce/article64.asp. Accessed December 8, 2019.

[12] Tim Parker, "Community Property State," Investopedia, June 2, 2019, www.investopedia.com/personal-finance/which-states-are-community-property-states. Accessed December 8, 2019.

[13] "Marital Assets Law and Legal Definition," US Legal, n.d., definitions.uslegal.com/m/marital-assets. Accessed December 9, 2019.

[1] "Marital Debt Law and Legal Definition," US Legal, n.d., definitions.uslegal.com/m/marital-debt. Accessed December 9, 2019.

[1] Zina Lumok, "What Happens to Student Loans in a Divorce," The College Investor, May 23, 2019, thecollegeinvestor.com/18291/happens-student-loans-divorce. Accessed December 9, 2019.

[14] Jeff Landers, "What Are the Consequences of Hiding Assets During Divorce?" Forbes, November 14, 2012, www.forbes.com/sites/jefflanders/2012/11/14/what-are-the-consequences-of-hiding-assets-during-divorce/#1290ed81190c. Accessed December 8 2019.

[15] Angie Gambone, "Penalty for Hiding Assets in a Divorce," Legal Zoom, n.d., info.legalzoom.com/penalty-hiding-assets-divorce-25071.html. Accessed December 8, 2019.

[16] Roderic Duncan, "How a Judge Decides the Alimony Amount," Nolo, n.d., www.divorcenet.com/resources/divorce-judge/how-judge-decides-alimony-amount.htm. Accessed December 8, 2019.

[17] Child Welfare Information Gateway, "Determining the Best Interest of the Child," Child Welfare, n.d., www.childwelfare.gov/pubPDFs/best_interest.pdf#page=1&view=Introduction. Accessed December 8, 2019.

[18] Denise Erlich, "Single Fathers, Single Mothers, and Child Custody Statistics," Erlich Legal, n.d., erlichlegal.com/blog/single-fathers-single-mothers-child-custody-statistics. Accessed December 8, 2019.

[19] "Child Custody FAQ: Answers to common child custody questions," Nolo, n.d., www.nolo.com/legal-encyclopedia/child-custody-faq.html. Accessed December 8, 2019.

[20] "Child Custody FAQ," www.nolo.com/legal-encyclopedia/child-custody-faq.html. Accessed December 8, 2019.

[21] Debrina Washington, "How Child Support Payments Are Calculated," The Balance, October 14, 2019, www.thebalance.com/how-child-support-payments-are-calculated-2997973. Accessed December 8, 2019.

[22] Lina Guillen, "No-Fault Versus Fault Divorce," Nolo, n.d., www.divorcenet.com/resources/divorce/divorce-basics/no-fault-versus-fault-divorce.htm. Accessed December 8, 2019.

CHAPTER 17

Other Aspects of the Law
You Need to Know

Every adult's life is affected by the law. But most adults have only a vague understanding of what the law actually says or what one can actually expect the law to accomplish. The knowledge they do have has been gathered in bits and pieces over the years. What they don't know can cost them a lot.

This chapter provides a general framework for certain important parts of the law that are most likely to affect you that have not already been covered in this book:

- The legal aspects of signing and/or breaking a contract

- Contract provisions to be wary of

- Your rights as an employee

- Lawsuits—including whether to file one, what to do if someone threatens you with one, and what to do if one is actually filed against you

- What you should do, and what to expect from the authorities, if you are the victim of a crime

- Whether you should have a will

ENTERING AND BREAKING CONTRACTS

. . .

Most contracts you will enter involve the sale or purchase of some physical item (referred to in the law as a *good*). If so, the contract is governed by a law that is common (with certain modifications) to all fifty states: the *Uniform Commercial Code* (UCC). Specifically, you will be dealing with Article 2 of that code.[1] Exceptions to this rule are real estate contracts, employment contracts, and contracts that involve providing services, such as financial transactions. These transactions are governed by state laws (other than the UCC). Most of the principles I describe here also apply to those contracts, although some of the specifics may vary.

There are a number of key elements of contracts that you should be aware of:

- A contract is an agreement that creates obligations on the part of both (or all) parties to the contract. Said another way, each party must give and get something of value, legally referred to as *consideration.* Consideration can be almost anything of value—money, physical objects, even a promise to do or not do something. Except in very limited circumstances, unless something is given in exchange for the promise, a promise by itself is not a contract, and a broken promise is not a breach of contract.

- There must be a so-called *meeting of the minds* for a contract to be formed. That is, if the parties truly have different understandings of what was being agreed to, or if one party did not recognize that he/she was being bound, then legally the contract never happened. To facilitate this condition, the contract has to unambiguously contain an offer ("I will give you this in return for that") and an acceptance ("I agree to that").[2]

- A contract does not necessarily have to be in writing to be a valid contract. A verbal contract can be a valid contract, although it might be, from a practical standpoint, unenforceable if there are no third-party witnesses.

- That said, almost all significant contracts *do* have to be in writing. If a contract involves any one of a number of criteria, it must be in writing to be enforceable. These criteria include any contract that lasts over one year *or* any contract for the sale of goods for more than $500.[3]

Contracts are broken all the time, for good reasons and bad. The term *breach of contract* refers to one party failing to live up to his/her obligations under a contract. What happens next depends on the severity of the breach and the parties involved.

- In a so-called *minor breach,* one party has failed to live up to some provision of the contract, but most of the contract can stay intact. In these cases, the parties usually work out a solution, such as an amendment to the contract changing a provision or agreeing to reduce the payment owed, etc.

- In a *major* or *fundamental breach*, the failure seriously impairs the contract as a whole, and the non-breaching party is allowed to terminate the contract.

From a legal standpoint, all the action takes place around a major breach. First, the failing party may claim the breach is not so strong as to impair the contract as a whole. He/she may claim the party who is terminating the contract is the one who is breaching the contract. Or the contract may or may not specify an amount of money that is due as a result of the breach (referred to as *liquidated damages*), or it may or may not specify a process for resolving disputes.

If the sides cannot agree, one or the other may initiate a lawsuit, and the matter may end up in court, which is ultimately resolved in a *civil trial*. To prevail in the lawsuit, the aggrieved party (now called the *plaintiff*) must be able to demonstrate that he/she has suffered some damage, caused by the other party (called the *defendant*), which is usually monetary but can also be other kinds of damage.

Very importantly, unless there has been theft or fraud involved, or the disagreements among the parties has risen to the point of violence, the police do not get involved in resolving disputes over contracts. The only legal remedy available to you in a contract dispute is to *sue* the other party in *civil court,* or if the contract itself specifies this, to submit the case to *binding arbitration* (which is somewhat similar to a civil suit in court, except the decision is rendered by one or more professional arbitrators who are experts in the issues at hand and whom you and your opponent select).

Unfortunately, as I describe below, lawsuits are a very blunt instrument. First, they take a long time to resolve. Second, they involve hiring an attorney, which makes them expensive to pursue. Third, should the lawsuit actually proceed to court, the emphasis will be on what can be factually proven, and many of the elements of a contract dispute often get down to "he said/she said." That makes the outcome less predictable than you might want it to be. That also is why most lawsuits never actually make it to court. Instead, they are usually settled out of court in compromises that both sides often find less than satisfactory.

JUST SO YOU KNOW
Only Sign Contracts With Parties You Really Trust

Because lawsuits are such a blunt instrument, are expensive, and in most cases end up being settled out of court anyway, everyone knows that the odds of a breach in a small contract (or small or medium breaches within a large contract) actually resulting in a lawsuit are low.

Therefore, entering a contract is overwhelmingly an act of trust in the other party. You may negotiate over the wording of the contract, but the point of that negotiation is to have both sides be clear as to what constitutes honest and diligent performance. The wording does not keep the counterparty honest and diligent.

Said another way, do not rely on the wording of the contract to protect you against bad behavior. It does not successfully serve that function. Therefore, *you should only sign contracts with parties whom you fundamentally trust.*

Now, honest disagreements can occur, and when they do occur, you would obviously prefer they be resolved more to your satisfaction than the other party's satisfaction. Your odds of that happening are better if you structure your dealings with two attributes in mind:

- First, keep inertia on your side.

  » That is, you want to ensure that, if both sides just walk away in frustration, you are relatively better off than the other party. For example, this is why contracts often require deposits or progress payments. There are other tools (for example, who possesses the physical product, including raw materials supplied by the other side) that can be deployed at various times during the process.

- Second, ensure that other relevant persons (such as future customers) can have visibility into what is happening.

  » Everyone wants to protect their reputation, particularly with potential future customers. A person will settle for an unpleasant outcome if the cost of pushing for a better outcome includes losing opportunities for future sales. For example, herein lies the power of sites such as TripAdvisor and Angie's List—they provide customers with a way to create visibility to their view of the vendor's product, helping to "keep the vendor honest" and prevent the vendor from taking undue advantage of them.

CONTRACT PROVISIONS TO BE WARY OF

Most of the contracts you will be asked to sign throughout the next few years will be prepared by the other party. Recognize they have been prepared to better protect their authors, not you. While you are often stuck in a take-it-or-leave-it situation with respect to the offered contract, here are a few provisions you might want to pay particular attention to:

- "Notwithstanding…" clauses

  » Be very wary if you see the word "notwithstanding…." That word essentially means, "Everything else we've promised in this contract does not count if the following happens."

» If you see this phrase—which commonly appears in several places in virtually any significant contract—it's time to pay very close attention. Chances are good that it's about to say something different than what you were expecting.

- "This contract contains the complete agreement" clauses

  » That phrase means essentially, "No matter what we have verbally promised we will do for you, and despite everything else we may have said about how great our product is, we are under no obligation to honor anything except what is written in this document."

  » If you feel there is something objectionable about the written contract—if the other party has added or left out something important and you disagree, insist that it be reflected in writing. Do not count on verbal promises—you never know what may happen down the road, or whether the person who made those verbal promises to you will even be associated with the other party anymore when some future problem arises.

- Binding arbitration clauses

  » Theses clauses say you agree that you will not sue the counterparty in court. They often then specify the rules and forums where any dispute will be arbitrated. Those rules and that forum will have been selected to favor them, not you.

  » You may prefer binding arbitration to court just as much as the other party does (since it often resolves disputes more quickly and less expensively than going to court), but make sure the specific terms in an arbitration clause are acceptable to you before you sign.

- Automatic renewal clauses

  » You already know what these are—in fact, you probably already have such clauses in various contracts you've signed in the past, covering anything from your cell phone contract to many of the apps on that very cell phone.

  » Pause for a moment and think about how comfortable you are with such a provision in this particular contract. Be doubly wary if the advance notice requirement for canceling the automatic renewal is either too long before the renewal takes place or is difficult to communicate.

- Last minute changes in *any* provisions.
  - » There is an old trick that some vendors use of slipping in some changes (in their favor) at the last minute. They are counting on you to be so anxious to get the deal done that you will not scrutinize the details.[4]

To be clear, I am not saying you should automatically walk away if you see these provisions in a contract—in fact, you will likely see some form of many of them in many contracts. Just be sure to read very carefully and decide for yourself whether you are comfortable with what they state. If not, then you should walk away.

YOUR RIGHTS AS AN EMPLOYEE
· · ·

A number of laws exist to protect you against being mistreated by your employer. There are laws at both the federal and state levels, and there are laws at the federal level that protect you unless the state laws provide even more protection.

Here are some of the most important laws at the federal level that relate to your employment status:

- Employers with more than 15 employees are prohibited from discriminating in the hiring process on the basis of race, color, religion, gender, or national origin (by Title VII of the Civil Rights Act of 1964). Further, if an individual can perform the essential functions of a job, that person cannot be discriminated against on the basis of their disability (per the Americans with Disabilities Act). The federal laws relating to this issue are enforced by the Equal Employment Opportunity Commission (EEOC).

- Unless your job is categorized as *exempt* (which means roughly "executive, professional as defined by having significant intellectual content and requiring specialized training, or administrative as defined by supporting management through independent exercise of discretion about significant matters"), your employer must comply with various limits on the duration of your workday, the number of breaks that must be provided, and certain salary and overtime requirements (per the Fair Labor Standards Act). You must be paid at least $7.25 an hour unless your job is one in which you earn tips (as of December 2019), and you must be paid at least 50% more than whatever your basic pay is for any hours over 40 per week. These laws are enforced by the Wage and Hours Division of the U.S. Department of Labor.

- Once you have worked at an employer for at least 12 months, your employer must allow you to take up to 12 weeks of leave (unpaid) for qualified medical purposes and have your job available when you return (per the Family and Medical Leave Act).[5] These laws are also enforced by the Wage and Hours Division of the U.S. Department of Labor.

You should also be aware of two other categories of protection by federal law:

- Your physical safety is protected by the Occupational Safety and Health Act of 1970. Apart from industry-specific rules, there is a provision called the General Duty Clause that prohibits any practice that represents a clear risk to employees. Thus, if you believe something is unsafe, you do not have to be an expert in the specific regulations of your industry to take action. The law is administered by the Occupational Safety and Health Administration (OSHA), which has a specific Whistleblower Protection Program to shield you against reprisals for speaking up.[6]

- The federal government also protects you against sexual harassment, although it does so by treating harassment as a form of illegal discrimination on the basis of sex.

  » The law is enforced through the EEOC, which defines sexual harassment as follows: "Unwelcome sexual advances, requests for sexual favors, and other verbal or physical conduct of a sexual nature constitute sexual harassment when submission to or rejection of this conduct explicitly or implicitly affects an individual's employment,

314

unreasonably interferes with an individual's work performance, or creates an intimidating, hostile or offensive work environment."

» More important, sexual harassment is more broadly defined than many people know. For example, both men and women can be charged, and one does not have to be a supervisor or have any authority over a victim to be charged as a harasser.

» Some, but not all, states provide more direct and complete protection against sexual harassment through laws such as Vermont's law requiring employers to adopt a policy against sexual harassment.

LAWSUITS
· · ·

The United States is viewed as a very litigious society, and the news media fuels this reputation by publicizing the most ridiculous lawsuits. The public perception seems to be that one can sue anyone for anything.

However, things are not quite as litigious as you might expect:

• First, the United States is not the world's most litigious society. That distinction apparently belongs to Germany. The United States is further bested by Sweden, Israel, and Austria.[7] That said, given there are between 195 and 197 countries in the world (depending on who is counting),[8] coming in fifth-worst in the world is still pretty bad.

• Second, the U.S. is actually becoming less litigious. According to the *Wall Street Journal*, the rate of lawsuit filing has dropped dramatically in the past 20 years. In 1993, ten people out of every one thousand filed a lawsuit. In 2015, that figure was only two people out of every one thousand, a drop of 80%.

• Third, the nature of lawsuits has also shifted. The majority of lawsuits (51%) now consist of disputes over contracts. Only 4% are the classic *tort*, where one party sues another party for a civil wrong that caused them to suffer loss or harm. And most tort lawsuits fall into one of three categories: auto cases, medical malpractice, or product liability.[9] The classic trope of one person randomly shouting toward another,

"I'm going to sue you," and then actually following through with the threat is not the norm.

Nonetheless, there are enough lawsuits around, and enough threats that someone is going to sue you, that you need to know the realities of lawsuits along two key dimensions: (1) the legal bases for filing a suit, and (2) the process of a civil trial (i.e., a lawsuit).

LEGAL BASES A LAWSUIT

One person cannot sue another person just because he/she is mad at them, or even because the person has been wronged in some way. There must be a *basis* in the law. The most common bases are:

- Contract disputes
  - » As I described earlier, the UCC (and similar laws for financial transactions and state laws for services) specifically provide that lawsuits can be filed for breach of contract.
- Family law
  - » This concerns the body of law governing divorces, custody of children, child support, etc.
  - » These matters rely on lawsuits as the basis of individuals bringing actions before the courts.
- Other statutory bases
  - » A number of laws, such as the UCC, provide for the right to file lawsuits. For example, most of the laws underlying your rights as an employee noted in the previous section have specific provisions that allow lawsuits against employers.
- Debts
  - » Lawsuits are specifically permitted for creditors seeking to recover unpaid debts.
- Property disputes
  - » Lawsuits are allowed over the use of land, boundaries, trees, noise, and ownership issues.

- Personal injury (torts):

  » These occur when one party sues another party for a civil wrong (such as negligence) that caused them to suffer loss or harm.

Each of these bases has its own rules for what factors must be in place for a person to have a *cause of action*. By way of illustration, let's examine what is necessary for a person to have a legal basis to file a lawsuit for another person's negligence. There are four elements:[10]

- Duty

  » An individual has an obligation to act in a manner conducive to the well-being of persons whom the individual can reasonably expect to be around them. For example, a factory owner has a duty to protect his/her employees, but does not have the same duty to protect a burglar from harm.

- Breach of duty

  » For a tort lawsuit, the individual must have failed in that duty, either intentionally or (more often) due to insufficient attention to the need to protect others from harm (referred to as negligence).

  » However, "duty" is not the same as "successfully protected." If it can be shown the individual failed, but had made sufficient efforts to protect everyone, then he/she is deemed to have not breached his/her duty.

  » There are some relatively narrow situations where the doctrine of strict liability is required—that is, the liability exists if the protection failed, regardless of whether the individual responsible made every reasonable effort to protect others.

- Causation

  » The failure must have led directly to the injury, or at least have been a large cause of the injury (even if other factors contributed).

  » There is a concept called proximate cause, meaning that the more that other factors played a role or the more time that passed between the failure and the injury, the less the injury can be blamed on that particular failure.

- Injury

  » The plaintiff must have sustained some kind of injury, although this injury is not limited to personal physical injury. Damage to property, pain and suffering, and emotional distress have all counted as injuries in lawsuits in the past.

THE PROCESS OF A LAWSUIT

While there are four official process steps in a lawsuit, it is more helpful to think of the process in six stages.

STAGE 1: The Threat

- Most lawsuits are presaged by a disagreement, complete with emotions ("I'm going to file a lawsuit!"). While there are no figures on this, many internet resources refer to the fact that far more lawsuits are threatened than actually filed.

- The less intense form of a threat is a verbal threat. Some people resort to the more intense form, that is, a letter from an attorney. These are sometimes called a *demand letter,* and they generally consist of a client's complaint (sometimes citing a vague reference to a law), the client's assertion of great harm done to him/her, and what the client wants you to do to satisfy him/her.

- Understand that thousands of letters like this are sent every day.[11] They are often deliberately manipulative, intended to frighten you into acquiescing. You should know they are quite inexpensive to produce, and many attorneys will send one without really looking into the case, but as a goodwill gesture toward their client.

- If you receive a demand letter, should you call an attorney? Every case is different of course, but calling an attorney can be expensive, and you don't want to spend that money unless this threat is serious. Whether you should take a demand letter seriously depends on a number of factors, including whether you believe the complaint actually has merit and how much effort has apparently been put into the letter. The shorter it is and the more boilerplate it appears, the less likely it is a precursor to real legal action.

- If you judge the letter to not be serious, I suggest you not reply to it. The problem with any reply is that what you send potentially becomes evidence. If you try to explain what really happened, or argue about the level of injury, you can accidentally undercut your case by admitting to part of what your opponent asserts. If your opponent is serious, you will almost certainly hear from that attorney again in a more thorough and sophisticated letter, but still short of actually filing a lawsuit. That attorney will have almost certainly advised his/her client that proceeding with a lawsuit is the most expensive route to any solution.

- If a second letter comes, and it is more carefully created than the first, then it may well be time to speak to an attorney.

STAGE 2: Negotiations

- For the reasons described above, the other side will almost certainly want to engage in a negotiation before actually filing a suit.

STAGE 3: Pleadings

- A lawsuit being filed consists of one party, the *plaintiff*, filing a formal document with the court, often called a *complaint* or a *petition*. The plaintiff must also formally deliver a copy of the filing to the party being sued, the *defendant*.

- The complaint provides the plaintiff's description of the events that led to the lawsuit, as well as how that caused harm to the plaintiff. The complaint must also establish the legal basis for holding the defendant responsible.

- The defendant then has a specified time in which to file an *answer*. It provides the defendant's own description of the events in question, challenging any disagreements as to the facts. Further, the defendant may file a *counterclaim*, which is essentially a complaint against the plaintiff, and therefore contains the same elements as a complaint (description of events and harm, legal basis).

- This can go back and forth, with responses, amendments, etc. Often a defendant will ask a judge to dismiss the case, asserting that the plaintiff has failed the tests required to establish the legal basis for the suit.

STAGE 4: Discovery

- Assuming the judge does not grant a dismissal, the process moves on to discovery. This is usually the longest, most expensive, and most grueling part of the process.

- Each side is given broad permission to seek information from the other side that may be helpful in its case. This may include documents, depositions (i.e., interviews of the parties and other witnesses under oath), examinations of the scene, etc.

- There are often petitions and motions to the court and hearings before the court, as each side contests the rights of the other to information; for example, claiming the information is irrelevant to the case and producing it would constitute a hardship.

STAGE 5: The Trial

- The trial proceeds in essentially the manner you have seen in television shows (although there are differences between criminal trials, which is what you typically see on TV, and civil trials, as we are discussing here). There are opening statements, then the plaintiff's attorney presents his/her case, complete with witnesses and evidence. Then the defendant's attorney presents his/her case. The verdict may be rendered by a jury or (if both sides agreed ahead of the trial) by the judge.

- If the court finds in favor of the plaintiff, it can then make any (or all) of several kinds of awards: *compensatory damages* (i.e., an amount that corresponds to the court's finding about what the monetary value of the actual damage was); *restitution* (somewhat similar to compensatory damages); *punitive damages* (a monetary penalty beyond the level necessary to compensate the plaintiff for his/her losses); and/or *specific performance* (in which the judge orders the losing party to undertake a specific action).[12]

STAGE 6: An Appeal

- If either party is unsatisfied with the verdict, it has the legal option to appeal the verdict to a higher court, called an *appellate court.*

- In an appeal, the appellate court reviews the proceedings of the original court; it does *not* conduct a new trial. It can affirm, modify, or overturn the original verdict, including the amount of damages awarded.

- On TV, it appears that the attorney for every loser of a civil or criminal case announces that his/her client will appeal the decision. That is not true:

  » A recent study by the Bureau of Justice Statistics found that only about 15% of civil verdicts were appealed (about half by each side).

  » Of those attempted appeals, only about 60% actually got a hearing (the others were rejected by the appellate court or actually withdrawn by the appealing party before the appellate court reviewed it).

  » About one-third of those appeals that were heard succeeded in modifying or reversing the original verdict.

  » However, even in most of those cases, the appellate court only ordered a new trial.[13]

WHEN YOU ARE THE VICTIM OF A CRIME
· · ·

In 2018, there were approximately 1.2 million violent crimes reported in the United States and about 7.2 million crimes against property (i.e., theft, burglary, car theft, vandalism).[14] Fortunately, both figures represented declines from the previous year.

If you are the victim of a crime, your first focus will be to tend to any injuries and provide any help you can to the police. Then, four questions are likely to occur to you: (1) What resources are available to help me? (2) How likely is my crime to be solved? (3) Will my insurance cover my injuries/losses? Do I have any rights as the victim?

AVAILABLE RESOURCES

If you are the victim of a crime, there are several resources to help you.

- First, obviously, if you feel you are in any kind of danger, you should call 911.

- If you are not in danger, you should look into a variety of victims' services. A good place to start is the Office for Victims of Crime (OVC), a branch of the Office of Justice Programs of the U.S. Department of Justice, at www.ovc.gov/help.[15]

  » It does not matter whether the crime against you was a federal, state, or local crime, because the purpose of the website is to help you connect with local programs run by both government and not-for-profit private agencies who can be helpful to you. Its directory contains information about over ten thousand programs.

  » More important, you may be eligible for crime victim compensation benefits, including reimbursement for medical services, mental health counseling, lost wages, and other costs incurred as a result of the crime. All states receive federal Victims of Crime Act (VOCA) funds from OVC to help support local victim assistance and compensation programs.

LIKELIHOOD YOUR CRIME WILL BE SOLVED

How likely are the police to catch the person who committed the crime against you? Obviously, the answer is highly case-specific, but unfortunately the statistics are not very favorable.

- According to the FBI, in 2017 (the latest year for which data is available), less than half of all violent crimes and less than 20% of all crimes against property were solved.

- Homicides had the highest clearance rate (62%), while burglaries and auto theft had the lowest success rates (13%).[16]

INSURANCE COVERAGE FOR INJURY OR LOSSES

If you have health insurance, it should cover any medical bills in accordance with the coverages and copays listed in your policy. And remember to look into the VOCA funds listed above that provide reimbursement for medical expenses if you qualify.

In terms of property, if your car was stolen, you will be reimbursed for the actual cash value of your car, but only if your auto insurance policy includes *comprehensive coverage*. Most policies do include this provision, but certain low-rate policies that are designed to meet only the minimum insurance requirements of the law may not include it—they are often limited to liability coverage or liability-plus-collision coverage, and do not include insurance against having your car stolen, in which case they will not reimburse you.[17]

If you are the victim of a burglary or other property theft, look to your homeowners' policy or renters' policy. Standard homeowner's and renter's policies cover your personal belongings regardless of whether they were stolen from your home or your car, or by robbery or pickpocketing. Both types of policies usually have a deductible.

Importantly, homeowners' and renter's policies from different insurance companies vary as to whether they will compensate you based on actual cash value or replacement cost value. The former reimburses you for the estimated amount that the article is currently worth, so it might be diminished by depreciation, which is an estimate of how used the article would be, given its age. The latter reimburses you for the amount it would take to actually replace the item today.[18]

There are two important caveats regarding your homeowner's or renter's coverage:

- First, some policies require that you file a police report in order for them to reimburse you—so be sure to report the crime.

- Second, some policies limit the amount of coverage. Therefore, if you have some items that are highly valuable, you may need a separate policy to cover these. These policies are usually provided by the same company that provides your homeowner's/renter's insurance, and go by various names, such as a *personal articles floater*. While you may be irritated at first to think you need to pay more, remember that the alternative would be to charge everyone the same rate for a basic homeowner's policy as would be necessary to cover the risk of that one family in town who owns the million-dollar necklace.

YOUR RIGHTS AS A VICTIM

The final question is whether you, as a victim of a crime, have any rights. In a majority of states, you do. They mainly come into play if and when a perpetrator has been caught.

Your rights typically include the right to be notified of all court proceedings; the right to participate in those proceedings; the right to be protected from the accused perpetrator; the right to have input during the sentencing process (in the form of a statement of the impact of the crime on you); and the right to information about the conviction, sentencing, imprisonment, and release of the offender.[19]

WHETHER TO HAVE A WILL
· · ·

With all the changes occurring in your life during your 20s, you might well ask if you need to go through the hassle and expense of creating a will.

There are two ways of looking at the issue:

- On one hand, if you are a woman, given that you were alive when you turned 21, you stand a 99.5% chance of still being alive at age 30; if you are male, the odds are 98.6%).[20] So, for roughly 99% of people your age, a will turns out to be unnecessary for the time being.

- However, for others, their families will be glad they created a will.

  » If you die without a will, you will be said to have died *intestate*. That means the *probate court* in the state here you lived (rather than you, through your will) will set the rules about who inherits any property and how long the process will take.[21]

  » Further, critical aspects of the process may be delayed if you don't have a will. To fully process an estate through probate court usually takes most of a year or more.[22] If your will appoints an administrator/executor, then that person (or institution) drives the process under the supervision of the probate court. If you die intestate, the state does.

  » This timing difference can matter, particularly if some of the beneficiaries of your will need access to some of the inheritance before the entire will can be settled (imagine, for example, that your spouse needs to cover day-to-day expenses while he/she waits for the rest of the process to finish). Your executor can petition the court to allow him/her to distribute some of your property sooner.[23] While the same thing can happen when the state is in charge, it will probably be much harder to accomplish.

Wills need not be expensive to create if your affairs are simple, as they are for most people in their 20. In fact, they can be purchased over the internet for less than $100.[24] It seems a wise investment, even if the odds of it being used are low.

ENDNOTES

1 "Uniform Commercial Code," Inc., n.d., www.inc.com/encyclopedia/uniform-commercial-code-ucc.html. Accessed December 24, 2019.

2 "The Basics of Contract Law," Rocket Lawyer, n.d., www.rocketlawyer.com/article/basics-of-contract-law-cb.rl. Accessed December 24, 2019.

3 Diana Fitzpatrick, "When Is a Written Contract Required Under the UCC?" Nolo, n.d., www.nolo.com/legal-encyclopedia/when-is-written-contract-required-under-the-ucc.html. Accessed December 24, 2019.

4 Adam C. Uzialko, "10 Common Contract Gotchas to Avoid," *Business News Daily*, April 12, 2018, www.businessnewsdaily.com/10686-contract-complications-avoid.html. Accessed December 24, 2019.

5 "Employee Rights 101," Find Law, n.d., employment.findlaw.com/employment-discrimination/employees-rights-101.html. Accessed December 25, 2019.

6 Daniel Kurt, "8 Federal Laws That Protect Employees," Investopedia, May 4, 2019, www.investopedia.com/articles/personal-finance/120914/8-federal-laws-protect-employees.asp. Accessed December 25, 2019.

7 Jack, "10 Most Litigious Countries in the Word," Jurors Rule, November 24, 2018, www.jurorsrule.com/10-most-litigious-countries-in-the-world. Accessed December 25, 2019.

8 Marques Hayes, "How Many Countries Are There in the World?" World Atlas, July 17, 2019, www.worldatlas.com/articles/how-many-countries-are-in-the-world.html. Accessed December 25, 2019.

9 Joe Palazzolo, "We Won't See You in Court: The Era of Tort Lawsuits Is Waning," *Wall Street Journal*, July 24, 2017, www.wsj.com/articles/we-wont-see-you-in-court-the-era-of-tort-lawsuits-is-waning-1500930572. Accessed December 25, 2019.

10 "A Brief Overview of Tort Law," Laws, December 22, 2019, tort.laws.com/tort-law. Accessed December 25, 2019.

11 Max Kennerly, "When Does a Lawyer's Demand Letter Become Extortion?" Litigation and Trial, July 19, 2013, www.litigationandtrial.com/2013/07/articles/attorney/demand-letter-extortion. Accessed December 25, 2019.

12 Travis Peeler, "Breach of Contract," Legal Match, June 22, 2018, www.legalmatch.com/law-library/article/breach-of-contract.html. Accessed December 25, 2019.

13 Marilyn Vos Savant, "What percentage of Appealed Court Decisions Are Overturned?" *Parade*, March 3, 2013, parade.com/37863/marilynvossavant/03-what-percentage-appealed-cases-overturned. Accessed December 25, 2019.

14 "2018 Crime Statistics Released," FBI, September 30, 2019, www.fbi.gov/news/stories/2018-crime-statistics-released-093019. Accessed December 25, 2019.

15 "Help for Crime Victims," Office for Victims of Crimes, n.d., www.ovc.gov/help. Accessed December 26, 2019.

16 "Table 25: 2017 Crime in the United States," FBI, n.d., ucr.fbi.gov/crime-in-the-u.s/2017/crime-in-the-u.s.-2017/tables/table-25. Accessed December 26, 2109.

17 "Does Auto Insurance Cover a Stolen Car?" Value Penguin, n.d., www.valuepenguin.com/does-car-insurance-cover-theft. Accessed December 26, 2019.

18 "Does Homeowners Insurance Cover Theft?" Value Penguin, n.d., www.valuepenguin.com/does-homeowners-insurance-cover-theft. Accessed December 26, 2019.

19 "What You Can Do If You Are a Victim of Crime," Find Law, n.d., corporate.findlaw.com/litigation-disputes/what-you-can-do-if-you-are-a-victim-of-crime.html. Accessed December 26, 2019.

20 "Actuarial Life Table," Social Security, n.d., www.ssa.gov/oact/STATS/table4c6.html. Accessed December 26, 2019.

[21] "What Happens If You Die Without a Will?" Find Law, n.d., https://estate.find-law.com/wills/what-happens-if-i-die-without-a-will-.html. Accessed December 26, 2019.

[22] Travis Peeler, "How Long Does Probate Take? A State Comparison," Legal Match, July 5, 2019, www.legalmatch.com/law-library/article/how-long-does-probate-take-a-state-comparison.html. Accessed December 26, 2019.

[23] "Preliminary Distributions from an Estate of Trust: The Basics," Simmel Law, n.d., www.stimmel-law.com/en/articles/preliminary-distributions-estate-or-trust-basics. Accessed December 26, 2019.

[24] "Last Will & Testament," Legal Zoom, n.d., www.legalzoom.com/sem/ep/last-will-and-testament.html?kid=_k_EAIaIQobChMI7djx2_HT5gIVyJ-zCh24WwDvEAAYASAAEgIWnPD_BwE_k_&utm_source=google&utm_medium=cpc&utm_term=online%20will&utm_content=368088641945&utm_campaign=EP%20|%20LWT&kpid=go_2017342920_75281997521_368088641945_aud-296264003243:kwd-24824491_c&gclid=EAIaIQobChMI7djx2_HT5gIVyJ-zCh24WwDvEAAYASAA-EgIWnPD_BwE. Accessed December 26, 2019.